Six Months and Fifty Years

A Memoir of 99.999 Percent Truth

by Mark Todd

Dorrance Publishing Co
585 Alpha Drive
Suite 103
Pittsburgh, PA 15238
Visit our website at *www.dorrancebookstore.com*

ISBN: 978-1-6376-4301-3
eISBN: 978-1-6376-4615-1

Six Months and Fifty Years

A Memoir of 99.999 Percent Truth

by Mark Todd

DORRANCE
PUBLISHING CO
EST. 1920
PITTSBURGH, PENNSYLVANIA 15238

THIS BOOK IS DEDICATED TO "THE BOY"

Touch has a memory. O say, love say,
What can I do to kill it
and be free in my old liberty?
John Keats

I wish to thank all of you that listened, loved and stood
beside me while I worked behind you. This book could
not have been completed without the constant love and
support of a man named Joel. Thank you. M.T.

NOTE TO READER: You will find as you read along there are notes left for you only, the reader. There will be suggested music downloads as you read. You will have to have an account of some sort with your service provider or use your favorite music app to download the music at your own expense, I am afraid. Should you choose to follow along with us and opt to download the music, you will have an enhanced experience. You will have a wonderful opportunity to find yourself "in the book" as it happens. Should you choose not to download the music for yourself, you will still enjoy the story. That is my hope for you.

On the title page of this work you have noticed that it is titled a memoir of 99.999 percent truth.

The, less than one percent of fiction to be found in this scribe is the last page.

The "man" in this Memoir is alive and well.

—M. T.

Today I received the first of many texts that were to follow. These texts were from a friend of mine. This friend asked that I share them, and the story that accompanies them, with the world in any way I could.

Initially, I accepted willingly. I really had no idea what to expect. Nor did I have a clue what these texts may contain. Upon reading several of these initial texts, I quickly became fascinated with the story that began to unfold. These texts were sent to me from an iPhone. The reason I mention that to you here is this: You, the reader, may find yourself a bit confused with this scribe. Follow along if you like. With some luck, you shall walk alongside an old man, the old man as a young boy, and another young man from South America as this story unfolds.

—J.S.

Banco De Bilbao Viscaya

Chapter One

There was a young boy who grew up among many people, yet he was always alone. He sought in his heart, day after day, that he should be loved. Or, at the very least, that he did not continually feel like a stranger among the other inhabitants on this planet.

One day, the man the boy thought he knew, his name was Jesus Christ, was taken away from him. *(IN TIME, READER, YOU WILL SEE HOW!)* It is an important part of this story. It was then the young boy had to search elsewhere for the love and affection he desperately needed as well as that astonishing thing called *touch*.

It is early December; a particularly dreary December. The kind of December that gets inside your bones. Marrow deep. This is the kind of cold that sneaks inside you and holds you hostage like a monster and leaves you questioning. *What is the point? Will spring arrive? Ever? Can I take one more dismal gray winter day?* Being prone to seasonal depression, the old man is struggling day after day to find meaning in his world. A reason to get out of bed in the morning has begun to elude him.

The old man has developed his fair share of health problems over the years that have reached a crescendo this December. Very much like the orchestra follows the maestro's lead as they reach the climax of the composition, they are not in charge. The pain, combined with the winter blues, has become a substantial problem for the old man.

The morning turned to afternoon with the usual fanfare.

Nothing.

Nada.

Shit.

As the old man sits on the white couch, gazing out of the only window in the room, at the frost covered rooftops of the monstrous complex he has recently moved to, he hears, from his cell phone, a chime. A *ding*. The man is not a techie. Nor does he care to be. He has never learned how to use a computer for anything. The man does not know how to type. The thought of creating a "new file" on a device of any kind gives him extreme anxiety. It always leads to feelings of inadequacy. There is a continual fear he might break something or lose something. As in the new file he has yet to learned how to open, let alone create.

The notification on his phone is an unfamiliar sound. "That is not my ringtone," he says to no one. Out of sheer curiosity, and the insane obsession we all understand today, the man looks at his phone. On the screen was a notification he has received a message from a dating app. It took the man two days to get the damn thing downloaded, then another week to answer all the ridiculous questions that allowed him to create his profile. That was at least two years ago. The app is rarely opened, nor does he receive many notifications from the site. He assumes it is due to his lack of presence there.

His phone annoys him. Basically, he has never cared for cell phones. He cannot tell what another person is really saying when he reads their text. Furthermore, when he sends a text to someone that might be rude or expletive, the recipient cannot often decipher his meaning in the damn text. Something critical is lost when texting is used by two individuals. So sayeth the old man.

Chapter Two

The man is intrigued as he opens the message. There is one word presented to him.

Hi

That is all. Simply, "Hi." The old man is very curious now. Not having the slightest inclination of any possible danger of viral infection, he responds.

Hi there!

He pushes the send button as a small bead of sweat begins to form on his right eyebrow. Within seconds, another message pops up on the man's phone.

How are jou?

The old man is brain fogged. *Who on earth would be texting me?* he wondered. Clearly a stranger. Yet there is no clue whom this person may be. He responds again.

I am well. Thank you.

He sends the reply off into space. He does not receive a response.

Chapter Three

There are two rooms in the dismal apartment. The man has tried to make it his home in the last three months since moving in. He still feels like a stranger here.

There are other figures who inhabit this small space as well. Many of them. They are seen by the man milling about his new home generally at dusk. Occasionally dawn. Mostly they are seen between three and four in the morning. During that hour, they are sensed somehow. They are *felt* like when you are sure someone is standing right behind you. You can sense an energy that is not yours alone. You turn around and there is no one there. Just an empty room. An empty apartment. The man sees them when he cannot sleep. They are seen only in one part of the apartment near the white couch as he sits in denial of his insomnia. He cannot understand why these people should be roaming about this apartment. It is not an old building, as one might think. They are ghosts or energies. Whatever they are, they hang out in this apartment without an invite, let alone an R.S.V.P. The man wonders in silence, since he first encountered another figure in his home, something untoward must have occurred at some random time. That is the way he thinks. There must always be an answer. Always.

There runs a set of train tracks directly to the east of his complex. The man is on the top floor of Building C. The monstrous complex numbers up to Building R. A quarter of a mile away as the crow flies. It may even be another country. The man has never ventured beyond Building C.

The trains that roar by carry passengers as well as cargo. The trains are very loud. They come and go every hour. A highspeed passenger tube takes over the tracks from eleven p.m. to seven a.m. The little apartment shakes and sways as they rumble by. It is the same feeling the man has in his hands early in the morning when the need for a drink is visiting.

Still, no response on the man's phone from whomever sent him the salutation. He decides it must have been a mistake.

A sense of longing settles in his heart. Outside the day has turned to shades of blue and purple, red, and orange. Gale force winds announce themselves at the window beside the white couch as the old man stares out looking at the frost covered rooftops of the other buildings near to his. It looks very cold, Much the same as a mother-in-law's tongue. Not much you can do about it. A bitter winter, indeed.

Chapter Four

Spain.

Madrid.

City Centro.

Alone.

Searching for a flower vendor.

Why?

Chasing a ghost.

No flowers anywhere.

Many hundreds of people.

Rain.

Cold.

No flowers.

Chapter Five

The old man feels an itch. It began shortly after he received the first message. From whom he had not a clue. It is a sort of deep inside the cerebellum itch. Thinking about the text somehow justifies his thoughts of sexual desires. A sexual warmth that begins at his knees. When relished, it warms the thighs and eventually progresses to a firmness that men know.

(NOTE TO READER: IT IS A SORT OF KEGEL THAT WOMEN KNOW. AN IMAGINED OTHER PRESENCE IN THAT SPACE THAT IS FORBIDDEN.)

The man needs some touch. Some affection. Truth be told, the man is randy. Copulating, or daydreaming about it, affords him an escape from his thoughts of aging. This horrible winter. Well-deserved, he has decided. An orgasm without guilt.

The man finds himself thinking these thoughts rather frequently lately. It really is a bit cumbersome. These thoughts that seem to take control of his brain, particularly when he is working. The man makes his living from his ability to understand the way a woman thinks in relation to design — interior, exterior, as well as everything related to home improvement. He also understands some medical arts due to working mostly with women for thirty years. He often directs women on certain cosmetic procedures.

It has become difficult to concentrate lately for the old man. He simply has other things on his mind.

As the man is driving home from work, still thinking about sex, he realizes his thoughts about sex are more about human touch than the actual physical act itself. He cannot remember when he was last held or caressed. Or loved.

Lost in thought, his phone makes another *ping* sound. It is a message notification. The same sound he heard for the first time a day ago. The man has viewed those two messages every hour since they first presented themselves. Like many of his female clients have said, "It's like an untreated vaginal yeast infection. It simply will not go away on its own." He has not been able to determine who sent the messages or why.

The man opens the new message. It is from someone on the dating app. Curious. The profile of the sender is locked. The man has tried many times to see who sent the first message. Each time he clicks on the profile button, the frickin app informs him this profile is private. What the hell does that mean? Why salute if you do not want a salutation in return? He has reviewed, investigated, scanned every inch of the app. At least as far as his limited understanding of the way the app works will allow.

The man placed a photo of himself on his profile some time ago. As he views his own profile, he does not recognize the man staring back at him. It is amazing what one year, or two, does to his face once he passed forty. Time tramples the face in friendship with the sun.

(READERS UNDER FORTY, BEWARE! USE SUNSCREEN. ALWAYS! LEST YOU WANT TO RESEMBLE A FRUIT ROLL-UP FOR YOUR DATING APP PHOTO.)

How disappointing it is this friendly stalker will not show themselves. The whole day has been a bit of a disappointment. Just another day of serving others. Advantage taken. Still, he is paid, nonetheless. The man wonders where these thoughts are coming from lately.

As he reaches the next stoplight, the seventeenth in the last hundred yards it seems, his cell chimes yet again. Once opened, the message is the same as the first. It is the same app.

Hi.

That is it. There is nothing he missed. He is practically seizure driven with anticipation and has no idea why. Plain old expectation knocking again. He types in a response while driving. Not good! He has had a prescription change for his vision every two to three years in the last twenty. His car veers slightly into the traffic on the right side. He realizes he has left his own lane entirely. There are a series of honks and angry mothers in Mormon assault vehicles everywhere, suddenly. Swearing and glaring. Some give him the finger. "That's rich," the man says out loud. The members of these women's congregations on Sunday morning church services surely never see this side of these sisters. The man does not care. He has a phone message to get to.

Man: Hi there.

Nothing comes back in response to the man's text. Not a frickin thing. The man is becoming agitated at himself for his transparency, feeling ashamed for hoping. Embarrassed at his longing. He is just so hungry for human touch. The old man does not share these thoughts with anyone. His loneliness. His desire for human touch. It has become an ache he can feel bone deep. If only an ibuprofen would help. He knows that a higher power of some kind is most likely aware of his thoughts lately. He convinces himself the big guy upstairs has been there himself a time or two.

As he pulls into his garage, a garage designed for a newt sized car, he engages the button to pull the side mirrors back like a horse doing the same thing with its ears just before it is about to buck. The ears of the car are safely pinned back against the car doors. The man has paid for not pushing that button twice before. Literally. A very expensive mistake he will not make again. He puts the car in park and turns off the engine. He is in repose. Sitting in the dark of the garage, in the light of early evening.

The man is in pain. His back. His knees. His feet. His feet have become a problem.

It began as a dull pain in his right heel. Then it became unbearable pain in the right heel. Pain that was left untreated for three years. At that point, the man could no longer ignore the pain. The podiatrist informed him he had plantar fasciitis. Helen Keller! He had never heard of such a thing. Many treatments were tried. A foot brace at night; gee, that was fun! Stretches and medication. The pain only intensified. The doctor performed a surgery to cut the tendon in his heel to relieve the pressure, and the pain.

Six weeks later, the man was able to remove the walking boot that had become as cumbersome as carrying a small humping dog strapped to your foot. The pain disappeared. Amazing. *Why on earth did I wait so long?* he wondered. Soon after, his left foot was in the same pain. He did not wait this time. Another surgery. The same procedure. He then was out of pain altogether in both of his feet. Truly amazing.

A year later, the man noticed a strange sensation in the pinky toe on his right foot. It was a queer kind of numbness. Two months later, the toe next to the pinky became numb. Along with the numbness, the toes began to burn. Very quickly, all the toes on the man's right foot were numb and burning. Describing the pain to anyone was difficult because it was such a strange thing to him. The best he could do was to say, "It feels as though I have hot, wet cotton balls in between my toes."

Life was becoming very painful again. Six months later, his entire foot was numb. He now was carrying an elephant strapped to his foot. Then the stabbing pain began. The jolting, searing pain began. He often felt as if he was going crazy.

Back to the podiatrist he went. This time, the good doctor told him he had neuropathy. After a series of questions and slight accusations insinuated by the man at the doctor, he was informed he would need to see a specialist.

Before the man could find a specialist on his insurance plan, a slight tingle emerged in his left foot. The same progression followed as on his right foot. At this point, the old man was becoming quite concerned. Within another year, he was in unbearable pain again. He no longer could perform certain tasks simple enough for most people. Work was very painful for him. Walking became dangerous on any uneven surface.

The man did find a specialist, eventually.

"You have peripheral neuropathy," he was told. "It is unfortunately irreversible. There is no treatment other than various medications." The doctor told the man he and his staff would need to do a series of tests to give a legal diagnosis.

Appointments were made and many tests were completed. Several weeks later, the man sat in a chair in the doctor's office, waiting for the doctor to reveal his test results. The man is uncomfortable with the doctor standing up to give him his test results for some reason. The doctor reaches for the man's file on his desk and opens it.

"I would feel more comfortable if you would sit down to talk about my tests, Dr. Ford," the man said.

"I am sitting down, sir."

Holy hell! The man wanted to crawl into a hole. There really is nothing to say when you blunder in such a way, so the man just stepped over it.

Slightly annoyed, the doctor informed the man he had diagnosed him with peripheral neuropathy. He, as well as the other three specialists at the university hospital working on the man's feet, informed him also that there was no treatment available for the condition. That it is progressive as well. "There are medications that are effective in alleviating pain in some cases. These drugs range from antipsychotic to antidepressants. There are also nerve blocking medications, though not necessarily experimental, they are often discovered in treatments we use for other ailments, such as insomnia and anxiety. Some individuals find no relief from any of these medications, while others insist that they are very effective in pain management."

Blah blah blah is what the man hears. Sounded to him like the doctors were guessing. The medication was prescribed and that was all they could do for him.

The pain was enough for the man to try these medications. Neurontin. Gahpabenten, Nortripty-line. Amitriptyline. All these were tried by the man at varying doses several times. They all made him feel very foggy. Not quite high. That would have been a bonus. No, not high, lethargic. These pills created a rubbery feeling in his legs. He stopped taking all of them. *It is, what it is,* thought the man. *I will just have to bear it all.*

The man has found no solution all these years later. His feet are the elephant in every room. They are very painful.

Despite the man's pain, he is ruttishly sitting in the dark garage. He knows not why he should be ruttish other than loneliness he surmises.

A soft *ping* comes from his phone. He opens the message instantly. On the screen there is a photo of a person with the most haunted expression he has ever seen on someone alive. The eyes are huge. The size of two tea saucers on a face. They are green. More a greenish, yellow gold.

(NOTE TO READER: CAN YOU RECALL THE FAMOUS NATIONAL GEOGRAPHIC COVER PHOTO OF THE AFGHAN GIRL? SHE WORE A SCARF AROUND HER HEAD AND NECK. THE FOCUS OF THE PHOTO WAS HER HAUNTING GREENISH, YELLOW-GOLD EYES. THE PHOTO THE MAN IS NOW LOOKING AT HAS THE SAME EYES.)

There are noticeable gray circles around the eyes. So dark, in fact, that the skin around them looks necrotic. The expression on the face appears void to the man.

He gasps out loud at the image. He feels breathless, suddenly. There is something about this picture. These few messages. This person. In the still of the garage, the man is quiet. His breathing is deep. The world outside the garage moves ever on. Like ants with an important message for the queen. The man is almost melancholic.

As he leaves the garage, he feels as if he is in a trance, due to whomever this person is. For the first time since moving in this little apartment, the man does not notice nor feel the climb to his door. Three flights of stairs. Horrible knees, bad back, and feet on fire. He is on autopilot as he reaches the pinnacle.

Once inside, he quickly makes himself a snack of cheese and crackers. He drops himself on the white sofa. As the air from the cushions of the couch is released upon sitting, he can smell Indian food.

I must have this creature steam cleaned, he immediately decides. He really does not know how to respond to the person who sent him the picture. He simply replies with a *hello*. He waits. He anticipates. There is no immediate response. Staring out the window, daydreaming, and now a bit satiated, he dozes off. There are visions of green eyes and a little girl in a scarf searching for him throughout the night.

Edward Arias

Chapter Six

Indians! The complex is full of Indians. Of the dot variety. The sun in the morning has yet to say "Get the hell up, old man," before the smell of onions, garlic, and curry accost his senses.

Red curry.

Green curry.

Hot!

These Indians are such beautiful people. They keep to themselves as if there is a lack of trust between the man and them. Maybe it is rooted deeper. Most likely, the man assumes.

The smell that infiltrates the man's clothing, bedding, carpets, and nose is a bit suffocating. The smell reminds the man of another odor. He has only recently connected the memory with the smell. It is the smell of the armpit. Warm and sautéed smelling.

(Do you remember, reader, in junior high school, those classmates who stand out in your head? They were not hot or beautiful. Nor were they the star player on any team. No. It was because they were hitting puberty and had yet to gain control of their armpit trouble. There was always a yellow stain in their JC Penney catalogue blouses and button up faux silk shirts just under the pit. The ever-present pit stains!)

The old man as a young boy sat next to a girl in class. It must have been English or math, both of which she excelled at. Tally Tooth was her name. Tally sat directly in front of the boy in their row. The boy's legs reached well beyond his given space provided by the education department of this small town. In fact, his ankles rested on the bar that crossed the front legs of Tally's desk when he was at his most comfortable in class. Tall and lanky, the boy was always trying to get comfortable in the tiny desks.

Tally! Toothy Tally! Tally had dandruff. A sort of waxy dandruff. Tally's hair was pitch black. Imagine the chunks of wax like scalp fighting for space in the black universe called Tally's hair. Tally always had a yellow stain under her pits. She wore a dress every day to school. The boy always thought of her as one of the Ingalls girls from walnut grove. There was always a smell about Tally the boy could not quite pinpoint. Kind of an oniony, hot garlicky, and sickly-sweet smell. The boy often smelt the same on adult women around town. Particularly in the hot summer months.

This was the late seventies. One never could be sure about odors.

Why did grown men drive around the neighborhood in windowless vans with no hubcaps? Why would someone create a fabric that retained the smell of biological matter even after it was incinerated? Holy hell. Polyester! Why were pants wider at the bottom than the top? Surely anyone could see they only made you look like one of the Manson girls without a gun. Tube tops! What the hell were they? The most unflattering article of clothing on the planet.

It was the summertime that the boy noticed a connection.

Tally.

Armpits.

Onions.

Garlic.

Heat.

Seventies polyester.

The connection was finally made one day when the boy was wandering around the most magical store within a fifty-mile radius. KINGS!

Kings was in town. Not the little place he grew up in. It was town! A mysterious drive he always thought, to town. Too far to walk. There were ten thousand people living "in town." There were only two hundred and forty people living in his little hamlet. Town was a mecca. Magic everywhere!

Kings sold many magical things:

Toys.

Bikes.

Candy.

Clothing.

Rubber balls.

Jacks.

Marbles.

Candy.

Candy.

(Oh my.)

Most of the items the boy was interested in were to be found in the basement of Kings. The wonderful Kings! The basement was where the boy could be found any time a trip to town was warranted.

Upstairs at Kings were the adult items:

Women's clothing.

Men's clothing.

Cologne.

Perfume.

Bras.

Underwear.

Blah, blah, blah

The basement was the place to be. It was on one of these visits in the summertime to this very store that the mystery of the smell of Tally was discovered. He was walking up and down the aisles upstairs. His mother told him not to go downstairs. They did not have time, she said. She was looking for something the boy was disinterested in. He wandered off, as was his nature. As he passed the perfume section, he stopped dead in his tracks. A smell caught his attention right where he stopped. The smell was:

Hot.

Garlicy.

Oniony.

Suffocating.

It was Tally! The boy smelled Tally. He looked to and fro, high and low. Tally was not in the store. He rummaged through the perfume bottles in front of him for the source of the smell. He was practically a Hardy boy. Truth be told, he much preferred Nancy Drew, but that was a bit of a digression. He knew he was on the verge of discovery. A bottle of something called "Taboo" was forcing itself on the boy. He picked the bottle up and placed the top under his nose and took a good whiff. The boy was sure he was about to have a cerebral vascular accident upon smelling the vile poison inside. He had an immediate rush of understanding. Tally was wearing "TABOO." Helen Keller, what a moment it was! All the women in the free world the boy had assumed had armpit trouble or menses odoriferous were spritzing themselves with "TABOO." could you just die? All was forgotten with a bit of "TABOO," and forgiven, apparently.

All those moments the boy had tried to put a finger on the odor. The mystery of Tally. (Though, in truth, the boy would not put a finger on it now without a moist towelette.)

It was that moment in Kings the boy decided it simply was the right women making the wrong choice. It was the seventies, after all.

After the boy regained a semblance of composure, he picked up a different bottle of liquid stink. The label said "ELSHA." When he inhaled the concoction, he was forced to lean against the metal shelving lest he have a myocardial infarction. It was the men's version of "TABOO." This day of discovery at the King's fine department store turned the boy's stomach.

These memories are very vivid for some unknown reason. The man, thinking of Tally from junior high as he sits on the white couch, gives him a small case of the giggles. And Kings! It has been a hundred years and several lifetimes ago it seems now.

The man is uncomfortable on the white couch. He is uncomfortable sitting in the dump. Period. That is how he refers to the apartment. "The dump." The couch is too short for the man. Short as in height from the floor. He recently purchased the couch to assuage his disgust in living in this tiny space. Each time the man rises from the couch, his body receives deep messages from his pain center in the brain. His lower extremities fight every thought of movement. It was either punishment or age or both. The white couch (as you, the reader, will learn in time) is also the source of some debaucherous activity. Activity that was recorded. Activity that has left the man with a sadness of sorts. Why and how did he allow it to happen? *(YOU, READER, SHALL SEE FOR YOURSELF. BE KIND TO THE OLD MAN AS YOU DISCOVER THE ACTIVITY THERE.)*

The man's knees hurt. His feet are now at such an inner nerve pain he can no longer accurately describe to others exactly what he is feeling. There seems to be no descriptive words left for him to use. Every day, every minute, every second, there is no reprieve from nerve pain. It is relentless. The pain is not even chased away with the drink. The man takes anti-inflammatory medication every four hours around the clock. The nerve pain is in his soul now. It sits patiently, awaiting a signal to flare.

Sitting on the white sofa, he takes off his second pair of shoes of the day. He must now take an extra pair to work with him every day so he can change them halfway through his shift. He knows not why but the nerve pain in his feet and legs is relieved for about twenty minutes when he does so. His work hours have had to be cut by close to half due to the pain. No choice.

The man is watching the Home and Garden channel as he stretches out on the white couch. There is a poorly done home renovation going on somewhere in the country. These TV programs require virtually no thought to watch. Just take off your shoes and feel no gravity on your soul.

As he rests, he cannot help but think about this delicate creature from another world. *What is it about this person that has me so moody? So intrigued,* he muses.

The man has always been cerebral. He thinks too much, worries too much. He often misses jokes because he is still wondering about "knock, knock" and all the possibilities a "knock, knock" could be, while the rest of the joke is being told. *Why can't he just let simple be simple?* he wonders. Simple is an illusion. Relative. Subjective. A Virgin Mary on a float.

The man is aware his thinking is not special. There are many who obsess about their troubles to a degree of insanity. Or incarceration. It is simply what chronic pain has done to his head. As a young boy, he was constantly at battle with his thoughts.

As the man sits in reverie of his youth, the storm that attempted to attack the whole of the valley moves on. The man looks upon with wonder from the window as the clouds move faster and faster toward a date the weatherman has chosen for another county.

(NOTE TO READER: HAVE YOU EVER REALLY LOOKED UP AT THE SKY JUST AS A STORM IS MOVING OUT? YOU SEE RAYS OF LIGHT FROM THE SUN AS IT PEEKS THROUGH THE CLOUDS. BEAMS OF DAPPLED LIGHT ARE SENT THROUGH THE ATMOSPHERE. AT TIMES, YOU ARE CONVINCED THE LIGHT IS REACHING OUT TO YOU FROM GOD OR WHOEVER OR WHATEVER, BUT DEFINITELY SOMETHING OMNIPOTENT.)

This is what the man is witnessing from his vantage point on the white couch. It is beautiful! Glorious! The sun is ablaze with color.

Blue clouds.

Black clouds.

Gray clouds.

Blue sky.

Black sky.

Stillness.

Beams.

Rays.

Peace.

The old man has a song on his brain. The storm has left him alone with these words tossing about in his head:

"How firm a foundation, ye saints of the lord, is laid for your faith in his excellent word!
What more can he say than to you he hath said, who unto the savior, for refuge have fled?

In every condition-in sickness, in health, in poverty's vale or abounding in wealth, at home or abroad, on the land or the sea—as thy days may demand, so thy succor shall be. Fear not I am with thee: oh, be not dismayed, for I am thy god and will still give thee aid. I'll strengthen thee, help thee, and cause thee to stand, upheld by my righteous omnipotent hand. When through the deep waters I call thee to go, the rivers of sorrow shall not thee overflow, for I will be with thee, thy troubles to bless, and sanctify to thee thy deepest distress. When through fiery trials thy pathway shall lie, my grace, al sufficient, shall be thee supply. The flame shall not hurt thee; I only design thy dross to consume and thy gold to refine. Even down to old age, all my people shall prove my sovereign, eternal, unchangeable love; and then, when gray hair shall thy temples adorn, like lambs shall they still in my bosom be borne. The soul that on Jesus hath leaned for repose I will not, I cannot, desert to his foes; that soul, though all hell should endeavor to shake, I'll never, no never, no never forsake!"

WELL, THAT WAS A SPEW, WAS IT NOT? READER? PRETTY HEAVY STUFF.

The boy inside the man was fascinated with these words as a young child. He waited and waited, but the promise of the words never found the way to him. It was lost, just as he was.

The man continues to be moved and inspired by the promise of his young naivety. He knows, however, that the promise was broken over forty years ago, and not by him. It's about to get real.

PERHAPS IT IS TIME FOR A BREAK, DEAR READER. SOME TEA, MAYBE? IT IS ALL A BIT HEAVY AT THE MOMENT. WE SHALL CONTINUE THIS JOURNEY SHORTLY,

The man leans back on the white couch. Back to the reality outside his head. Something snaps him out of his thoughts. A car, or a tenant below, perhaps. He looks once again at that beautiful face. Even as the evening comes to a close, it is that face he envisions as he crawls into his California king.

The morning has arrived, as it has for millenniums. The man has made it to work, although he is brain fogged due to the obsession of the recent text and that damn face that haunts him so.

As he eventually drifted off to sleep last night it was that face that lulled him off to dreamland. *This person is a ghost,* the man has concluded, *sending random texts to me.* Sending a photo. There never is a text response. It is becoming more than a bit of an obsession, he is beginning to realize. This tormented ethereal creature. The green eyes. The dark circles. There is a promise of hope in the whites of the eyes, somehow. The face has no age. It may belong to a fifty-year-old or a twenty-year-old. He cannot determine if he is looking at a male or female. That drives him to distraction.

For reasons unknown to the man, he becomes teary-eyed looking upon this face. The person in the photo looks sad, yet there is a scandalized corner to the mouth. The lips are perfect by any standard. Full and symmetrical. The man can almost see the amount of blood coursing through the folds. *They are Tarragona,* he thinks. The color that occurs naturally but is artificial looking. The neck is slight and long, giving the figure an air of ease and grace. The man is fascinated with every inch of the image.

Another uneventful workday has ended. Half the day is spent daydreaming, the other spent daydreaming. On the drive home to his apartment, the man has the image of whomever open on his phone sitting on the passenger seat.

(Note to reader: I feel it necessary to say at this point you may find a misspelled word or two in this scribe. Chances are in your favor that you will. Please understand, this is a story of truth. Much is inspired by the beautiful country of Spain and North America. There are many memories here for you to read. Some of these may be difficult to read due to the content. For that, I am sorry, reader, if you find yourself uncomfortable. Simply skip over certain moments, if you must. However, these are my truths. There are no lies nor false memories. Even now, as I write to you, dear reader, I can see some of the material is very difficult, particularly for me in my memory.

You will read about explicit sexual encounters between men. If you have a sensitivity to such encounters which, by the way, are natural and surely God-given, then you shall miss an interesting tale.

As was mentioned to you earlier, you will have an opportunity to listen to music as you progress through the work. Some of the music will be explained as it happens. Some of the music may be suggested simply because it is amazing and happens to be on the playlist of the old man in this story. The suggested music is nothing more than great music there for you to have a break from your day, from your head, and from your everyday life. Just listen. Sit back, place the earbuds in your ears, and turn the volume up to its best sound for your ears. Get coffee, tea, water, or a cocktail perhaps. You choose. Then just listen!

Here is the first suggestion in music, dear reader, for you to download. Simply because it will make you smile. If this song does not make you smile, well, just smile. Close the pages of this book and lighten your heart.)

> **Music Download:**
> **"Oh, Heavenly Day"**
> **Patty Griffin**

Chapter Seven

Madrid, Spain; Centro City

The old man walks along a cobblestone alley. Just wide enough for his shoulders to pass through. There are storefronts lining both sides of the narrow street. It really is not a street by today's standards. Probably no later than the 1900s. It is very small, this street. The doorways for every shop meet the man's chin level. There are hitching posts still intact every fifteen yards or so.

As he moves up along this marvelous street, he sees the daylight is diffused due to the closeness of the architecture. There are gas lamps lit; a soft yellow hue is his guide along the way. The man is convinced he could find a shop on this street to purchase a wand. Certainly, there is magic around every corner here. Anyone with their eyes open could see it.

Just ahead, the man notices what he assumes to be a father and son. The boy looks to be about ten. The two are bound for something as evidenced by their brisk walk. The father has his hand placed gently on the child's shoulder as they walk. The old man is moved by the tenderness the father shows his child.

The old man himself has an enormous father. Six foot, six inches tall and well-proportioned from stem to stern, as is said. "Flora and Fauna" is much funnier off the tongue to say, reader, however, nothing to do with his father. His father is a stern and uncommunicative man.

The old man often thought, as a young boy, that his father did not care for him.

A memory floods the man's head as he is resting his burning feet in this little alley in Spain. The father and son have just left his line of vision. He is alone here with memories of things said to him as a child. For an unknown reason, the memories are very unpleasant. Memories that accompany a guilt that cannot be extinguished. To this day, the man understands guilt but little. How is it that the parent's choices and attempts at ignorant childrearing can carry with it such eternal power?

As the man stretches his swollen feet and legs, thinking he really should let these thoughts go. He simply cannot. All these years later, as a grown man, he understands the actions of his parents as more puzzling than a Rubik's Cube.

It is said and read and heard many times that parents do the best they can. That they have no guide or rulebook. As the rain begins to fall cold and hard on the man in this alleyway, he acknowledges his own prior thoughts on the matter. "It all sounds like bullshit to me." He has never bought the story of any parent attempting to validate what they understand later in life, when their children are adults, to be merely an excuse for, "Sorry, children, I messed you up forever, but I did the best I could."

The man's thoughts on the matter are a bit irritable, as you can tell, reader. It is cold. It is now raining very hard. The rain in Spain does not stay mainly on the plains, as he can testify. Standing under the only dormer the man can find, he hears a lonely guitar coming from his earbuds.

MUSIC DOWNLOAD

"LA GUITARRA"
B-TRIBE
SPIRITUAL SPIRITUAL ALBUM

The man is among thousands of Spaniards as he wanders aimlessly around the city of Madrid. There is beauty in everything he sees. Everyone is wearing dark, or black clothing. Scarves are tied up snugly under their chins. Most of these people have on gloves. It is quite cold here today. It is noon and the crowd around him is beginning to swell at a surprising pace. There were a mere hundred people fifteen minutes ago. Now there are five or six hundred milling about. Shopping, lunching, going about their day.

The man has walked as far as he can; he must rest his feet again. The cobbles, though smooth from thousands of years of foot traffic, are uneven. It intensifies his pain. He stretches them out, and attempts to massage them a bit. It never really helps for more than five minutes. The man walks off kilter because of his foot pain. Walking this way causes his hips to hurt. Indeed, from behind he assumes he must look like an eighty-year-old man. He is a bit embarrassed when all around him are beautiful and seemingly healthy people. A single salty tear reaches his mouth. He feels a quiver in his lower lip. His breath is stolen directly from his person. Somewhat like an asthmatic might feel during an attack of public un-breathing.

Narrow Alley

Chapter Eight

Back to December! Back to the first six months!

Face.

Green eyes.

Ghost.

It is early evening. It has been two days since the first message was received. He is bored. He is searching for anything to occupy his brain in the small apartment other than watching the television. The man does not enjoy watching television. The only time he can really concentrate on any chosen program is when his life is in order; when his work is running smoothly and his apartment is clean. Well, at least when the toilet is clean.

"Holy hell, I must get out of this apartment right now," the man says out loud. The bookstore, the gym, anywhere will do but here.

He is in his closet, (no chuckling at the pun, reader) changing his shoes when he hears his phone chime from the bedroom. There is an immediate tingle in his back teeth that moves through his entire body. Not surprising, he is no longer bored. He intuitively knows the message is from the same individual who has held him captive for two days. He picks up his phone and heads to the white couch. As he looks out the window, it is crystal clear outside. Everything is tinted with a soft, early winter glow after the storm. He feels as if he is looking through a viewfinder. All the trees, houses, and cars, everything looks backlit. It is surreal.

The phone is hot in his hand. He realizes he has a death grip on it as he sits down to get comfortable. His phone informs him he has received a new message. As he opens it, he feels like it is Christmas morning and he is about to open the "BIG GIFT" that he asked for when he was a young boy. The message contains the same picture as before, however, there is a second message after the picture. It is a greeting and a name with it. The man's brow furrows as he reads it. "It couldn't be," he says aloud. It is a common enough name, but he was expecting something more…exotic? A name that matched the face. Like perhaps Sojourn or Mejia. He expected a name he had never heard before.

Edward!

How are you? I'm Edward.

This is the message. *Why the name Edward?* he wonders *Edward, really?* The man is a bit miffed. Who names their child Edward? *No, it must be pronounced with several 'rrrrrr's' off the tongue,* the man thinks.

The man waits for more messages to come. There are none. The man gets in his car and drives nowhere in particular. He is hoping for much more conversation with this *Edward,* but after an hour with no communication, the man needs to get out of the dump. He figures Edward will text him eventually. Clearly there is something building up here. The man will wait.

Chapter Nine

After a long, restless night and a long workday hoping for messages that have yet to arrive, the man is now standing at the bottom of the three flights of stairs that lead to his door, looking upward. These stairs inevitably will lead to pain in his extremities, as well as pain in the brain when he reaches his door. A silent prayer is performed and he is off. He has learned he must not stop at any point. *Keep your head up and your denial low and get the fuck to your door, old man.* This has become his mantra.

Once at the apartment door, the man thanks the gods of cartilage and reaches for his key. Holy hell. The apartment key, once again, is in his left pocket. He has in his left hand and arm at this very moment mail, grocery bags, and his work crap he halfheartedly decided he would attempt to complete at home. He is also carrying a package wrapped in brown paper and tied up with strings.

(Note to reader: Who among you can resist "brown paper packages tied up with strings"? Certainly not the old man!)

The man is right-handed. It is impossible to retrieve the key from his left pocket with his right hand. The key, the magic oddity that will allow him entrance to his own curried hole.

He is thoroughly irritated. He must put all his items on the stoop so he can access his left pocket. "Fuck," he says out loud. He thinks it is just a typical lack of proper thought delivered to such a simple action that can set him off. Ugh!

The smell of onions and garlic is so pungent as he enters his hole that he stops in his tracks for a millisecond. He throws up a little in the back of his throat. Gag reflex. He has not eaten his evening meal and already needs a Prevacid just from the wafting pontiferous odor oozing from the apartment below.

The gag reflex is not unfamiliar to the man. He recalls the reason now. Cocaine. Many years of cocaine and alcohol abuse. That was many years ago, however, like oxygen to a fire, there never was one without the other.

As the man is putting away his groceries, he hears that chime from his cell phone. There is an immediate reaction to the sound reader, a grin; yes, cheesy as it may be, the man is smiling from ear to ear.

It is half past four in the early evening and dark outside in North America. Another winter night ahead.

He has not yet turned on the house lights. The tiny dump is depressing enough. In the dark it is practically a suicide in the making. Lights on, check. Food cooking now, check. The apartment is aired out and the smell of India is pushed back as far as India will allow.

Now, on to far more important matters. The message that awaits his reading! Where is the cell? He has checked his pockets thirty times at least as he wanders the apartment in search of the portal to anywhere other than this apartment in this ugly month of December. The portal is, of course, his phone, and now it seems to agree with the old man and has vacated the dump. The phone is not in the garbage can. It is not in the fridge. Not in any of the cupboards. It must be in the car. That is the only option left. Wait, how could it be in the car? He heard the message chime inside the house. Holy Helen Keller. "I'm going to lose it," the man says.

"You little fucker." He sees his phone on top of the fridge. "Really?" He remembers leaving it there clearly.

The man takes a seat on the barstool near the fridge and powers up. There is another message on the dating app from Edward, he assumes. He hopes. Once opened, the message Edward sent to him last, was sent to him again, with his name. There was another message as well from Edward.

Edward: i from Colombia.

Colombia? What the hell? Colombia? The man is most confused by Edward's message. He says the word aloud, "Colombia." He then tries it again. Enunciating each syllable. "CO-LOM-B-AH." The man giggles at himself as he looks over his shoulder to ensure no one can see or hear him talking and giggling to himself. This is the last thing the man expected to hear. He has, in the last two days. imagined all kinds of possibilities about this person's identity. Colombia. *How in the world did Edward find me? Of all the people on the planet, me? An oversized, clumsy, overly emotional man from a simple, small farming town in North America.* He decides to respond to Edward and perhaps get an answer to that very question.

Man: hello. How are you?

The man has little time to regret or to be nervous. There is an immediate response.

Edward: I fine

The man is trying to keep up conversation.

Man: what's up?

He supposes this is the next logical thing to say using the lingo of computer conversation. He has never asked anyone before in a text "What's up?" It looks silly written. However, this is what he sent.

Edward: no ting

The man giggles aloud. "No ting." He is not sure if the word is simply misspelled or a grammatical issue.

Edward: how jou?

The man's first instinct was to type back, "I good," just to be a smartass. However, he refrained which is odd for the man.

Chapter Ten

The sun! El sol.

El sol plaza.

Spain.

Madrid.

Rain.

Day after day.

Cold.

There is a feeling here, in Spain, the man most certainly did not anticipate. The architecture is burnt. The rooftops are ablaze even in the cold rain of April. The clouds above the man's head as he wanders the city seem to move faster than any where he has seen before. Changing shape, telling a new story every few minutes as if confused of conviction. These clouds somehow add to the man's moodiness.

The man can see his reflection in the windows as he walks by. The image he sees is not what others seem to see. He is very tall. Some say he is handsome. He would not agree. Though his perceived attitude may suggest otherwise. When the man looks too deeply into his eyes, he feels shame. Even at his age now. The person looking back at him is a child, the child he used to be. The man cannot see backward nor forward. For reasons unknown to the man, as he observes the city of Madrid, he will relive his past.

His mind is occupied with thoughts of self. Wondering, as he walks among the race of Spaniards, if they think the same as he. He will never know in supposition.

The man's feet are on fire as if he were a fiddler on the roof. They will not still.

Gilt.

Bronze.

Warrior.

Edward.

Feet.

Knees.

Burn.

Dance on the ridgepole.

Chapter Eleven

The hot tin roof for the man, as he was a boy, was a refuge for him. It was just that, a hot tin roof. The roof was attached to the shop the boy's father used for his workshop. It sat some thirty feet in front of and just to the north of the family home. The front of the shop sat perpendicular to the main road that meandered from town to town along the west side of the valley. The road hugged the foothills along its journey for many miles. This was the only road in this lonely little place. One in, one out.

The winters here were brutal. The town did not have a snow removal system due to its small size and the unaffordability of the proposition. There were many winters in the bitterness of the months of January and February, where the road was completely iced over. It became the nearest ice-skating rink for the boy. Wearing ice skates, a size too big, and older than the back of your head, he skated up and down the middle of the road. Past the high school, then the church, circle round and back home again as fast as he dared to go. On these occasions there was nary a car to be seen coming toward or behind him. Any moving vehicle would now be found in the burrow pit. Not moving anymore.

The shop of his father was huge to him as a boy. It was of whitewashed cinder block construction. It was very high. The roof seemed to touch the sky. The boy thought of it as an oasis that was his alone. Many of the windows were broken which was cumbersome in the coldest winter and hottest summer months. The boy often thought of suggesting to his father that if he were to put some kind of wooden box together and attach it to the outside of the window ledge, he could put flowers in it. He never did dare make that suggestion to his father for fear it would only confirm what he already thought about his son. There was one solitary window on the back wall of the shop. It was very small and required a ladder on the outside wall to see inside the shop. The odd sized window always gave the boy pause. He could not grasp why it was so small and placed where it was. It gave the boy the creeps when he looked at the window. Something untoward occurred at or near that window; the boy always knew but never spoke of it to anyone.

There sat an orange trailer proudly on blocks just beyond the creepy window. The trailer was a mystery to the boy. It sat defunct in every way. Where it came from had never been clear to him. Inside the trailer there was nothing but smashed in cupboards. Stained stove top. A queen-sized bed. The boy could see unpleasant activity on the bed, so he rarely entered the trailer.

On the north side of the trailer, connected to the shop, was the café. (Yes, reader, I said café.) There was, at some point in history, a wooden sort of cabin styled café built onto the north side of the shop. The café, the shop, and the house were all built long before the boy and his family took residence there. The café was thus called for no other reason other than his parents called it that upon moving into the property. It had always been "the café."

At some point in time, the café must have been operative. The front of the café faced the road just as the shop did. The walls were covered in a beautiful tongue and groove knotty pine. There were two large windows at the front facing the road. Surely not coincidental. The boy always wondered which came first. The house, the shop, or the café?

The café was also large. It was about the same width as the shop, but it was longer at the back by another twenty feet or so. Both the shop and the café were sealed together, although there was no passage from one to the other. The café seemed a magical place to the boy. He could hear the chatter of folks eating there. Many diners there must have been on their way farther north and stopped in for a chicken fried steak with mashed potatoes and milk gravy. A biscuit certainly, cream peas, definitely, and then a slice of sour cream pie, and coffee to finish. There must have been "regulars" as well. Farmers mostly, "shooting the bull," as it was called in that little, sad town in North America. (Reader, "shooting the bull," if you don't already know, means taking a break from your very long day of farming, and then you sit and bullshit/gossip about anything and everything with any willing participant until your very own cows come to get you with swollen udders begging for a pull.)

The boy imagined the café as sort of an inn like the one in the movie *White Christmas*. The time period was not clear in the boy's head. He imagined a singer there in the evenings, her hair was pinned up on both sides. She did not share her personal life with any of the patrons. Only the cook knew who she really was. This was a gig that would allow her to feed her children.

"Somewhere Over the Rainbow," she softly crooned. "Fever" was the next selection. Then she was on to "It Might as Well Be Spring," rounding off the evening with "Dream a Little Dream of Me."

The boy could visualize her every move. Her every note. Even the clothes she wore was a creation of the boy's imagination. He giggled as he watched her perform in his head.

The crowds had left the café. There were no songs left to sing here. There was no equipment, no tables, no chairs. There were no checkered curtains with yellow stained sheers underneath. There was only rubbish strewn about the floor. The floor was not even a floor anymore. There were holes, gapes, and fissures that must be navigated as one moved about the haunted place. The walls in many areas of the café were still intact. They were beautifully crafted, panels of pine shellacked to a high gloss. The light that streamed in through the broken windows reflected off the varnish and caught the boy's imagination.

The boy played in the café daily at the age of ten. He was alone. Always. The café and inhabitants there, the woman and her torch songs, were his property. They came only to him. He was not aware that his behavior was less than normal. The people he saw there were his friends.

The boy's father worked in his shop next to the café. The boy was careful not to let his father hear him visiting the ghosts of the café. He did not want this imaginary marvelous place tainted by his father's words about him talking to no one. His friends there, the bubble he lived in, in this space always disappeared when anyone without the ability to see what was right before their eyes came inside.

His father was a very talented man. That was what the boy heard frequently. He was afraid of his father, so he did not recognize that he was given many of the same talents at birth. His father was a mechanic, an auto body fellow, and a painter of cars. These were the things he was doing when his child was next door talking to ghosts.

Inside his father's shop were rows and rows of paints and chemicals. Things most boys found fascinating the boy surmised. Most of the "stuff" bored him inside the shop of his father. The café, another matter entirely.

Then there was the roof, The rooftop of both buildings. The hot tin roofs, Both the shop and the café had a flat roof surrounded by a two-foot retaining wall of cinder block and tar. There was a slight incline from the café roof to the shop roof, but it was a simple maneuver. In truth, it was the roof that the boy loved most about these two buildings.

The old man cannot help but smile as he remembers himself as a young boy, hiding out on the roof. He had a wonderful vantage point from atop the white cinder wonder. From there, he could see the high school across the street. The junior high was in the same building as the high school. As the boy reached junior high, the roof became a regular haunt for him. He could see the school. He could see if Eddie were there.

The only way to get to the roof of the shop/café was by climbing the tree that grew alongside the café on the north side. A trash tree. A Chinese Elm, it was. The boy knew the tree well. The family did not own a ladder tall enough to reach the roof, so the tree, trash or not, became a trusted friend to him.

An irrigation ditch ran directly on the north side of the tree. There was no available space between the café wall and the tree, and no available space between the tree and the ditch that ran full and fast all summer long, bringing with it lifesaving water to crops farther east from the shop and café.

Getting to the tree was difficult when the water gate was open at full turn. The boy knew the sound of the rushing water was far more frightening than the depth of the water.

The old man giggles at the thoughts he had when he was a boy. This was one of those moments in his childhood where he knew the truth of the ditch and was not scared of it.

The ditch was two feet deep. Just to the boy's knees. A fact he knew because he fell into the ditch once and the water, though fast, only reached his knees. His imagination told him the water was above his head. The sound of the water was just a red herring. *Ha! No fear here,* the boy thought as he smiled at the truth.

He was alone as usual. As he preferred. He carried with him, in his left hand, his bag of magic. What was inside the bag was not for others to know. (Sorry, reader.) The bag was made of raggedy old carpet or tapestry. The bag once carried very important musical compositions for the piano, cello, and violin. That was what the boy chose to think. This magic bag once held magic music now held the magic of the boy's childhood. Things that soothed him. His very own secrets. Secrets that were touchable and not hiding in his head.

I will tell you, reader, one or two items in the child's bag, simply because it is too delicious not to share a secret or two of this kind. One item in the bag was, of course, glitter. The boy could not pass on glitter. Ever! (Unless it was multicolored. It clearly had to be monochromatic to make it into this bag.) Another item was glue, of course. Plain, old, white glue. However, the lid of the glue had to be special. The tip must be made of rubber and be mitered at a forty-five-degree angle for this little mister. This allowed the unguent the best opportunity to perform. It was an entirely satisfactory day when glue was used.

There were other things in the bag, many things. The old man has not taken the liberty of telling anyone what they are. They are the boy's secrets. The two of them share them together. They are joined in deoxyribonucleic acid. Joined in memory. Joined in joy and in pain.

The old man speaks to his younger self occasionally. It is usually to warn him of an impending danger, or to comfort him. The boy is never comforted. He seems to be locked on a roof. Sometimes the man needs to walk with the boy. The boy does not like to be walked with. The man gives him his space.

The boy was up on the roof, safe, for now. It was hot. The portion of the roof above his father's shop was flat and covered in corrugated tin. The roof retained the summer heat and could burn much the same way of a frying pan when touched too soon after moving it from the burner.

The boy always wore his gym shoes on the roof. There were small sections of roof where someone at some time had patched holes with black tar. It certainly was not done in the years the boy lived there. Money was not available for nonsense roof repair. The tar was soft and malleable in the summer sun. The boy pulled a wad off and moved it back and forth between his thumb and index finger. He found an unexplainable satisfaction as he squeezed it like the white bread his mother bought when she did not have the time or desire to make her own. It was always best when wadded up into a ball before tossing it at your uvula.

He put the wad of tar in his mouth and gnawed on it for a very long time. It did not break down in his mouth. The tar had the consistency of gum. It didn't taste like gum, however. It tasted somehow like earth.

The boy loved to lick the sidewalks just after a heavy rain in the summer. At any time when it began to rain, his back teeth felt a longing for it.

(NOW, READER, YOU MAY FIND THESE LAST FEW INSIGHTS INTO THE BOY A BIT PECULIAR. JUST KNOW THERE REALLY WAS NOT MUCH THAT ENTERTAINED HIM IN THE SMALL TOWN.)

The old man still feels an urge in his back teeth when it rains. Although the teeth at the back of the man's mouth are not his own. True, he has paid for them, or is currently paying for them each month when the bill arrives. However, there is no root attached to these teeth by way of information, reader, yet he continues to have a longing, an ache, for the sidewalks when it rains.

The boy chewed his tar as he opened his bag. He was continually watching out for the school bully across the street at the high school. It was not a school day. There was no reason the bully should be at the school. The boy was terrified of him. Perhaps the thought of this bully infiltrating this personal part of his life, the roof, the summer, was what had him hypersensitive to his presence.

It was not long ago, in fact, at the end of the last school year, that Eddie removed the fire extinguisher from its rightful place on the wall in the high school hallway and beat the boy about his head, knocking him unconscious. The kafuffle occurred because Eddie called the boy a fag one too many times. Eddie hunted the boy. He waited outside of classrooms he knew the boy was in. Eddie was three years ahead of the boy in class, yet he seemed to find some perverse pleasure in teasing and taunting a boy in junior high. On this occasion, the boy found the courage to say something to his tormentor. Eddie called him a fag; the boy called Eddie a prick. The boy woke up at some point on the floor of the hallway after he was knocked out by the fury of the redneck asshole's hand attached to a fire extinguisher. These were the kind of boys who would, and did, kill those they judged to be queer in the boy's day. He never spoke up for himself again.

The boy had no memory of the next several minutes. Neither does the old man. Shortly after the boy took consciousness back, he was instructed to go home. No questions were asked. Bullying, at that time, was looked upon as an event to make the weak feel stronger, or to look upon themselves and recognize what it was they couldn't see in themselves that the bully could. The bully was generally rewarded in this moronic place and time.

The boy crossed the only street in town and walked the short distance home to his mother. The boy pissed himself as he entered the side door that led directly to the kitchen. His mother was mad at him. He could sense it before one word was spoken from her lips. She sighed. He shut the door behind him as he peed himself again. She informed him she had been called by the school principal. She was expecting him home. She admonished the boy, asking him what he had done to provoke the other boy.

The boy could not speak. He stood there simply wanting a hug he knew was not coming. His mother told him she knew he used a dirty word.

(IT IS TRUE, READER; THE BOY CALLED HIS TORMENTOR OF SEVERAL YEARS A PRICK IN RESPONSE TO BEING CALLED A FAG.)

Endure.

Insecure.

Skinny.

Smart.

Abused.

Unvalidated.

Mute.

Dirty.

Lost.

Alone.

The boy's mother asked him what word he said to the bully. What did he call him?

The boy peed again.

He couldn't speak.

His mother said the word out loud, "Prick." His mother was very mad at him.

The boy did not understand his mother's reaction. He decided he deserved to be beaten unconscious. The boy took what his mother gave him by way of verbal punishment with a low head. He left the room as soon as he felt it was safe to do so.

The old man tells the boy to walk on. *Go hide. Go to your roof. Go alone. Find your magic bag.*

The boy left by the kitchen door. The door that led to the chicken coop. There were no visitors today, so the boy had no fear of touch. The boy did not understand his mother. The old man does not understand her either.

The boy had a sister of whom he had always been afraid. She was three years older. There was no need to mention her anywhere in this scribe other than here and now.

The boy's sister heard about this bullying incident from someone outside the family. She was not living at home at the time. She had moved on to bigger things; to find her dreams and to explore young adulthood. She happened to be at home for a holiday break when the "shit" went down. She was vividly livid at the news. She marched herself across the street to the high school on the next school day on a hot afternoon. She ascertained from the office exactly where this Eddie was to be found right that very second.

"Well, little missy, I believe Mr. Frickelmeyer is in Mr. Abbot's class studying geography at the moment," the office clerk said as she retrieved a number two pencil from her set in order to log in the foreigner from across the street.

The boy's sister wasted no time. She confidently marched down the hallway to Mr. Abbot's geography class. It was in session. She opened the classroom door without saying a single word. Once at Eddie's desk, she lifted him from his seat by the back of his head. She calmly whispered in his right ear, "Walk out of the classroom into the hallway, now." The moment Eddie's topsider crossed the threshold, she proceeded to beat the shit out of him.

Now, reader, you must remember this was a very small town indeed. Eddie Frickelmeyer knew exactly who was relieving him of his pride, as did all the jowls that were dropped and watching the brutal penance happening in the hallway of Mountain Side High School at that moment.

As she was finishing her tutorial to Eddie, she made a comment in his left ear. The right ear was a bit bloodied from her newly manicured fingernails done not two days prior. "If you so much as even look at my brother again, you will be killed." Verbatim!

The boy did not witness his sister taking care of familial business in the hall that hot afternoon. She did not ever mention it to him. The story was told to him by many other students who had witnessed it. As legends often are.

North American Winter

Chapter Twelve

The man is absentmindedly putting his groceries away once again. It seems that is all the man does lately. Work, eat, buy groceries so he can eat again. He puts the ice cream in the fridge and the heavy cream in the freezer. Neither placement will prove effective. The man has other things on his mind. It has been a few days and the man cannot seem to stop thinking about Edward from Colombia. He has no clue as to whether Edward is a good guy or a total ass. There is something happening to the man, something of which he is not in control. His emotions. It is a very uncomfortable feeling at his age. He is used to being in control of most things in his life. Or so he thinks. The daydreams of meeting Edward, of marrying a South American in South America tumbles about his brain on the delicate cycle. He has never been married. He has never wanted to be married. These thoughts of marriage and long-term love affairs are new to him. They are quite intimidating, but also very intriguing. What would he wear to his own wedding? Where would the ceremony take place? He will need an interpreter, of course. *Holy hell,* he thinks, *what am I doing? I am thinking like a schoolgirl with a first crush.* The man can feel the blood rush to his face as he clears some of the fog from his brain.

Should anyone be looking at him at this very moment, they would see a smile beginning at one lobe and traveling to the other.

His phone vibrates in his pocket as if on cue with his thoughts. It is Edward, he has no doubt. Looking at the screen, the message is not what he expected.

Edward: so horny!

The man practically coughs up a lung. This is the last thing he expects to read from Edward.

Edward: I send a picture for yew 🐙

The man looks at the photo Edward has just sent. Holy hell! The Latino is naked. He is erect. He is holding his erection with one of his hands, the other is resting on his hip. Edward is standing in what appears to be a bathroom. The loo is rather large from what the man can tell. The room is tiled with a grass green color that appears to be wall to wall.

Edward's body is completely shaved. No armpit hair, no pubic, no leg, no butt hair, and no facial hair other than brows and lashes. Edward is staring straight at the camera. He is not smiling. The look on his face is a look all men get while engaged in sexual activity. The black circles around his eyes seem to be more obvious in this photo. He looks as if he has not slept well. His skin is a translucent white, and he looks very skinny.

(I WILL SAY IT HERE AND GET IT OVER WITH, SINCE YOU MAY BE WONDERING, READER. HIS ERECT PENIS IS HUGE. I WILL NOT MENTION THAT AGAIN. HE IS UNCIRCUMCISED. DID I MENTION HUGE? SORRY. I APPARENTLY LIED ABOUT NOT MENTIONING IT AGAIN.)

Edward is also gifted with the stereotypical "Latino butt." It is very large and very round and rests high in the air. His body looks androgynous in the photo. However, there is little question about his manhood. No pun intended there.

The man is terribly aroused. He stares at the photo for, how long? He does not know or care. He has never been attracted to shaved men. He has never been turned on by uncircumcised men either. He always saw a carrot, not a penis. Grooming and trimming are a must to get the maximum benefit from a man, but a complete body shave? Never. Somehow, on Edward, it makes him look more vulnerable. A bit sadder. These adjectives endear him to the man even more.

The man has not a frickin clue what to say back to Edward. *Should I tell Edward what kind of thoughts I am having about him? No, not yet. It is too early on in this…thing.*

His phone chimes again.

Edward: he is horny

As the man reads the text, it doesn't fit; it is out of context. He cannot tell what the issue is.

Edward: I like

Okay, clearly Edward is using broken English. The man is hesitant to reply. He does not want to make Edward feel ignorant, yet he wants to know what Edward is trying to say to him. "Screw it." The man decides to respond without changing his grammar.

Man: the photo is very sexy Edward. You have made me erect. I think you are beautiful. Where are you now?

Edward: I at my grandmother's house. In bathroom

Man: no, I mean, you said you were from Colombia. Is that correct?

Edward: I am in Colombia. I am Colombian.

The man is a bit confused about it all. Edward is in South America. He is in North America. *How did my profile cross his path?* The man is quite intrigued by it. He giggles softly to himself.

Man: how did you find me? And why?

Edward: I use search engine and filter To see what I like. You picture came up

Search engines? Filters? The man is truly lost now.

Man: I am sorry. I still do not understand. I am afraid I am not very good with phone Apps. or computers. I really have no interest in it so I have never learned.

Edward: ja ja ja no problem.

Edward: I like big and tall guy

The man's skin on his back begins to act up. It's cold and clammy. It has been a long time since he was interested in talking with someone. Interested in getting to know them. He does not visit with anyone on this site nor has he been on it for some time. The last time he opened the app, he was looking for some intimacy. Okay, he was looking for sex. However, he always felt old and awkward talking to others on the site. When he logged in the last time, there were many younger guys looking for "daddies" as he remembers. That is what most of the men called him. It made him a bit uncomfortable, so he did not open the app much. The man placed his profile on the site himself. He is sure many of the other profiles are false. People hiding their true selves is easy and give some a feeling of euphoria. These men can say whatever they want, be whomever they want without consequence. Edward must have liked what he saw.

The man plays around with the filter himself and can now see how Edward found him. Mystery solved. It really is very flattering.

Man: what do you do in Colombia Edward? If you do not mind me asking.

Edward: I am in Colombia at my fathers House. Is holiday vacation for me.

Man: where do you live in Colombia?

Edward: I live in Spain. I visit Colombia.

Man: Spain, that is nice. Did you grow Up in Colombia?

Edward: jes I grow up in Medellin Colombia I move to Spain after graduation in Colombia. I receive college degree in Journalism.

Man: that is impressive. Is your family all living in Colombia?

Edward: jess, my father and his wife, my stepmother and a little half-brother is living here wit me?

Man: oh, I see. Is your biological mother still alive? I am sorry Edward if this is too personal. I would like to get to know you.

Edward: is no problem my sexy. My mother she live in Mexico City. She divorces my dad long time.

Man: do you look like your mother or your father more?

The man has no idea what to say to Edward. The man knows nothing of Colombia other than the drug trafficking.

Edward: I look like my mother more than father

Man: may I see a pic of them? I am curious to see who made this beautiful man named Edward.

Edward: of course. All for jou

The man receives a pic of a woman in her twenties. She has long, black, wavy hair. The picture is very low quality. The image is unremarkable in any way. She resembles Edward very little.

Edward also sends a pic of his father and current wife. The woman in the photo looks to be thirty years younger than the man, Edward's father, the man assumes. There is a young boy of maybe ten or eleven in the photo, and standing next to the young boy is Edward. It looks very recent. Edward looks disinterested in the photo.

Man: your father is handsome. He and I Look about the same age. That is a terrifying thought for me.

Edward: ja ja My father is fifty.

There are many things one could say about this admission. The man is mortified, honestly. Edwards's father and he are the same age. The man feels a bit sick. He knows Edward is very young, but he is nonetheless very forward and very sexual with his attitude toward the old man. The man chose not to see the gap in age. Until now.

Edward: if my dad look like jou i would, I can't say it.

Man: say what? Tell me?

Edward: it's a sin

Man: what is?

Edward: I would go to hell if you were my Dad because what I want to do with jou.

The man knows it is time to turn back now or there will be trouble. The boy tells the man to run away. The man is already in too deep.

Man: what will you do this evening?

Edward: no ting no plans

Edward: what you do?

Man: I am going to go to the gym and then I need to go to the grocery store. I Would like to talk to you when I am Finished if you like.

Edward: I want my sexy

The man assumes the conversation is over since Edward does not send him another message. The man will finish his day as he usually does. Except for looking forward to talking with Edward later. He feels the need to exercise hard this evening. Harder than usual. The gods of wrinkles and crepe must be appeased so he will look and feel younger. There seems to be a reason now. The man smiles as he thinks, *Time will tell.*

He cannot concentrate. Edward is everywhere. The music on his playlist reminds him of Edward. The other Latinos with big butts who are also working out send him over the edge. Particularly when any one of them does a squat.

The man is having far too many naughty thoughts inside this testosterone infused man cave where he is lifting weights.

The market did not help clear his brain in the slightest either. He purchases enough food for a small country. Here and there, throwing in a Spanish item or two, he has no idea what they are. The man thought he would try some Spanish cooking. Holy hell!

Driving home from the market is a blur. The man is thinking about a vacation to Colombia. All the amazing things and people to see there. *Wait a minute, where is Colombia? Exactly? Is it a destination spot for many? Come to think of it, I cannot think of any reason to see Colombia. Other than Edward, obviously,* he muses. *Holy hell, get it together, old man. Concentrate on the task at hand! You do not even know the Colombian. There are a million reasons why nothing can come of this.*

He is mentally trying to clear his head of his daydreams. He is feeling a bit peckish he realizes as his stomach growls. A rather beautiful Indian child with topaz-colored eyes darts across the road as the man pulls into the apartment complex. Such beautiful people. Such lovely food. It just tends to linger everywhere. On white cotton couches especially.

The man has a dear friend who grew up in India. She is Tibetan. She tells a story of her people fleeing the Chinese regime years earlier. How the walk down the high slopes of the Himalayas must have been grueling for many of these immigrants fleeing their homeland only to find themselves in India. A beautiful, overpopulated, smelly, dirty, shack ridden land. Caste in every direction, other than yours. The Ganges! The river of life. Cattle wandering freely in and out of dwellings and markets leaving their fecal trail for the righteous to enjoy.

Wow, the man has just been to the mountains of Tibet and on to India in his head. He is hopeless, he has decided.

The man does have another tale to tell of this trek from the high plains of the Himalayas to the Indian lands made by a royal family of sorts he met in North America and became close to, however, that story will have to be told another time. That was long before Spain.

The man begins his ascent to the peak he must climb to reach the white couch. *What in the hell was I thinking? The third floor? The stairs are not even regular stairs.* There are seventeen steps at first. Rather steep! They must be taken sideways. One at a time, and slowly. He then reaches a landing just large enough for an Indian child to sell you curried lemonade. Then another seventeen stairs await. A bit steeper than the first set of stairs. At this point, the feet and the knees no longer cooperate with the man's brain. Another landing. This one is just large enough for the brother of the first Indian child selling lemonade to put up a display of his goods for sale. Two boxes of chicklets! The gum is placed in a beautiful and very colorful silk handkerchief. Most likely a present of his mother's. Given to her by her mother, who came from Dharamshala or rama-lama-ding-dong or such.

"No thank you," the man tells the child as he attempts to start his breathing again. "I've had new chicklets permanently screwed into my gums not more than a year ago." The man bares his teeth for the child to see. The young child has no clue what has just happened and runs away as fast as he can. The man cannot help but giggle as he continues this walk to plant his flag.

Finally, the door! Damn, his keys are in his left pocket again. He becomes irritated at his transparency. He simply is incapable of learning from his mistakes. There is always a hope that things will be different this time. The left hand and arm will naturally hold whatever he is carrying leaving his right hand, his dominant hand, free for anything. Is an autonomic move. His right hand reaches inside his right pocket where he expects the key to be so he can open his frickin door with ease. Never once in the man's life has that happened. He cannot reach into his left pocket with his right hand. The laws of this universe and this existence seem to have nothing to do with his wants. After several seconds of shifting items, the man retrieves his key from his left pocket and finds his way into his apartment.

It is the same space as usual. Somehow, when the man comes home, he expects to see the ones he sees at four in the morning. He does not see anyone. He can, however, feel they have been moving about; there are changes in the air, shifts really, here and there. More stale than fresh.

The man sets his food items down and immediately takes off his shoes. *Why has Edward not sent a message?* he wonders. There is something strange about that boy. The man is a bit perplexed. He cannot quite pinpoint his unease. At that very second, his phone chimes.

> Edward: I hungry

> Man: did you not eat dinner yet? What time is it in Colombia?

> Edward: it is 11:30 now

> Man: it is very late. Do you always eat this late?

> Edward: no eat. My father has no brought dinner home yet.

The man finds this an odd statement. Edward's father has not brought dinner home yet. Why doesn't Edward get himself something to eat? The man puts the thought inside a file in his brain and leaves it alone for now.

Man: when will he bring dinner?

Edward: I don't know. I hope soon.

Man: I would gladly make you dinner if I were there with you right now.

Edward: sexy man. I want.

Man: what do you like to eat? What is your favorite food?

Edward: pasta!

Well, thinks the man, spoken like a true homosexual! Of course, pasta!

Man: I love to cook. Right now, I would be making you a light meal of romaine lettuce, a miniscule amount of grated fresh garlic and a large amount of parmigiana topped off with a chicken breast and salt and cracked pepper. very light and very simple.

Edward: omg I want 🐙

Chapter Thirteen

The man is lying on his bed, unable to sleep. This is nothing new for him. He has had insomnia since early childhood. As he lies there, his feet do a continual dance. If he allows them to lie still, the pain is intolerable. There seems to be a battle between each foot for the most comfortable space under the sheets. Both feet are fully aware they are in charge of the man's every waking moment. Even in sleep, the battle between the right to be in charge often brings the man to consciousness.

The man's brain is simply not going to shut down tonight. There are so many things Edward said to him today that have him most curious. Why is Edward staying with his father? The man assumes it is because of circumstance as well as finances. Or the lack thereof. However, Edward is an adult, and yet he awaits his father's return for food. It almost seems to the man that Edward feels as though he should be served. Edward is starving and yet he will not take care of the matter on his own. Why does he not go out and get his own food? Why does he not cook a meal on his own accord? These are the questions racing through the man's head at breakneck speed as he lies atop his California king.

Edward also said he has a younger half-brother who is also in his father's house. Are they not social? Do they not spend time together shopping or calling on other family members? It is after all the holidays. Christmas is just around the corner. Over the river and through the woods. You know, reader, right? The man cannot help but think of his younger brother as he ponders Edward's relationship with his sibling.

The man's younger brother's name is Adam. A truer friend could not be found this side of the Mason Dixon. The man has many bittersweet memories of his brother. He was short in stature. He was a portly child. So cute. Adorable, really. Adam was born with huge tootsie brown eyes. Adam was incorrigible. He was a fibber. He was very smart. Being the youngest child of so many, he learned early on how to manipulate those around him to get what he needed. Mostly it was someone to play or giggle with. Someone to love and to be loved by. There were many athletes among his siblings. Most of them excelled at their chosen sport. Adam did not fit into any of those molds. The man has often thought that the two of them were peas in the proverbial pod.

It is true that the man was only fourteen months his senior and nearly two feet taller than Adam, and easily seventy pounds lighter, but the two boys were kindred from the beginning of their advent to life. There is a bond that cannot be broken with some people in life, reader, my hope is you have the opportunity in your life to know someone like Adam.

The two boys shared a bedroom for a great deal of their childhood. For nearly five of those formative years, they shared red and blue carpeted bunk beds their father made. They were marvelous, these bunks. The walls of their bedroom were also covered in the same carpet. Wall to wall, I kid you not, reader. Shag to boot! Could you just perish? The man remembers now that the carpet must have been remnants as he visualizes the patchwork. It was certainly unique, nonetheless.

The man has no idea if his brother knew of his troubles, or if he sensed he was different from him. The man as a child was afraid. Afraid of his own shadow, his brother Adam provided a much-needed comfort for him. A safe place. A beautiful place just for him. The two of them giggled at night until their bellies hurt. They talked about everything. Everything except girls. The boy knew nothing about girls, and his brother Adam was too young to care yet for them.

The winters were brutal in this small town. The summers could be hell. The family home did not have air conditioning and frequently did not have heat in the winter. The man's bedroom he shared with his brother as a child was on the second floor of a hundred-year-old farmhouse. There was zero airflow inside. Cracks and crevasses in most of the windows. Gaps in the panes that would make an orthodontist pass out.

During the harshest winter months, the two boys often shared the lower bunk together. To cuddle. To giggle. To stay warm. I believe I have mentioned to you before, reader, the family was not wealthy. The source of heat for this drafty old house was coal. There were many times it could not be purchased. Therefore, no heat. The house became frigid.

These winters in western North American could be unforgiving at that time. The snow would drift often to six feet or more. The boy's bedroom faced north which also happened to be the direction the wind blew in from in late winter with a vengeance. The boys often woke up from their spooning to see a snowdrift that nearly reached their second-floor bedroom window. They could not resist. First things first upon awakening, PEE! They opened the window and christened the bank with their names in pee. In cursive! Have you ever? It was divine not to have to walk all the way downstairs to use the only bathroom in the house. The house that slept eight to ten people. You would have had to put on your ice skates to get to the bathroom anyway, it was so frickin cold. The open window seemed much more sensible to the two boys.

The summers were just as hateful some years. Late summer in this house, particularly upstairs, had a smell to it. A hundred-year-old smell. The air upstairs in summer dared us to make it move. It was often as lazy as we were in those hot months of summer. If you knew where to look on the upstairs level, you could see creatures riding the dappled rays of light coming from the windows. Almost as if they were fighting for dominance along the light runway.

One of those late summer mornings, the two brothers awoke from their heat stupor called sleep. It was Sunday morning, the old man recollects, near eleven a.m. The two boys were home alone; which is odd, the man thinks now. *Where was everyone?* Church services were mandatory for all. The man's parents were very religious. *Pious, is a better word.* Indoctrinated. Pick one. Thinking upon this in adulthood, the man is clear these demands by his parents to pummel organized theological poison into their children's souls was not based on reality. At least not the boy's reality, nor the man's.

He was forced to go to church for three hours on Sunday. Tuesday evening, it was an hour and a half, and then frickin primary on Wednesday afternoons. Not to mention seminary, years later. The thing is, he was never given a choice. His father was not a safe presence in the man's youth. He knew his father was cheating on his mother. Often. The boy was afraid of his father. The boy felt shame when he was around him. The boy felt dirty. Not safe! His father was never abusive to him, but the boy witnessed what anyone of today's standards would call abuse toward his older brothers. The shame he felt was simply a reaction to his inability to be like his other brothers. Thinking back on it the man realizes, like his mother, his father was too young to raise children effectively without procuring life long consequences.

Sunday morning, with Adam, alone in the house. Just exactly whose idea it was to do what they did that Sunday is still a mystery to the man as an adult, as well as his brother in his adulthood.

A decision was made. The two brothers, of ten and eleven years young, dressed themselves in their mother's and sisters' clothing and became two old spinsters of the 1800s and decided it was time to saddle Karen, the sway-backed mare, and get themselves to the chapel.

The man cannot remember exactly which outfits they chose on that hot Sunday morning. It is very likely the man's choice of dress did not fit him. He was very tall, even as a child. His brother Adam, much shorter than he, probably looked stunning in his church garb. The high heels fit his feet, the man now remembers with a smile. They both tried to find "pioneer" looking dresses and a shawl. Oh, how they laughed while getting dressed. Deep, hard, belly laughs! Adams legs looked quite shapely when he put on his heels.

Off they trudged, two little leaguers in full drag, in a hundred-degree weather, to catch the sway back Karen. "Lord, help the mister, that comes between me and my sister." (You know that one, reader?) Adam could not walk in his heels. He very nearly broke his ankle several times. Which, of course, was hysterical. It was not long before these two young she-males were dripping with sweat, in their church clothes, to boot. They decided they could pull their dresses down to their waists while trying to lure the sway-backed mare into the stall to be saddled; any respectable pioneer woman would do the same.

They marched right past the place they pretended was not there with their head held high and their corsets down low.

Karen was finally lured to the gate with a promise of a nibble (which she did not get; they did not have a treat for Karen). The two boys also decided they would not saddle Karen. It was far too much work in the summer sun, so they just put on a bridle. Try as they did that morning, they were laughing so hard they could not get on top of her. The boy could clearly see his brother's weight was too much for the delicate gold heels he chose for church that day; by the way, the heel was bending forward and then backwards. Something was coming loose. It was not just the heels.

Karen was eventually mounted. The younger of the two sat in the front of his older brother. They both had a death grip on the bridle as they walked around the yard. One of them was speaking with a

British accent to enhance the character, while the other brother chose to employ an East Coast sort of Katherine Hepburn mock. The couple fell off their ride to the chapel more than once.

To this day, the man remembers that afternoon as possibly the hardest he has ever laughed. Who better to share it with than his brother Adam.

Chapter Fourteen

When the man was a young boy, he often wandered the foothills near his home. There were not many places that gave the boy respite from his head. The rooftop, as you now are familiar with, reader, was one, the other was the foothills that hugged the mountain range along the west side of this valley. The higher up you hiked, the more beautiful the view. The plant life also became more complex. The trees turn to the coniferous variety. The rocks turn to boulders and then to castles that jutted off the mountain side in every direction.

The boy preferred to play alone on the lower foothills. Among the deciduous trees and the brooks that babbled along as they spoke to him. The boy felt comfort there. He would never take another person with him. This was his secret alone. He enjoyed the freedom of self-expression the land offered him. There were no homes, no farms, just raw freedom. The boy rarely, if ever, saw another human being when he was exploring these hills. He was the only haunt for miles.

The man has always felt like a stranger around his family. Around all people, really. He remembers thinking this when he was very young—five, six years old. He felt displaced. He felt as if he had been loaned to this family. He never knew why.

Intuitively, the boy knew better than to ask anyone in his family if they felt the same way. Certainly, it was not a safe topic to bring up to a parent when one was very young. They would have been most concerned the child's elevator never really reached the top floor.

Like most everything in the boy's life, he hid in plain sight. He did not learn to speak his mind. Speaking your mind was dangerous territory in those days, if you were anything like the boy in this story.

A slow-moving darkness seeped its way into the boy. Much the same as the fog made its way through the little town in late February. In time, it numbed him. He became shy around adults, better described as very uncomfortable.

The boy walked the foothills when he became depressed. The energy inside the family home was often a bit stressed. He had knowledge from early on that his mother was in over her head. He could sense her stress in everything she did. He could also sense her joy in all that made her smile. She was a complex woman; a girl, really. She did marry at the age of fourteen. Nonetheless, she was complicated to the boy, making him feel on edge often. Near the age of six, the boy began to pee himself whenever she became angry. She had a habit of sighing when she was mad. A deep sigh signaled the boy's bladder to release its contents. If she called to him from another room in a tone he quickly recognized as anger, he'd peed his pants.

The man can now remember pissing himself at school as a child when his mother called on the principal or a teacher to discuss him. The worst of the peeing came when she reprimanded the boy, or hit him, or pulled his hair, or disciplined him in any way. It was those times when he would void his entire bladder on himself. It was hot on his legs. It smelled. The boy was mortified at his inability to hold his urine. He began taking an extra pair of pants and underwear and hid them in safe places so he could clean himself up after one of these occasions. He was very careful to choose clothing his mother would not notice if it went missing. A set was placed under a log in the hills. Another was placed up on the roof under a loose cinderblock. The last were placed in a hidden cupboard in the wall in the bedroom upstairs that was silent. These hidden securities helped him to feel some control. There were times when he had to sit with wet pants and underwear and cry on the inside and hide in sight inside his head.

The man has spent a great deal of time trying to figure out why this had happened. How it had happened. He never peed in his bed. Ever! Only in his clothes when his mother was angry. To this very day, the man has no clue.

There were many siblings in the home of the man and the boy of this story. Each child had a sibling very close in age; either just above or just under. The boy was the fifth born. There was always a cousin or two staying there as well, mostly through the summer months.

There were several years when the boy's parents decided to take in and foster Indian children (feather, not dot) as part of a church program designed to give the Lamanites a (chance) to escape the situation their own homelives on a reservation afforded them. Mostly abused socially, and possibly sexually, and most certainly being raised by alcoholic adults, these beautiful children became part of a history they had no clue about. Dictated by many and fostered in an air of insouciance. The trouble was the parents of the boy often could not feed their own. More of everything was required to house these Lamanites, and the resources simply were spread too thin as it was.

The boy paid them no attention. Not out of unkindness. They were older and not particularly interested in him either. The boy had the hills and the rooftop. That was all he needed. He often daydreamed about these escapes of his when he was stuck inside the family home for too long. There was too much noise when everyone was home at the same time. There was too much noise in the boy's head. Crowds only made him feel more insecure. He had a continual feeling everyone knew the secret he himself had yet to put together for one reason or another. At every opportunity, he would run away to the hills. Away from his family and their perceived ignorance.

One of his favorite things to do as he escaped and walked the mile or so to his hideout was to look for colored glass. Broken glass. Bits and pieces. Small enough for him to put in his magic bag. The only bits worth keeping, or worth entry to his bag, were the old ones worn around the edges from years of trample. Transparent. Translucent. Particularly pale blue. Light purple or red.

The boy could be seen frequently walking the only road in or out of the small town with his head down the entire walk. The other inhabitants of the town surely thought him odd. They did not know, of course, that he was searching for magic.

The boy knew his parents were concerned about him. He could tell they did not understand him. He was different from their other children in many ways. There were moments of whispering between the parents when they were not aware he was around the corner listening. The boy was a bright child. A perceptive child and creative. Perhaps this scared people.

At the early age nine or ten, the boy's parents asked him to get in the back seat of the station wagon. (Reader, I believe it was an avocado-colored Chevy Impala. Nonetheless, it was a massive car for three people.) The boy could sense something was wrong immediately. They asked him to put on some "nice clothes" and his Sunday shoes. There were times his mother spoke to him in such a distinctive way he knew not to question her. Just obey! The boy felt like he may pee. At some point, he was told he was being taken to a Doctor appointment.

The boy was far from stupid. He knew this was not the whole truth. Never had both his parents taken him to see a doctor for anything. You did not go to the doctor in this family, unless you were dying. There was no way to pay a doctor.

Putting on his Sunday clothes, he noticed there was a quiet reverence to the way they all got dressed that morning. It was a summer morning, and somehow there were no children around the house.

The boy stole a moment to himself back in his room. He began to cry. He peed his pants. He was afraid and alone, yet he did not know why. He must have done something wrong. They knew what he was thinking when he was alone all the time. Only, the boy hadn't told anyone his secret thoughts. And God, well, he was not available. The boy knew that God was ashamed.

The boy was sitting in the back seat of the Impala. He was wearing a mustard-colored sweater and matching corduroy pants. Sunday shoes too. His feet were wiggling at a hundred miles an hour. He was sitting on his hands trying not to urinate.

The doctor's office was in the larger town east of the family's which meant driving the long winding road, past the Whatzits and up the big hill that sometimes made the boy sick to his stomach. He was afraid of the bridge and the river that ran wide and deep underneath it. The boy was afraid to even look in the mirror. His siblings all seemed normal and happy to him. *Why am I so sensitive?* Tears welled up again in the lid beneath his blue eyes.

The boy's parents did not talk very much on the drive which simply confirmed what he had been thinking. *What have I done?* He was worried it had something to do with God. The boy knew they were perplexed by his depressive, solitary place in this family.

In town, the boy's father circled a block, looking for parking. He eventually found a spot directly in front of what the boy assumed to be the doctor's office. It was a small nondescript building, a flat, gray color with a horrible mint green edge surrounding the roofline. Only that decade dared such a blatant anti-feng shui, the boy thought to himself. Sitting in the car in front of the building, the boy could see it was nothing more than a glorified single wide. *Holy hell! I cannot be treated for whatever my parents think I need treatment for in a single wide.*

His parents got out of the car and attempted to act as if this was the most normal thing they had done that day. They waited for the boy to get out of the back seat. The boy didn't want to get out. He was terrified. He was shaking. His hands were cold. His feet felt like ice blocks and just as heavy. He thought he may throw up. He did, just a little in his mouth. He swallowed the bitter truth along with the bile. He must get out of the car. He followed them into the trailer. No one had said a word in the last five minutes.

As the boy passed the entry to the trailer, he noticed a plaque on the wall that read doctor something or other, along with his parents' religious affiliation at the end of the description. It mentioned he was qualified to judge anyone. That was what the boy read. He was a doctor of psychiatric medicine, *"ordained by God and your parents," is what it should say,* the boy thought.

The boy was directed to sit down in the small area that was once someone's living room. He sat down. His mother was talking to a woman behind a desk, and his father stood behind her. She was doing all the talking, as usual. She was choosing fate for all. His father certainly did not say a word. His wife would not allow him to take care of whatever situation she had decided the boy was experiencing. His parents disappeared through a door behind sister so and so's desk. The boy sat all alone in this single wide where he was sure the murder of a spouse had happened over the wrong choice of Hamburger Helper. It clearly did not help her make a great meal, as was promised.

His stomach was beginning to cramp. His heart was broken. His world was broken. He felt the size of a pea alone on that big sofa. His back began to sweat. He entertained thoughts of killing himself. His skin crawled all over the room returning to his body dirty. He needed to pee, but he did not. He kept his head down and his mouth shut.

Sometime later, his parents emerged from the door with a short, middle-aged, balding man walking behind them. The boy's father and mother sat down beside their son. She smiled nervously at her child. The doctor extended his hand to the boy and announced himself. He then turned around and told the boy to follow him. As the boy stood up, he felt a warm sensation in his crotch. Hiding tears and piss was somehow very important with a man like this, the boy's intuition told him.

They both passed by Sister Missionary Flora Flockhart, as her badge on her modest dress announced. He entered a small room with two burka loungers and an oversized desk in the middle of the room. He stood in the middle of the room as he heard the doctor lock the only entrance or exit to the room. As the doctor moved toward his rightful throne of judgment, he instructed the boy to sit. The boy had no idea what was going on. He had never seen this kind of doctor.

The boy sat and stared at this pitiful creature. The boy could almost feel the disgust this man felt toward him. Whatever his parents had told him, the boy was sure the doctor did not approve.

The doctor, after a few minutes of stare downs, jumped right in. "Why do you like to take baths?" he asked the boy. "Why do you walk around the house after a bath with the towel wrapped around your head, as a woman would? Why are you? Why are you not? Do you like it? What do you think about girls?"

Question after question.

The boy peed his pants at the first question. A full bladder pee right there on the Naugahyde burka. The doctor was judging the boy. He had no compassion for the confused child in front of him.

The boy was terrified beyond reason. The doctor did not have the ability to recognize the permanent harm he was nourishing in the boy's body and brain. More pee! The doctor was mean. He used the word "God" and "Jesus" many times. The boy was sick. He wanted to die. He was so small and lost and helpless!

This was the first time these people took God away from the boy. It would not be the last.

Foothill Arch

Foothills

Foothill Friend

Foothill Friend

Foothill Friend

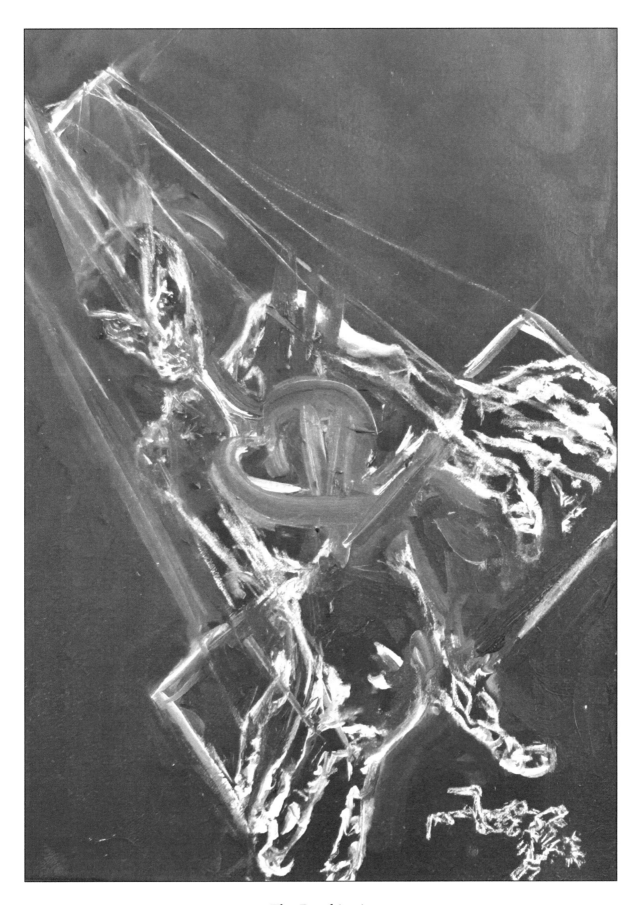

The Psychiatrist

Chapter Fifteen

The man wakes to the sound of the transit train as it angrily grumbles along its route. His thoughts instantly turn to Edward. It is two hours later in Colombia. However, he knows Edward is still asleep. The clock on the bedside table says 7:01 a.m. The train is a few minutes early today.

After a series of stretches, yawns, and the acceptance it is indeed morning, the man heads to the head. Then directly to the coffee pot.

Sipping his coffee and mentally preparing for the day, the man feels a tingle in his nether region. He is excited about life for the first time in a very long time. Edward has wedged his way into his psyche. The man likes it. "If only he would text me," he whines to himself.

The man heads toward the white couch to open the blinds. The light that enters the apartment is dull and gray. There is a blur of white, angry flakes committing suicide at his window. It is clearly bitter cold outside. The window is frosted.

He has been mentally having a conversation with himself since he first opened his eyes this morning. He wants to text Edward. He does not do so because somehow Edward makes him feel old. Maybe it is not Edward. It could be anyone under thirty, and he would feel old. These warning signals are everywhere, but the man chooses to ignore them. The thing is, the man does not want to seem like an old pervert seeking Edward's affection until he knows for sure what Edward's intentions are. The man has no idea what Edward sees in him in the first place. No idea what he wants.

The man has never been aggressive in any of his relationships. From sexual encounters in the past, he has finally learned he will never allow himself to be pushed around or degraded in any way, nor dominated again. In such cases as this, the man firmly takes the aggressor by the back of the head and informs them he will not accept degradation, roleplay, or violence, so if another man aggresses toward him once again, he will squeeze the back of his head. That is always enough!

The man does, however, prefer the other party make the choices of eating establishments, of dine-in or out, a movie, those sorts of things.

The morning coffee is finished. The man is a one cupper. The white couch is lulling him back to unconsciousness. He is not due to work for several hours yet. The weather has not improved. It is December and the man has not put a single decoration up. He just cannot find a reason to do so. This apartment has no character. The man simply cannot feel the holiday spark that generally initiates his desire to decorate for the season. The apartment is so sterile and lacking in architectural interest that he cannot imagine where he would even put a tree.

From the white couch where he sits, there is a chime coming from his phone. It is the only sound he has wanted to hear this morning. That familiar noise that instantly makes his heartbeat faster. Edward is awake! The notification is from the dating app. There is a message from Edward.

Edward: good morning

Holy hell. Someone is playing a set of tom toms inside the man's chest as he reads Edward's words.

Man: hi, good morning!

Edward: as you wake?

The man cannot quite figure out what Edward is asking him when he uses this phrase. He does not ask. In time, he will. He answers the question in the hope that Edward's response will give him a clue.

Man: I am doing well this morning. You?

Edward: I good. Do you speak Spanish?

Man: no, I am sorry I do not. I have taken several Courses in the language but it has never helped

Man: you speak English well Edward.

Edward does not respond to his text for several minutes. The man wonders if he has offended him. He sits back down on the white couch after pacing back and forth as he texts Edward. Minute after minute passes. The man is looking at everything he said to Edward in his texts to see if there was something he missed.

Edward: I like you profile

Edward: is sexy

Edward: I want

Man: thank you. I think you are very sexy!

Edward: what are you doing now?

Man: I am sitting on my couch having some coffee. I soon will have to get ready for work.

Edward: will you work long time?

Man: yes, probably till five or six in the evening.

Edward: will you unlock?

The man is lost. Unlock what?

Man: unlock? Unlock what?

Edward: your pics

The man has totally forgotten he has placed four or five personal photos on the app. In fact, he forgets they are talking on the app. He is nervous. He cannot remember which photos he put there. The man clicks on his personal file and locates his personal photos. They are locked so they cannot be seen by anyone using the app unless the owner of the profile unlocks them for a specific person.

The photos are fair. Not overtly naughty. There is no full nudity. A couple photos are of him with his shirt off. He is in shape. There is another pic of him standing in his bathroom in his underwear. He is also wearing a semi-erection.

Those are okay, he decides. At least he is not too embarrassed to look at them.

Man: I just unlocked them Edward

Edward: so sexy

Edward: OMG! 🙊

Edward: I horny

The man is not sure if he knew about this feature on the app, the sending of private photos, or if he has simply forgotten. He can see that Edward's photos are unlocked now. Whether he has unlocked them for the man or someone else, he does not know. He clicks the private photo icon on Edward's page. There are six photos. Three clothed, and three nudes.

Edward is a beautiful man, to be sure. The clothes he wears are stylish and very slim fitting. His style is what the man would call "preppy." Topsiders, his socks showing. Peg-legged slacks. Tight. Very tight. A long sleeve button up shirt with an attached sweater around the neck. It is not the sort of fashion statement the man would have made at the same age. In fact, this is the very look the man and his friends despised in the early eighties. At that time, it was certainly considered to be a far too mainstream, "wanna-be" kind of look. However, it is clearly not the eighties anymore, and the truth is Edward's dress only makes the man recognize his age more. Albeit the sexiness that Edward pulls off naturally.

Edward has beautiful black hair, styled in the day's fashion. A severe part is shaved in at the parietal and there is a natural fade to all the edges. Edward does not smile in any of the photos. All the photos seem to be taken around the same time. The nude photos are very suggestive. Edward is standing in a bathroom that is from the floor to the ceiling in a green tile. A forest green. In two of the nudes, he is fully erect. He has a very large tool! Uncircumcised. This would generally be a turn-off for the man. Not in this case. For whatever reason, it has the opposite effect. Edward is holding his member firmly in one of these photos. The man assumes what he is doing with that piece in his hand. In the other picture, Edward is naked; it is the same event as the other pic, but in this one Edward is bent forward slightly, spreading his butt crack ever so much. The man can almost see the suggestion of what lies behind those perfectly rounded, smooth, ample butt cheeks.

The man is turned on, to say the least. Edward is extremely thin; however, he has been given a beautiful body.

The man wonders as he looks at these pictures why there is no smile. There is not even a hint of humor nor playfulness. His eyes are hauntingly circled in black skin and seem sad to the man. If Edward did not have perfectly clear and creamy skin, the man would have guessed him to be a heroin addict. Or meth head. That he had not slept in six months, at the very least. And yet, he is stunningly beautiful.

The man has back chills. He can feel the sweat beading between his shoulder blades. He can also feel a wetness at the tip of his penis.

> Man: wow! What else can I say? The photos on your profile give me impure thoughts for sure. Damn!!!
>
> Edward: i unlock completely for jou
>
> Edward: jou like?
>
> Edward: i horny now 🙈
>
> Edward: the naked pics are right now
>
> Man: what? You took them just now?
>
> Edward: for jou. Completely for jou
>
> Man: you will drive me crazy. Now I am so aroused Edward.
>
> Edward: will jou exchange pics wit me now?

Right to Final Jeopardy, the man thinks. He is nervous at the thought of exchanging pictures with anyone. Especially naked pictures which is what Edward wants to see, he is sure of it. *Which photos should I send?* The man is not ready to send explicit photos. Not yet, anyway. Which year should the photo represent? Should they be real, untouched? Or should I photoshop what time does to those who are not aware of the toil the sun takes on the skin?

He grew up in a time when the sun was to be worshipped. He would lay in the sun for hours. In North America, the sun was its hottest during the months of July, August, and often September. He had a secret that gave him the darkness he wanted. IODINE. He mixed iodine with the tanning lotion. It never failed to turn him into an Oompa Loompa, but he thought he looked smashing!

The man remembers the feeling of the hot sun in August on his crotch as a teenager. Not quite a little boy anymore, but hardly a man yet. He would lie on the roof naked. It felt sinful to even say it. The world of body shame and nakedness were united in the mindset of his parents. Especially his mother. It was forbidden to do such a thing. The boy knew it had nothing to do with God. It had only to do with the whim of his mother. She was more concerned that he would be seen by a neighbor lying naked in the sun than to explain to him how beautiful his body was, and to be proud of it. Not to mention how natural it was and felt to have the sun kiss your entire body. No. Her hang-ups were At&T's worst nightmare.

In adulthood, the man can see how silly he was in his thinking then. How scared he was. His mother would not have climbed the tree that was necessary to gain access to the naked sunbathing roof for love nor money. Yet, he always felt like he was sinning.

Those moments of freedom in his life, the freedom of self-expression, up on a hot tin roof became priceless to his soul.

When the sun touched his genitals, it warmed him from the inside. There was nothing sexual about it. When the boy moved his sac and allowed the sun to reach the little fold of skin that traveled the stretch of highway to his anus. He giggled at the sheer warmth of it. Sex was never anything other than what someone stole from him. This was purely natural, and the boy felt healed when the sun gained entry to those uber white places.

Each year that passes, the man finds it harder and harder to remember the simple joys of child-hood. A song. A smile. The fascination of recognizing your body growing. Your mind expands. A longing for truth that never materialized. As a boy, he only wanted simple things. He wanted to know the feeling of an uncomplicated touch from his mother. The man wants to remember a time when lemonade was fresh. The man wants to have a foothill to run to, but they are all gone.

The man decides to send Edward a very simple picture of himself that was taken about a year prior. He is shirtless in the photo, standing with other men he cannot remember now. He was at some sort of festival in the hot summer. This is the photo he has chosen because he does not look his age. The light is great. He is tan. His chest is toned, and his nipples are paying full attention. The man sends the photo to Edward.

> Edward: so sexy. I want 🐙
>
> Man: thank you. I think you are very sexy. I think about you more than I care to admit.
>
> Edward: I will stay with you all day
>
> The man begins to tear up. (Big surprise, huh, reader?)
>
> Man: it is a deal. we can text all day if you like. If you are free?
>
> Edward: I want 🐙
>
> Man: I must shower and prepare for work now Edward. I could talk for hours with you but I must get moving here.

Edward: no problem my sexy.

Edward: we shower on camera later together

The man, sitting on the white couch, is practically on fire. Shock is a better description of feeling. This young man is apparently attracted to him. It has been a very long time since he felt wanted sexually. Spoken to in a sexual tongue. A Latino tongue. Holy hell! If anyone could see his person sitting on the white couch at this moment, the arousal would be clear. Now, how to get up from this behemoth without bending something so straight?

The man tries to focus on his work. It is proving to be impossible. It has been only four hours since he and Edward last texted. It feels like several weeks have passed to the man. As he walks about his workspace, he cannot help but smile as if he had a deep secret to tell everyone. The truth is no one really cares when you are in that phase of a relationship when you constantly smile. Or talk incessantly about the object of your obsession. We all easily become annoyed with the twitter pated. So thinks the man, so he keeps his secret to himself. He has told no one of his lightheartedness. It is enough that he knows. He cannot wait another second. He must send Edward a message.

Man: hello, Edward

Edward: hi my sexy

Edward: what you do

Man: hi there! I am at work. I wanted to say hi.

Edward: OMG!

Edward: i miss

Man: you make it difficult to concentrate!

Edward: sexy. How are jou? Work is busy?

Man: I am well Edward. Work is work. What are you doing today?

Edward: noting. I stay home today.

Man: are you home alone?

Edward: jess

Man: did you eat anything today?

Edward: no yet. I make something now. I hungry

Man: good idea. Go eat please. It is not my business but I wonder if you eat enough. I do not like to think that you are hungry.

Edward: jess I know I am very skinny. I hate. I tell jou a secret when you work finished.

Man: I cannot wait!

The man reads Edward's profile again. He states he is twenty-three years old from Medellin, Colombia. Graduated college with a journalism degree. He writes that he lives in Spain currently. He is looking for daddies, older men, professional men, jocks, and fit men. NO FEMME! Sounds like Edward is looking for someone with money. The man is slowly putting some things together.

The man wonders about Spain. What is Spain all about? He will ask Edward.

Chapter Sixteen

The man's family, his parents, that is, were both born and raised in the big city south of where the boy grew up. It was another state entirely. Two or three times a year trips were made to this city to acquire goods or services not available in the boy's tiny town. His extended family all lived in the big city, so naturally seeing them was always on the trip itinerary.

Some of these trips the entire family went together in the old white station wagon. At other times, there were just three or four who went.

They always drove the white station wagon. It had faux wood paneling along the sides. When in motion at any speed above forty miles an hour, the large barge tended to sway in and out of its designated lane. Reeling it back in was like trying to calmly reel in a marlin.

Like most children, the boy had a favorite place to sit in the car. The back seat. The very back seat. The seat that folded up as if by magic. It was a bit of magic to get yourself inside the cubby initially, but it was always an adventure. Made of white Naugahyde that made you sweat in the summer and chilled to the bone in winter. Of course, there were holes in the seat itself. At some point the marvelous thing called duct tape was applied to the holes in the upholstery creating a patchwork look that befitted the family. The seat was just large enough for two small children, so it was generally the two youngest who sat there. When the boy sat in the seat, he was facing backwards, so he could only see where he had been, not where he was going. It was warm from the exhaust system that ran underneath the car. The boy could feel the road moving by under his feet. The seat was tucked so low in the back of the station wagon he almost felt invisible. Almost.

Magic

Warm

Exhaust fumes

Treasures hidden smiles formed

Then there were times when these trips involved only one or two children, and possibly only one parent. It entirely depended on what the trip was for.

On this trip, the young boy was accompanied by two of his older brothers. As the old man remembers this event, he cannot recall which parent was driving or if they both were in the car. It is not clear to the man exactly what they were all traveling some hundred and thirty miles south for. He remembers what happened on this trip. The horrible events that took place. He cannot figure out why meeting Edward should coincide with these childhood memories. He is emotionally spent now. These memories flood his brain very randomly. They come and go much the same as the wind does at his window as he sits on the white couch thinking about the white station wagon and the visit to the city.

The man is not eating well. The spot in his inside where the ugliness lies is regurgitated almost daily now. If only he could puke the memories into the toilet along with the piss shame of the past, maybe they would dissipate entirely.

As these thoughts play tag with each other in his brain, the chirp of a bird is heard at his window.

Birds

Birds

Tweeting

Calling

Mocking

The old man begins to cry again. The young boy inside his memory is eleven years old. He and two of his brothers were in a park in the big city south after the three-hour drive in the white station wagon. This park was humongous to the boy's eyes. There were large open spaces in this park where many people played soccer or tossed a frisbee to each other. There were also many dark, secluded areas which the boy could sense ugly events that transpired there.

The old man is almost trancelike as this memory plays itself out in his pants. The man cannot remember why they are at this park. He has no memory of either of his parents being there with them.

The boy's brothers were playing ball which held no interest to the boy. As is his usual practice, the boy wandered off to explore. To be alone. To hide in sight from himself and others.

He walked along the paved paths in the park. There were trees that seemed to reach the sky as the boy stood at the base of a cottonwood tree and looked up toward the tree top. It was a beautiful place. As he moved farther into the park, he could hear what sounded like very loud angry birds. Squawking and pecking for order. The boy knew the sound of birds when they were pecking at each other. When they were attempting to establish a dominance over their assumed peers.

Just ahead, he could see a huge enclosure of some kind. There were structures as well as many people milling about inside this place. It was a zoo. A bird zoo. There was a sign just ahead. This was an aviary, he discovered. He did not know exactly what an aviary was, but he assumed it was like a zoo for birds. The boy looked all around him. He had wandered very far from his brothers. The aviary had a large iron fence surrounding it. The iron was painted black and must be old because he could see rust all over it. The fence must be there to keep other people out. Or maybe it was there to keep the birds in. The thought of being locked in made the boy uncomfortable. As far as he could see, the iron fence went all the way around the aviary. As he peered in through the iron bars, that had to be as high as the top of a high shelf in his father's shop, he could see exotic unfamiliar trees inside the enclosure. With both his hands clutching the iron bars, his face pressed through the gap in the bars, as far as would allow about from his left cheekbone to his right cheekbone. These trees looked like they were from the jungle, yet the boy knew they couldn't be. The winters here were not as severe as they were at home, but they were harsh just the same. Trees of this nature would die in winter, he knew.

The day was sunny and very bright. The boy was giddy as he looked through the iron bars. The smell of the air was heady with the scent of cottonwood trees.

There were beautiful birds everywhere. Some of them were in cages. Some were in huge net enclosures with telephone poles holding up the nets. He could see a little swampy area where pink flamingos strut indecisive of a leader. He had never seen a flamingo. They looked bedraggled and old. They were not as pink as he hoped or imagined. To the left, just inside from where he was standing, there was a California condor perched on a large log. The bird was huge and plain brown. It had a bald head that gave the boy the giggles. The skin on the head looked like it could use some lotion. If only he were inside, maybe he could help put some bag balm on the condor's head so it would not be so dry. The sign describing the bird informed him these birds were an endangered species. It looked like a vulture from the nature shows he watched sometimes. He was surprised to see how big the creature was in person.

To the right, in very small enclosures were several prey birds. The cages were so small the boy must swallow the lump forming in his throat due to his body's reaction of sadness and the beginning of tears as he saw the cages that couldn't possibly allow these birds to feel at home. He suddenly felt a longing for flight.

The boy was completely lost in his imagination. He had no sense of time. Real or imagined. It was some several minutes before the boy realized there was a man standing very close to him.

The boy first became aware of the man due to the odor of his breath that carried to the boy on a wind shift. It was sort of dry smelling and hot. Like when he would crouch down and crack the oven door just a smidge to peer inside to see what his mother was cooking. Sometimes it was hot, stinky air that wafted to his face. There was another smell about this man. Feces. The smell was somehow familiar to the boy. The boy needed to pee suddenly.

The stranger asked the boy if he liked birds. Softly, the boy replied that he did. The boy felt a sense of danger. A knowing inside himself. He let go of it. The sun was shining bright. It was warm. There were people all around. What harm could befall him on this beautiful day? His big brothers were there. Somewhere. He pensively scanned the park for any sign of them.

The stranger asked the boy if he liked budgies.

The boy stifled a chortle. He had never heard of a budgie. He thought the man must be full of budgie poop. *(WHATEVER THAT IS!)* That must be the smell around him.

"A budgie is a parakeet," the stranger informed the boy. "We call them budgies where I come from in Australia."

The boy thought he sounded strange. It sounded interesting to the boy. He told the boy he visited this park every day to check on the birds. That the birds were mistreated here and they needed a better caretaker.

The boy knows nothing about all that. Some of the birds looked a bit portly to him, actually.

The stranger asked the boy if he would like to see his budgies? "My house is that little yellow one right there just across the street." He pointed in the direction of a row of houses. Small. Built for a single family. Most likely in the post-war era when the homes were dark, small, and stuffy. If you were raised in one of these homes in an Asian or Indian family, then it would smell like the man's apartment does right now.

The boy was curious about these budgies. He was naïve, at best. He also wanted friendship. He had never related to children his own age. The things they said to him were boring, juvenile, and simple. His own family, as kind as they were, do not seem to see the things the way he saw them in the world. The boy wondered when he was around these other pink children, fattened from their parents' larders and the udders laden with heavy cream from the Holstein Friesian on the family farm, what did they know about:

Art

Magic

Light reflection

Guilt

Jolly Ranchers

Fermat enigma

Paradigm shifts

Madeleine L'Engle

The Wednesday witch

They knew nothing of talking to their clothing. The worst thing about these children was they offer him no candy.

No, the boy did not relate to those in his age bracket. He was curious about this man's birds, however. The stranger did say he could take a budgie home with him and a very special cage to keep it in.

The boy had not listened to that inner voice in a long time. Not since that day in the doctor's office when his parents were trying to fix him. It's that voice that guided him in times of trouble. That voice that lay deep inside his soul. The voice that spoke when he, alone, couldn't.

There was a deep rumbling now in the boy's soul. Unfortunately, that voice box was severed in a chicken coop.

"Okay," said the boy.

The stranger led him away from the iron gates. The stranger walked with confidence in the direction of his home.

The boy could not have known this then, but the little yellow house was directly across the street. No more than a hundred yards from where the boy first felt the wind change. The change that carried the smell of feces and dry mouth.

There were people everywhere on this sunny day in the park. Families, teenagers, grandmothers and grandfathers. Many were riding their bicycles in the park. There were many young people riding that new oddity, the skateboard.

The old man has no memory of which day of the week it is. Or even what time of day. The old man, sitting on the white couch tries to recollect. He clearly remembers the bright sun, and that it was very hot. A large tear reaches the man's chest plate with a splash as the memories solidify in his head.

The boy made eye contact with a woman in a car. She had stopped to let the stranger and the boy cross the street. The stranger walked ahead of the boy. As the boy looked in the eye of the driver, he sensed something. She sensed something; he was sure. The boy was becoming unsure of himself.

As they approached the house, the boy noticed all the windows are dark. Too dark to be natural. He had a feeling in his insides:

It was familiar.

It was shame.

It was pain.

It was dark.

It smelled of poo! Even from the sidewalk. The stranger retrieved his house keys from his right pocket. This man had not said one word since they left the iron gates. Once the door was open, he turned to the boy and smiled and gestured with a nod for him to go ahead inside.

The boy moved closer to the threshold. Pensively, he peered into the room as the stranger held the door open for him. The boy could hear the stranger breathing through his nose. He could feel the breath on his neck as the stranger shifts himself closer to him. It was a sour, foul mouth. The boy poked his neck in farther so he could see inside the dark room. He could hear birds. Many, many birds. The air was hot and smells of lice. And bird poo. That was the smell of the stranger the boy now realized. The smell that was familiar to him. Bird poop!

The old man in memory and the young boy in reality both begin to sweat down their backs. The old man is going to puke. The young boy is going to pee.

There are moments in all our lives when time stands still. Utterly still. Just before an accident. Just before the death of a loved one, or even the death of a stranger. That moment you walk into a viewing of another human being in death. That ridiculous ritual many Christians insist upon to witness the death mask of:

Suicide

Alcoholism

Murder

Age

Disease

The air becomes still. If you listen and are aware, it is the flight or fight moment inside all of us that is saying, "Get away. Run, you dumbass. What else do I have to do to get you to see you are in trouble?"

The boy had lost faith in himself. He no longer trusted this voice.

The old man is in deep repose. His younger self is in deep bird poo!

The hair on the back of the boy's neck was standing straight up. His senses had become heightened. Tunnel vision hit.

The man pukes again.

The boy felt two large hands around his neck squeezing tighter and tighter. His lower legs were on fire from being kicked inward by the stranger. There was dappled sunlight coming through the filthy blinds that did not close entirely. There were feathers softly surfing the light rays.

Bird poop

Human feces

Fear

Another's fear

Pee

Dirty linens

Soul void

Queen bed

Living room

Boarded fireplace

The old man is rocking back and forth on the white couch.

Sobbing

Screaming

Bleeding

Run

Run

Run

The boy couldn't run!

The old man is well aware. Don't you wish you could speak to your younger self, reader? To give that child some sugar when all they have is acid. Or to warn him. Or tell him he will not recover should he choose to continue the silence. Over, and repeatedly.

It is a script best not rehearsed, thinks the old man, caught in between memory and inaction.

The stranger squeezed the boy's neck with one hand as he was lifted off the floor. He shut the door and tossed the child on his filthy bed. The boy was raped for an hour and forty-seven minutes. The boy heard the things happening to him, for some reason, but did not feel them so much.

Tearing

Tissue expansion

Pissing

Budgie whaling

Singing at

Laughing

Nothing new

The boy survived the physical torture by watching and listening to the birds. Their white eyelids blinked at a fevered pitch as the stranger moved faster and faster. Somehow, the budgies comforted him.

The man has thought on occasion in his life when recalling this event that those birds were sent for him. Not the bloody chickens. The chickens were mockers!

The yellow caged birds made eye contact with the boy as he was being used as a butcher block. It turned out to be a false comfort, however. The boy and the man have learned there is no eyelid of faith. Birds mock on and on!

The boy was bleeding heavily. He could feel the warmth of his blood on him. He smelled iron. He smelled poo. His own poo, as well as the stranger's and the birds'. The boy could also smell the presence of the last child bedded here. The sheets neither looked nor felt as if they had ever been laundered.

At some point in this dark abyss, the boy heard his brother calling his name just outside the rape house. The voice was strong at first. Then it faded away like an ice cream truck as you realized you did not gather your coins fast enough as the pervert driving the good humor box leaves your street.

The old man has no memory of what happened between his brother's voice calling his name and much later that night.

The boy inside the man remembers.

The stranger moved off the boy without a word. He simply stared at his filthy crotch in disgust.

The boy was covered in blood and poop. He was sticky. The boy did not know what the yellow, creamy stuff running down his legs was. The boy felt hot and ugly. He felt guilty and was full of shame. The boy lay there embarrassed at his naked form. The stranger was somewhere in the house. He could hear a faucet running somewhere. The boy found his underwear in the top drawer of the stranger's dresser. Apparently, he planned on keeping them. Terrified he would come back, the boy put them on, then his pants. The birds were singing a sickening happy song the boy did not know. He vomited all over the stranger's bed and pillow.

The boy ran. The sun welcomed him as he passed the door jamb into the light. He did not realize he was sobbing or that the blood could be seen all over his body. He couldn't move very quickly now. He was starting to feel the pain in his backside. Each time his heart beat, there was a fresh ooze of blood coming from his butt. The boy needed sutures. He put his hand on the rape spot and felt a large tear.

The boy got himself to the only landmark he knew in this park. The bird zoo.

There was too much blood. He must clean it up somehow. What would he say? How to live? How to clean?

Just ahead of him there was a garbage can. He was sure people were watching him as he rifled through the garbage looking for something to stop the bleeding. There was a discarded 7-11 bag. Inside he found a handful of napkins and a hotdog carton smeared with different sauces. The smell of the hotdog and condiments made the boy puke over and over again until only yellow stuff came out. He took the napkins, though they were covered in mustard and ketchup. The boy had little choice. He must stop the bleeding. After finding a shaded secluded area in the park, he gingerly pulled down his clothing. His pants were entirely bloodstained. It would not come out, he knew. The boy shoved the soiled napkins into his newly created place on his body to poop. The napkins burned. The mustard inflamed the swollen tissue even more.

Within ten minutes of resting, the bleeding had stopped. *Now, what to say to my brothers?* They would be angry for wandering off. He did not even know where to find them. He sobbed at the thought of a kind face. He was filled with sadness and shame at his choice to go with the stranger. He knew not one of his brothers would ever do such a thing. He was spent of emotion. He was terrified to face his mother. Would she know? Did someone tell her? Would she think he deserved this? Did she already know how dirty he felt on the inside? It was too much to bear.

The boy wanted to find a way to kill himself before his brothers found him. He did not know how to kill himself. *Maybe if I just run away.*

Mom

Dad

Brothers

Sin

Passing the sacrament

Taking the sacrament

God

God is gone

God, why'd you run away?

Compass less

Mute

Adults

Relatives

The boy had retreated into his head. That was the only way he knew to kill himself. To hide in that space where there were lots and lots:

Shiny things

Colored glass

Animals

Trees

Green things

Magic things

He could hear his brothers approaching, rather, he sensed their approach. He was locked inside his head.

What happened next, even the boy inside the old man had been blocked from memory. There was no recollection of his brothers scolding him nor of any conversation. No memory of getting in the car, where they went, or with whom they were staying.

The boy was certain of one thing, as is the old man. Neither one of them spoke of the rape. Ever! Neither one of them had the ability to speak the truth. The child was alone, yet again. His body was taken with no return of affection. No tenderness. No touch.

They would both spend the rest of their lives giving to others. Sharing and loving, and on an endless search for touch that is not stolen.

(NOTE TO READER: YOU MAY BE WONDERING IF THIS MAN IS SCHIZOID. THE BOY AND THE MAN ARE THE SAME BEING, YET THEY RELATE AS TWO SEPARATE INDIVIDUALS AT TIMES. I ASSURE YOU, READER, NEITHER THE BOY AS A BOY, NOR THE OLD MAN AS AN OLD MAN HAS MENTAL HEALTH ISSUES. NO MORE THAN YOU DO, DEAR READER.)

Aviary

Budgies

Chapter Seventeen

Finally, the last client is seen. The workspace is tidied up. As much as the man cares for it to be today, anyway. He is finished for the day.

He is thinking about Edward, of course. Absentmindedly, he leaves the studio and heads to his car. "No keys. Holy hell." Once retrieved from his studio, he is back sitting in his car, staring off, totally absorbed in his thoughts.

Colombia. Spain. These locales seem unreachable, far off lands. He has traveled very little in his life. Well, in Europe, anyway. Out of sheer curiosity, the man has googled both countries and has become fascinated by everything he has researched. Beautiful people to be sure, as well. The man mentally notes it is 7:30 p.m. in Colombia.

Man: hi Edward.

Edward: my sexy

Edward: how you work today?

Edward: finish?

Man: yes, I am finished for the day.

Edward: what you do at work?

Man: I design home interiors. I also do some informal life coaching as well as advise women and men on cosmetic surgical procedures that they are interested in receiving.

Edward: I love. Im good at all design my friends say to me.

Man: well the image you present, the way you look, I will bet you are good at many things.

Edward: ja ja ja i have eye for fashion

Man: I do not like to buy clothes. They never fit. I hate to go into a dressing room. I am always the biggest thing in that little closet with terrible lighting.

Edward: ja ja ja your body is big and long. Its beautiful.

Edward: if you would come to Cartagena, I could help you pick some clothes.

Man: that is close to Medellin. where you are?

Edward: jess. It very close. It a beautiful old colonial city. We could stay there together a week

Man: that sounds amazing. Are you serious though?

Edward: jess. It very cheap. Colombia is no expensive. We have beautiful hotel. A car if you want. i arrange everything. We eat good. I have sex all day wit you.   i want kiss you all day. We can show affection to us. There is no one there that know me.

Man: this all sounds wonderful. I will have to look more into it when I get home. It would not be for a while if I were to come. I am self-employed and I would have to plan a bit.

The man sits and waits for Edward's reply. After ten minutes, he heads home. He wonders if he offended Edward. The man is feeling a few walls go up on his end. Why would Edward care if anyone knew him? He seems intent on Cartagena. Almost urgent. It seems a bit odd to the man, but so do most things. Twenty minutes later, Edward replies as the man is resting his feet on the white couch.

Edward: look. *I send you information.*

There are four attachments with Edward's text message. They all contain glossy pictures of beautiful hotels and B&Bs. There really were endless things to do and see in Cartagena. It would be a spectacular trip. And to meet Edward in person and stay together there.

Of course, all the usual doubts pop up in the man's head. All the things that have stopped him from taking risks in the past. Work, money, time. *What if we get there and I want to smack Edward upside the head the whole time? What will others think? People around us. They will think I am Edward's Daddy, to be sure.* That does not encourage the man to go. There are no specific prices on most of the information. Which cannot be good. He decides to investigate it all further and see what his work schedule is like in the next month or so.

Man: *thank you Edward for sending that information. Holy hell it is a beautiful place. I will look further into costs and flight information tonight. who knows? It does sound amazing.*

Edward: *jou can give me your credit card information i will find the best deals because i speak Spanish. I will book it for a week from now.*

The man is a bit taken aback by Edward's boldness. The truth is, it totally turns the man off. There is not a chance in hell he would give his credit card information to anyone in South America. In Colombia!

Obviously, if Edward were to book anything with the man's card, he would also include himself on the man's dime. It is obvious Edward does not have any money. He does not work. The man has already decided he is not up for paying for a week's lodging, meals, and entertainment for someone he just met, not even in reality. It is all cyber meetings. Even if he had money to burn, he would not do that. Not at this age.

As he looks over his work schedule, he can tell it is impossible anyway. He could not get away for at least eight weeks.

Man: there is just no way that I can make it happen in a week's time Edward. I would love to, but it is impossible. I have clients that have booked appointments with me for several months. I cannot cancel a week's worth of appointments. I am sorry.

Edward: ok but remember that i dont have much time left in Colombia. I want see you here. I want to get away from my dad. He is machismo and very strong in his head.

Edward then sends the man a picture of his plane ticket to Spain. A one-way ticket from Bogota, Colombia to Madrid, Spain. It is dated just over seven weeks from now.

Man: wow that is soon. I will continue to see if I can make it happen before you leave for Spain. We can talk more about it.

Edward: jess. Can i watch you shower tonight?

Man: yes. I am nervous about it.

There is no response from Edward. The man is home staring out the window. It has been a gray, sunless sky all day. The pollution in winter in this valley traps itself as if covered with a blanket. Yet the blanket only traps in the cold air and it remains motionless, depressing, and bitter on these winter days here. There is no warmth under this blanket. It is very near Christmas. There is a sense of urgency in the thick, soupy sky. The man feels none of it. Cartagena is another matter altogether. The sun! The warmth! The water. Shit, damn, hell! The man knows inside he will not make it there. Lack of money has him a bit down. But then there has always been a lack of money. There are many reasons why at his age. After nurturing a business for twenty-five years, there is a lack of funds. However, that is another story for another time, reader!

Just then, another seed is planted in the man's brain. *I could meet Edward in Spain in the spring.* At that very moment, the man knows this will happen. The timing is perfect. He will have nearly three months to ready himself. He would much rather see Spain than Colombia. He will prepare mentally from this second on to ensure that it becomes reality.

Man: hi Edward. I have finished eating and I am now relaxing on the couch. What are you doing?

Edward: my sexy.

Man: how are you?

Edward: i good. You tire? Long day at work

Man: yes, my feet and knees are in much pain.

Edward: i would massage for you 🐵

Man: that's very kind of you to say. But you are not here.

Edward: it is true what you say.

Man: I am going to take a hot shower. That will help with the pain.

Edward: i shower with you

Man: what?

Edward: i shower here at my grandma's house when you shower at your house. We film it live
so we see together.

Man: I have never done that. Maybe you will not like my body? You have mentioned it before,
taking a shower together I mean. I guess I thought you were kidding.

Edward: i already know you body

Man: how?

Edward: your pics on the app.

Man: yes, but I am not completely naked. You cannot see my whole body.

Edward: you are beautiful and sexy man. Let exchange cock picks first. Will you?

Man: yes, I will

The man answers Edward's question before he even really thinks about it. This is all new to the
man. He has never had a cyber sexual relationship. It is extremely erotic.

What pics shall I send? Panic mode! The man receives another message from Edward.

Edward: completely for jou!

There is a picture of Edward completely naked in the green bathroom again. He has his back to
the camera, and he is bending over forward.

The man is very hard in the y fronts. Not true, reader. The man is wearing a thong. (*YES READER,
A THONG. MANY PEOPLE THINK THEM EIGHTIES BAD. AMERICANS GENERALLY ASSUME YOU ARE FROM EUROPE IF YOU
WEAR A THONG. THE MAN JUST LIKES THEM. THE SECRET IS OUT.*)

Holy hell. He must choose a pic to send. He chooses a safe pic. He is wearing lulus, of course. No shirt. There is no face in the pic. The man never takes selfies, and he certainly never takes pics of his face. It seems so silly and serious that he just giggles on those rare occasions where he did take a face pic.

The man is in the best shape of his life. He carries a 6'5 in frame along with 260 pounds of pure muscle. He is very toned, and he is very large in every way. What the man does not have is the skin of a thirty-year-old. Time and choice rob your skin first.

He decides that will be the one to send. Off it goes, soaring through "the cloud" the ever-mysterious human created anomaly.

Edward: so sexy

Man: thank you

Edward: send naked pictures. I want see all of you

The man realizes he is not going to get out of this easily. He will have to send nudes and lighten up a bit sexually if he wants to keep Edward interested. He knows about regret. He will no longer regret the things he does, only the things he does not do.

Once again, the man must decide in the way of photos for Edward. The man is convinced he looks better, a bit younger in the pics, where he has a bit of a tan. Even cellulite looks better with some color on it.

As was mentioned prior, the magic hour or hours, were between one and three in the afternoon when the boy was free to visit the roof and the sun. The pigs had been slopped, he had just finished milking some 150 cows, and then bottle-fed all the calves. Finally, he moved the sprinkler pipes manually in the alfalfa fields, came home to weed the garden, and then eat. The early afternoon was his. So, from one to three, the boy lay in the sun.

The story is told better simply by looking at his skin.

Memories of lying in the sun generally trigger the need for vodka. The thoughts of using are as random and unexplainable as a circus popping up out of nowhere in a farmer's field unannounced. The man would find it much easier to send naughty pictures of himself if he had a tumbler full.

Sitting on the white couch, the man tries to remember exactly whose decision it was that became the catalyst for him quitting his drinking of alcohol. Was it the group? His mother? Himself? After three years, it has evaded him.

His picture gallery is scrolling furiously. Holy hell, some of these must be deleted immediately. What was I thinking? Some of the pictures look good to the man. A few of the videos also look sendable. He chooses a video for Edward first. This video, without becoming too graphic, is of the man lying down receiving oral sex. It is very naughty (that is all you get to know, reader.) There is sound on the video which the man was not aware of till this moment as he proofs it. The man is embarrassed at hearing it again, but alas, it is what happened.

With the video sent, it is getting late in the evening. The man is hungry and getting tired. His feet are barking louder than usual tonight.

He sits down on the white couch with a simple meal of soft-boiled eggs, sliced avocado, and tomato on a chunk of toasted sourdough. Salt and fresh cracked pepper, naturally. A large wine glass full of water and ice rounds off tonight's meal.

Edward: OMG! 🖤 🖤 🖤 🖤 🖤

Edward: the video is amazing. I watch over and over many times. I want so much you.

Edward: who is man wit jou?

Man: he is just a friend. we only call each other when we need to be touched. We call it a "booty call" here.

Edward: you are amazing sexy.

Edward: you have big dick. How big?

Man: I do not know how big it is exactly.

That is a lie. There is not a man on this planet who does not know the exact measurement of his penis. Some begin the measuring from the bottom of the scrotum to the tip of the penis. That way, if he has a small member, it will measure two inches longer than it is, therefore, comforting the individual. Some men will measure it soft. Do not ever mention the size of your penis if you've measured it when it was soft. Really? *(As you men know, the penis can often be a grower not a show-er.)*

The man knows exactly what the measuring tape tells him when he measures. Unfortunately, that is not public information and will not be volunteered here.

Man: yes, it is big.

Edward: i equal

Man: yes, I have seen it, it's big and thick. What are you doing now? Where are you?

Edward: I at my grandmothers .im talking wit jou.

Man: oh, I assumed you had gone back to your father's house by now.

Edward: my father's house is next grannys. I like to spend time here because it's quiet. Also, my grandmothers house is a meeting place for family and friends so it feels happy here. My grandmother is almost eighty-five. I like to be here if she needs help with anything. There are also two aunts and uncles that live on the same street. I visit with them all day. we coffee. I don't like my stepmother and my dad is machismo in his thinking and strict. So i stay at my grandmothers as much as i can.

Man: wow! That is sharing a lot with me thank you Edward. There is something that has been puzzling me though. May I ask you?

Edward: of course my sexy. I tell anything

Man: I do not want to offend you but I'm just so curious. Sometimes when I text you, you reply to my texts immediately. At other times, it takes five minutes. You speak one way, in most texts but then in another, it is completely different. It has made me very curious.

Edward: ja. i use a translating app. Sometimes it takes longer to be translated. Sometimes the app gets it wrong and my response does not make sense or it says something that i did not mean or say. When i dont use the app my spelling and grammar is terrible. I speak only a little english.

Man: oh wow. How did I miss that one? That makes sense now. Shit I cannot believe how ignorant I am at times. Thank you for enlightening me.

Edward: no problem my sexy. What you do now?

Man: I just had dinner. Now I am relaxing.

Edward: you feel better now. I happy

Man: I do thank you.

Edward: i want

Man: you want what Edward?

Edward: to see jou. Will you shower wit me

Man: how will we do that?

Edward: on the app we call and turn it to video and watch each of us. I cant talk loud.

Hmm. This has the man most perplexed. Why can't Edward talk out loud? It must be so he does not disturb his grandmother's rest. Inside his head, the man thinks it may be something less transparent.

Edward: jou wil have to set up your phone so we can see you in the shower. I turn mine on put it in a glass it stands up an see through the glass.

Man: ok I have set up my phone in a glass. It works quite well. I have never done this, so I am a bit nervous. Are you ready?

Edward: Jess I want see the whole thing. I want see taking off clothes and all. Just act natural it will be sexy. Push the connect video icon on the bottom of the screen. Do you see it?

Man: Yes, I can see it. I did not know what it was until now.

A notification came to the man. "Edward Arias wants to video chat with you. Push *accept* to take the call or push *decline* to end the call. Push *report* if you want to report this user."

The man can see the incoming video call on his screen. He is panicked. He has no idea what to push. He tries the green one. Edward's face appears on the screen. The man has not taken a breath in two minutes. There are awkward seconds where Edward is staring and not saying anything. The man said "Hi "to Edward several times but clearly the man has not done all that is necessary to interact with the caller.

A typed message appears below Edward's live face.

Edward: turn on your camera and microphone.

Holy hell, I am an idiot, the man decides. He must seem incompetent. Or, worse yet, old. The man locates and turns on the camera and sound. Instantly, the man can hear the shower water running just behind Edward.

The man says, "Hi," again.

"My sexy," replies Edward.

The man is surprised at the sound of Edward's voice. It is deep, baritone, and is extremely accented.

"Wow, it is great to see you and to hear you. It makes it much more real for me."

"I equal," Edward said. Edward is standing in the green tiled bathroom of his grandmother's house mentioned before in his scribe. He is naked. He is not shy. He is not covering his genitals. The skin on his body is olive. Quite olive. Green almost. Of course, the color of the bathroom tiles reflection would make anyone look semi-ill.

Edward asks the man to get undressed slowly. "I want see all," he says.

The man very nervously begins the ritual of undressing. Untying his shoelaces. Real sexy! He feels silly while being watched doing these routine tasks. Taking off his shoes. He then undoes his belt. The man can see himself in the split screen getting undressed. Edward is on the other half staring and touching himself. The camera angle is too high for the man to see his own crotch. The man is completely naked now. He steps into the shower and adjusts the temperature to his liking. He replaces the phone and glass on the shelf in the shower with him. Edward has done a similar thing and is now rinsing off his body. The man watches him. He is a beautiful man, for sure. Edward smiles at him. He quietly asks the man to lower the camera a bit. The man can see his entire crotch on his side of the camera now.

"So sexy," Edward says. He copulates to completion. It does not take Edward more than a minute to ejaculate. The man turns off his own water and tells Edward he is finished. Edward continues to shower. The man dries off and puts his clothes on. He takes his phone from the glass. Edward is now washing his hair. The man allows Edward some privacy and disconnects the transmission.

The whole thing made him uncomfortable. He did not expect that. Nor does he know why. He decides to get a snack and wait for Edward to finish.

       Edward: Hello

       Man: Hi Edward

       Edward: you okay?

       Man: Yes, I am great. Thank you. you look beautiful all wet.

       Edward: All for jou my sexy. You are amazing. Why you leave?

Shit! The man does not even know why himself. He does not want to hurt Edward. It is not about him. He simply was uncomfortable. It seemed an invasion to the man. An invasion on Edward's person. What to say now to Edward?

       Man: I did not leave. I am here.

It is a lame excuse, but it is the best he can do now.

       Edward: Ok my sexy.

       Man: It is getting late. Did you eat?

       Edward: I no eat.

       Man: Did you eat today?

       Edward: Jess this morning.

       Man: That's it? For the whole day today?

       Man: Why have you not eaten?

       Edward: I tell you the truth.

The man is waiting.

       Man: Edward?

       Edward: I have problem with food. When I was young boy. I see doctors and I was very sad. My
       father is mucho machismo and I fear him. He no no I'm gay. No friends or family I tell. My father
       has government job. I have no courage to be honest wit my family. I stay at my grandmother's
       house. So I can talk to you. I want to go away. Please come and we can go to Cartagena!

Man: I'm so sorry you have had to deal these problems in your life. I want you to know that even though we just met, actually we have not met. But since we started texting each other I have become very close to you. I feel strongly about you and you have made me feel alive again. I thank you for that. I have no answers about your family situation. It is very personal for we gay men! You will deal with it when the time is right for you, or maybe you never will tell anyone in your past. That is a shame if true. However, I feel like I did not deal with my feelings when I should have, and it caused me such sadness and self-loathing as a young man.

Edward: Is true. I feel equal about you.

Man: Its late. I am going to go to bed now Edward. Sleep deep! Thank you for sharing your life with me.

Edward: Jess. You sleep well my sexy. Goodnight.

Man: Goodnight.

Chapter Eighteen

The man lies in bed for hours unable to sleep. His mind is on Edward, of course. *Clearly there are some major fear issues with his father. He did not actually say his father was mean. He said "macho or machismo,"* the man thought. Which, to him, simply meant his father was set in his thinking about what a man is and what a man should be according to his beliefs. The old man had gone through it with his own parents when he was forced out of the closet. He remembers it as being a very uncomfortable time in the house for everyone.

He has many happy memories as a child as well. He is reminded of his mother. These happy memories are not complicated, as many are, where she is involved. There were simple joys. The man smiles naturally as he remembers his mother in those moments of happiness and the thought of the frequent treats she held just for him. She loved her son. She showed it in many ways. She loved treats, candy, and chocolate. Her child also had a weakness for this sweeter side. As she well knew.

She would occasionally procure a hard candy from her purse and slip it to the boy. Occasionally, she had something sour she found in the bottom of her purse. Always lint covered, but the sour candy was still a treat when she presented it to the boy. Always at unexpected times. Waiting in a line with her at some governmental agency for this or that. Waiting for the doctor, she would slip him something. Or sometimes, when all the children were together, she somehow magically placed a hard tack in his hand. There was never enough for all, so he always felt whole and complete in those tender moments with his mother.

There were other times in the boy's life he desperately needed to tell her his thoughts. About the things that were happening to him at school. The bullying. The shame and disgust he felt inside. He wanted to share all his secrets, but he knew she would be mad at him for his truths. All these moments and events that shaped the boy into the man he became were kept inside himself building, fermenting into a poisonous stew. These moments were not safe to discuss with her, or anyone, for that matter. The boy knew his mother and was aware she was not a safe space when these untoward events happened. The boy felt his mother would assume any negative event occurring in his life must be the result of something he did to encourage it.

One such event the boy did not speak of for many years.

The boy clearly remembered the population of this small town as does the old man he grew to become. There stood directly in front of the boy's home at the edge of the dry lawn, the town population sign. *Pop, 368* is what the sign told those traveling north on this, the only highway. It was a constant reminder to the boy he was going nowhere. Neither were any of the other 367 people the sign indicated as living in this town. This seemed to be the final destination for most of the townspeople. They seemed content in this place, to the boy. That always made him itch for somewhere else.

The old man remembers everything that happened to him in that small, moronic Mormon town. The boy had no ability to speak to anyone about the things happening to him. It was made known to him he would be killed or stabbed or choked about the neck until dead on more than one occasion from many of the rednecks who decided that self-expression was to be stamped out. The boy made them nervous. He had no idea of it then, but now, as an adult, he can read the writing on the walls, and particularly in between the lines.

It was a sunny day in October when the boy of this story received a beacon from one of his siblings to come to the phone. That he had a call.

The man, now in memory, has no idea who called him to the phone, but he remembers answering the call.

"Hello," the boy of thirteen said in to the receiver. There was a long pause on the other end of the call. The boy could hear breathing. The boy began to sweat. A bead formed at his nape and was about to race to the finish line at the small of the boy's back. The boy felt as if he may pee. *Please no more peeing*, the boy pleaded with himself. He covered the mouthpiece with his hand as he loudly asked everyone in the room, "Who is it?" As was often the case, he did not receive an answer.

"This is Bishop Wardwinds calling. I need to speak with you. Come to my office at the ward house."

The boy was terrified. He felt all alone in a world of many. He put his Sunday clothes on for the second time that day. He left the house by the back door. Walking past the place where he did not look at now, the boy was becoming anxious. There were a million thoughts racing through his head as he walked past the shop, the high school, then just ahead another thirty yards the ward house.

The ward awaited his entry, as did the bishop. As the boy entered from the back of the building, he immediately could smell vacancy. There was no one in the church other than himself and the bishop. Generally, there was a sister cleaning or generally acting busy rushing about the hallways or the kitchen. Apparently, all the righteous, the pious, and narcissistic had all gone home for Sunday dinner and a nap. The bishop's office was at the front of the ward house next to the chapel just off the foyer. The boy timidly peered in the office. A diminutive man was sitting behind a desk.

The old man can see this memory playing out in his head as if in slow motion.

Time was indeed moving very slowly for the boy as well. The bishop asked the boy to sit, without looking up from his work. The boy sat in the chair facing the bishop. He peed himself a small amount as he sat. The face of this messenger of God looked at the boy; he had no smile nor greeting for him.

The boy felt like he was the size of a dust bunny. More pee. The bishop stared the boy down for what felt like an eternity. There was an uncomfortable thickness to the air in the office. The boy imagined himself swimming out of this room. If only he liked to get his hair wet, he giggled inwardly.

The bishop opened his mouth to speak.

More pee.

"I have received information that you are unworthy," the bishop said. "You have lain with another boy. You are condemned. Unclean. Immoral. Do you know how your heavenly father feels about your sin? Do you know where those of your type will go in the end? You will go to hell."

Lots more pee!

(NOTE TO READER: THE BISHOP IN THIS PART OF THE TALE IS REFERRING TO A TIME NOT LONG BEFORE THIS VERY MEETING WITH THE BISHOP. THE BOY AND ANOTHER SLIGHTLY OLDER BOY HAD EXPERIMENTED WITH EACH OTHER. NO DETAILS ARE WARRANTED HERE. USE YOUR IMAGINATION, READER. THE OLDER OF THE TWO MOVED AWAY FROM THE SMALL TOWN FOR REASONS UNKNOWN TO THE BOY. BEING OF THE MORMON FAITH, THE OLDER BOY FELT A NEED TO CONFESS WHAT HE CONSIDERED TO BE A SIN COMMITTED BY HIMSELF AND ANOTHER BOY. HE CONFESSED HIS ACTIONS TO HIS NEW BISHOP. THIS NEW BISHOP FELT A NEED TO TATTLE. HE CONTACTED BISHOP WARDWINDS. BOTH BISHOPS, FOLLOWING MORMON DOCTRINE AND PROTOCOL, CALLED EACH OF THE BOYS INVOLVED TO THEIR RESPECTIVE OFFICES IN ORDER TO HAVE THE "MORALITY" CONVERSATION AND TO INFORM THEM BOTH THAT KINGDOMS WOULD NOT BE AVAILABLE TO THEM IF THEY CONTINUED THEIR SAME SEX ATTRACTION.

IT MUST BE SAID ALSO THAT WHATEVER THE OLDER BOY SAID TO HIS BISHOP IS PURE SPECULATION. WE WILL NOT BE PRIVILEGED TO KNOW. THE LIPS OF THE BISHOP BRICK BRETHREN ARE AS TIGHT AS A BAPTIST MINISTER'S WIFE'S GIRDLE AT AN ALL YOU CAN EAT PANCAKE BUFFET. AN ASSUMPTION IS MADE HERE BASED ON THE CONVERSATION THE YOUNG BOY WAS FORCED TO ENDURE WITH THE SELF-RIGHTEOUS BISHOP WINWARDS.

THE BOY OF THIS STORY PAID A GREAT PRICE FOR A GROPE AND TICKLE, AS THE OLD MAN COULD VERIFY. HE TOO HAS PAID OVER AND OVER AGAIN. LIVING IN ZION DOES NOT GUARANTEE REDEMPTION IF YOU ARE OF A DIFFERENT JELL-O MOLD.)

The old man remembers this event well. It has scarred him for life. This was the second time God was taken from him.

The bishop continued with his condemnation speech. The boy no longer was really listening to what the bishop was saying. All that he saw and heard from that point on in the office was a black forked tongue spewing forth hatred.

At some point, the boy stood up from this seat of judgment. He felt extreme shame and guilt. He was crying. The boy was unable to hold his head up. If he kept his head down, it seemed easier for him to be invisible, along with his feelings of self-hate. His pants were wet. The trouble was, once again, the boy had nary a soul to talk to. This secret he had buried his entire life thus far was just spoken out loud. Not even by him! It would be one thing if the boy had a friend to confide in, to tell his secret thoughts. It was an entirely different matter to have the mouthpiece of God call you out. The boy did not even know what a closet was. He certainly never had one, let alone hang out in it. What the boy feared most had just happened to him. God found out who he really was. Surely, God now saw what a mistake he had made in the creation of the boy. God ran away. The boy was left to navigate this world alone without a compass once again.

The boy thought, as he left the ward house, it was one thing to have your family know how filthy you were, but to have God run away was too much for the thirteen-year-old. The boy wondered how he would ever sleep again.

Out in the raw light of early evening, the boy felt naked. Exposed. As he walked aimlessly forward, away from the bishop and the smell of the ward house, he thought of his family. His mother and father. His siblings. All his aunts and uncles and grandparents. What would they all think if they heard about it? The bishop informed the boy he would have to start the process of excommunicating the young boy. His family would definitely hear about it in the case of the excommunication of a thirteen-year-old boy.

The boy could not get away from the ward house and that odious little man fast enough. He was paralyzed with fear. Where to go? If he went home, his mother would involuntarily make him pee again. He could not talk to her about what the bishop said to him. His mother was on the side of the bishop. This the boy was sure of. The notion of seeking comfort from his father was as foreign as his father himself. He could not go home. There were far too many prying eyes there right now.

As the boy struggled to put one foot in front of the other, the sobbing began. These were sobs that came from his soul. The boy was a wreck. The boy walked on in his own darkness. God was gone! He should die, he thought. God was telling him to die. The boy wandered aimlessly toward the back of the high school. He was looking for somewhere to hide from himself and from God.

Just ahead the school dumpster presented a solution for the boy. This was where the boy belonged. With the rest of the trash. As he reached the big blue dumpster, he peered around to ensure he was not being watched. He raised the huge lid and crawled into the filthy hell he deserved. He burrowed down deep among the school stench and sobbed. His identity was lost completely now. He lay in the fetal position. His halo had fallen to his ankles like a shackled prisoner. He wanted help. He wanted a mother who was not available. He wanted touch from anyone. He dozed off at some point. Upon awakening, he became sick and vomited. Over and over until bile was the only offering his stomach would provide. He eventually became aware enough to stand. He climbed out of the dumpster unaware of the time of day.

When he first crawled in his new home, the sky was dark. It was now dark as he climbed out of it as well. His head hung low; the boy walked the short distance home. He quietly walked upstairs to his bedroom and lay his head down on his pillow and tried to figure out how to kill himself. There was a darkness that entered the soul when hope was gone. Joy was nothing more than someone's name. The darkness nestled into the boy's pee place of shame. It took residence. It had never left.

The man is wide awake in his bed. His thoughts are many. He is thinking about his mother. The memories of his childhood are ever-present for a reason he does not yet know.

His mother often took the boy into town when groceries were needed, or gasoline was imperative. It was on these outings that both mother and child came together in pure love. Maybe she felt a sense of freedom. Freedom from her chosen responsibilities. Raising six children. Freedom from her husband. She could be a girl again. She, at that time, was not much older than the boy. She could easily have been his older sister.

His mother made her choices in life. The man will never have the privilege of knowing the child who was his mother before she married his father. But the boy did always sense a freedom in her smile and an ease in her soul when time was spent together just the two of them that was not present in the daily drudgery of life's choices as they drove off, headed anywhere but back.

The only market in close proximity was actually not terribly close. The road that delivered them to said market was hot and wavy in summer and pure hell in winter. The road turned and curved sharply in many areas. There were speed limits posted here and there, but there was no police force, nor the money to support one, nearby. There was not a soul to enforce the posted signs of speed limits or the liberties taken by other drivers, so it often felt to the boy as if this road was a hazard to drive on. However, it was the only road leading to groceries or petrol. Oftentimes, vehicles came barreling around these corners at warp speed. It always made the boy nervous. It made him nervous as he became a man as well.

The first noteworthy landmark in this small North American town along this drive was a small cemetery where the boy spent many hours alone among the dead. The pain of his life went away when he walked along the stones that marked the lives of those now trapped in a smaller space than the community they lived in. It was a peaceful place for the boy somehow.

A bit farther down the road was the elementary school where the boy first discovered light, reading, dodgeball, and the joy of school lunch in the country. Wow, school lunch! The boy knew every day when school was in session, he would have a full stomach. They gave him two milks too.

A mile or so from the school laid the railroad tracks. The boy loved that spot of the drive. There were cattails growing alongside the tracks. He marveled when he saw them. To him, they looked like hot dogs growing up from the ground. They never failed to stir his imagination, as well as his funny bone. There were always yellow and red cardinals hurtling about. As much as the boy loved to see the birds in this area, he still was leery of them. The boy did not trust birds.

The closest house next to the train tracks where the hot dogs grew from the ground was where Weston Elm lived. Occasionally, the boy would play there with Weston. They were both in the same grade. Weston wanted only to play stupid games. To dress up like Star Wars characters and save some girl from some sort of trouble. The boy did not like Star Wars. He really did not care for movies in general. The boy always felt the director of movies often stole his imagination right in front of him. He had to pay money he worked all summer for, milking cows as they swung their poop covered tails hither and thither inevitably hitting his face, only to give it to the pizza faced trollop working the ticket booth.

(JUST SO YOU ARE AWARE, DEAR READER, COWS ARE NOT THE BRIGHTEST ANIMAL ON THE EARTH. TRUTH BE TOLD, EVEN THOUGH WE RELY ON THEM HEAVILY, THEY ARE DUMB AS A ROCK.)

In truth, Weston's mother made creamed potatoes and peas that were sheer starch stimulatingly scrumptious! Weston was merely an excuse for the boy to gain entry to the kitchen of his mother.

Another mile along where the mother and boy traveled lay the city dump on the east side of the highway. The boy remembered going there often to scrounge. The boy's father and his father's cousin, Elbert Ron, would occasionally go together to the dump to scrap for metal. The boy knew not why he attended some of these outings with his father and Elbert Ron, but he did. Probably to search for light reflection.

The boy would never forget, nor would the boy, who is now a man, the strong smell about his father's cousin. When he thought about that smell, he was instantly reminded of Elbert Ron's mother; one of the boy's favorite relatives. Her name was Elnapress. Elnapress Eastunder. The man always smiles when he thinks of Elner. Even now as he is having these memories run through his head, he is smiling as he thinks of Elner. And her eyebrows! One cannot think of Elnapress without thinking about the wonder that were her eyebrows (as you shall discover shortly, reader).

Her son Elbert Ron and his dirty hands and fingernails made the boy nervous for some unknown reason. He was a kind man. A bit strange, the boy always thought. He and the boy's father could often be seen hanging out at the shop. Elbert's hands always made the boy think of an onion. He knew somehow, no matter how much he peeled the dead skin off, there would always be another layer to deal with.

Elbert Ron's mother, however, fascinated the boy. In truth, he loved her very much. She was utterly impeccable. When the boy had the opportunity to be around Elnapress, he stared at her continually. He was amazed at her ability to detail herself. The manner of her dress and hair and her make-up application was nothing short of a miracle to the boy. Most of the women in this minute town cared very little for their appearance. At least that was how the young boy viewed them. Elnapress was entirely different. She had a fashion sense the boy recognized as purchased from a catalogue. It certainly was not available in any of the stores the boy had ever seen. Definitely not at King's fine department store. Elnapress did not wear taboo either. She always had a distinctive smell about her person. It took the boy many years to discover the source of the smell. It was not found in any department store. It was frickin moth balls. Could you just perish, reader? That discovery took place at Skaggs Alpha Beta one day while shopping with his mother. Much the same as his discovery of Tally's pits in Kings fine department store.

This discovery was in a grocery store a mere fifty yards to the north of King's fine department store. While browsing the isles, the boy recognized a smell from the cleaning aisle. It was in this very aisle the boy discovered the source of Elnapress's odor. It was moth balls. Holy Helen Keller! Who had ever seen a bag of moth balls? Furthermore, what the hell were they used for? The boy was convinced what he saw was a bag of Horehound pioneer candy. Vile as it was. No, he read the package and discovered that these balls were designed to ward off moths. Really? Who knew?

Elnapress drove her own car. Elnapress worked. Like really, worked. A job. Elnapress wore suits, stylish polyester suits that did not require ironing. She always wore a silk scarf about her neck that matched her ensemble, the boy noticed. Elnapress wore a barrel curl set of pitch black. Teased and back-combed it was till the cushion at the root was impenetrable. The boy would often walk circles around her as she sat at her little kitchen table in an attempt to see if her set was even from every angle, whenever he was visiting. Elnapress loved the cushion the beauty operator put in her hair, but more than that, she loved the smoothing out process after the cushion was placed just so. Any shape was a delight if it was symmetrical. One week it would look like a Ferris wheel. Some weeks it resembled a spirogyra. However, the football helmet was the "do" of choice most often for Elner, the boy decided. It was sheer heaven to the boy. A quarterback's protection, it was. The color of the set was matte black. Uber matte. Most likely created from the coal bin out back of her kitchen. Extra hold deluxe aqua net super spritz was what she used in between her weekly shampoos to shellac the set to unmovable earthquake standards. This the boy knew because he snooped under her faux oak cabinetry in her bathroom one day in late October.

Elner also wore high heels. Even while sitting at leisure in her home, she often could be seen wearing heels. During the day! Who could resist staring? Not the boy. That always gave the boy the giggles when Elner caught him staring at her. She always responded in kind with a "wink" or a small smile reserved especially for him.

Then there was her make-up. Elnapress was not one to shy away from anything a spatula could not fix when it came to her face. She wore eyebrows of architectural precision. Inside Elner's make-up kit you would find:

Shellac.

A spatula.

A cake knife.

A jack hammer.

A ruler.

Tarantulas (false eyelashes).

A rouge broom.

A level.

A sharpie.

And measuring tape.

These implements allowed Elner to replace her eyebrow that had been plucked tweezed and mowed for so long there was no longer a follicle left intact. Elner responded to this unfortunate hair loss with the tools mentioned above. The boy was almost afraid of her eyebrows they were so perfect.

Elnapress was a strong, loud, and independent woman, the boy always assumed. True or not, was of no importance here. She welcomed the boy into her home and her heart at every opportunity, and the boy, as well as the boy who became a man, would never forget her.

Do try to follow along please, reader, with the old man and his random memories and shifts in thought. There are often jumps in time, and from memory to memory in this tale. This is just how the old man and his brain work, and it would not be true to change this process. We are back, reader, to the trip into town with the boy and his mother.

Another sharp turn and they were now passing the Whatzit's house. Shortly thereafter, the river bottom valley was laid out before them.

Always mystical, to the boy. Often in winter there would be a low-lying fog in this area that blanketed the road creating the illusion of driving into heaven. There were Russian olive trees everywhere you looked. Beautiful and pale green. They perfumed the air with a heady, almost sickly-sweet smell. The river was a no go for the boy. Never in his life did he go there. There were goblins and witches and, most terrifying, the unknown things in the river. Nessie? The boy was not so sure, so he stayed to his neck of the woods when he needed solace.

NEVER THE RIVER BOTTOM!

Once the car cleared the bridge on the east side of the river, the road took them on a steep incline. Straight up and up and a few curves as they went, and then farther still until the road finally leveled out. Then the boy finally exhaled.

The boy's mouth began to water with the possibility of a slapstick or a handful of Laffy Taffy. The safety of his mother was close.

No peeing.

No deep sighing.

Just a simple day.

No fear.

Green.

White car.

Oil burn smell.

No air conditioning.

The two travelers passed the slaughterhouse on the south side of the road. The boy couldn't look in that direction. It was the place where a large bolt was forced into the bovine's forehead and they died. Eventual murder. That was all it was to the boy. He felt sick. He ate meat. He was aware of the dichotomy. He was still nauseous.

Houses lined up in the same shape as in any big, small town city in the western states signified they were entering town.

The car needed oil. It needed petrol. The father of the family often brought home what all of them called "clunkers". These were cars on their last rim. Who knew where he found them? They always came. This car was no exception. The car begged for oil every time the ignition was activated. It loved oil. The boy could hear and smell the constant requests from the little Monza. The boy's mother chose the gas station to the left of the only streetlight in town and pulled next to a pump.

The boy knew the routine. There was a small, black, plastic attachment that allowed white trash to use regular gasoline instead of unleaded when it was pushed over the metal end of the petrol gun. Therefore, it was cheaper. Much costlier for the government apparently. The "doohickey" was kept in the glovebox. Of course, there were never gloves in there. He retrieved it and got out of the car. He felt as though he had a gun in his hand and was about to rob the petrol station. There was simply an unspoken knowledge in the family that this was illegal. Or was it? Who could say? The boy assumed most everyone used the "doohickey." A penny saved.

The old man knows now how important, if not boring, a penny saved truly is. His mother was very proud, and probably very embarrassed, at the consequences that accompanied the lack of funding.

On they went to the market.

Sheer joy.

Items everywhere.

For sale.

To touch.

To smell.

The boy had excitement in his soul. He knew his mother would stay at his side and ask for his input about choices made. She would buy him a treat. Usually, he chose a coconut or a lemon and, of course, one piece of candy.

The boy wanted something exotic this particular day. A coconut was usually what he chose. He would hammer a large nail into one of the bowling ball holes and then crack open the magic. The milk inside the hairy wonder, he did not love the taste at that young age. But, in his mind, it held the magic travel juice. If he drank it, he could go to exotic locations all around the world. Of course, it simply brought him home again. He loved to imagine a different ending. The raw coconut would be chewed upon all day. It tasted better than tar!

As they meandered up and down the aisles, he was always awestruck there were so many items for people to eat. It seemed like a fantasy to him.

He sensed his mother's nervousness at the inability to provide. It was always a bit of a buzz kill. She did not know her son could sense her every pretense.

Her choices.

Her roughness.

Her meanness.

Her sighing.

Her beauty.

Her love.

Her heart.

Her child inside.

She was a child without the gift of childhood. The boy knew this even at age nine or ten.

She always gave him a treat.

Candy.

Something shiny.

A ball.

Rubber.

Coconut.

Limes and lemons.

Or even just a drive into town to buy illegal gas.

The two finished their outing and returned down the hill to home. The boy loved his mother. The boy was afraid of his mother. These private moments with her were better than coconuts.

The Wardhouse

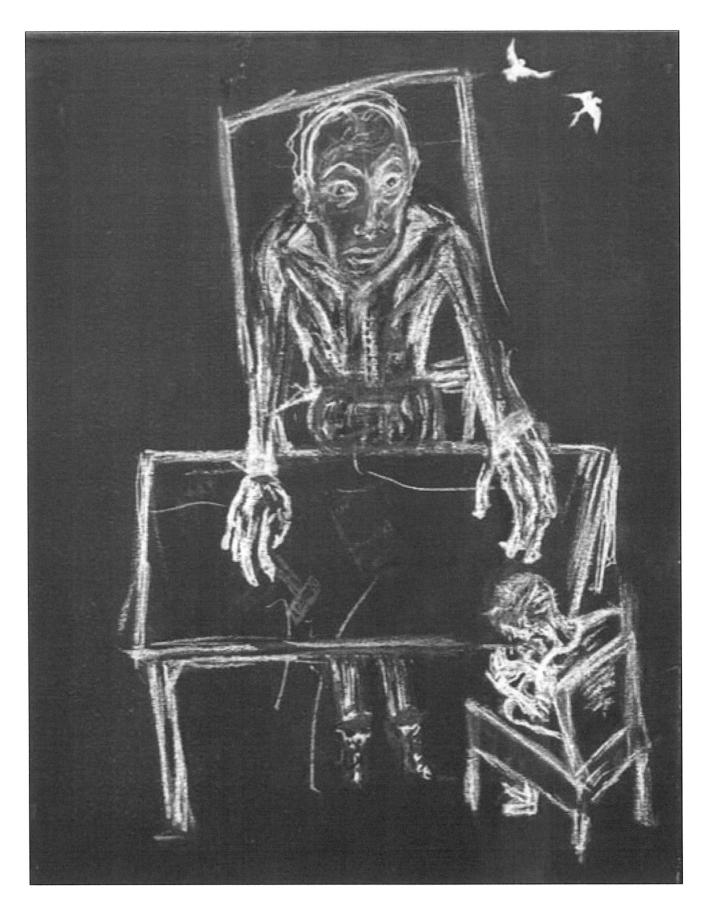

Bishop

Dumpster

Chapter Nineteen

The man has not slept well. His memories kept him up most of the night. He is out of his bed at 6:30 a.m. A horrible time of the day for him. He finds his phone and opens it. There are messages from Edward. The app icon says he has three unread messages. He opens them immediately.

> Edward: OMG! My grandmother fell. She go to pee and balance was lost. She hurt her hand.
> Why you no answer?

Edward sent a picture he had taken of his grandmother's wound. The next message was an hour or so later.

> Edward: I have helped my grandma. She is sleep in chair with all the lights on. I'm tired. I sleep
> now. 🙈

Holy hell! The man is fully awake now. The photo attachment Edward sent was a pic of his grandmother's hand. Edward is holding it in the picture, and he has zoomed out. Both he and his grandmother are in the shot. She is asleep. He has her hand in his. He looks very tired and malnourished, to the man.

It is early for Edward now and he is asleep, the man is sure. He feels compelled to send him a message.

> Man: Good Morning Edward. I just got up and saw your messages. I am so sorry I was not there
> for you. It looks like she is ok? You are sleeping I am sure. So, when you wake, please let me
> know that you and she are ok.
>
> P.S. I wonder where you sleep at Grandma's house? Do you know P.S.? I am very naive probably
> about what you understand. I wish I spoke Spanish! I am sorry.

The man starts his day as usual. Breakfast and a quick shower and teeth brushing, then heads off to work. Aside from Edward continually on his mind, the day is uneventful and satisfying. He wraps up his space, locks the glass doors, and heads towards his car. As he unlocks the car, he cannot resist for one more second the urge to talk to Edward.

Man: I hope all is well with you Edward.

He does not have the nerve to text Edward what is really on his mind. He waits a few minutes. Nothing. Edward generally responds within seconds. Not so much in the last few days. It seems so odd to the man to think it has been a few days. *That's it! Holy hell, man, get ahold of yourself.*

The Christmas rush is everywhere as the man is driving home from work. The traffic is terrible. The man decides to stop on his way home and procure a cappuccino from the coffee shop near his work. It is just so yummy. Dark, black, and bitter with milk foam on the top. "Double dry skinny cap," is what the man has asked of the barista. It makes him giggle to say that order out loud.

Nearby, there is a sixty-foot cottonwood tree absolutely covered in clear sparkling Christmas lights. It can be seen from a mile away. He decides to take a few pictures of this beautiful monstrosity for Edward to see. Somehow, he does not think this sort of thing is budgeted for in Colombia.

Coffee finished, pictures taken, he has had enough. It is a very clear night. The air is colder than usual. It is 5:30 in the evening. The sky's the color of ink. It is time to think about what to have for dinner. The man loves to cook, but he is not motivated tonight. Cooking for one is not appealing tonight. He will rummage through the fridge at home for something. There lay ahead of him the climb up to Everest. It is forever on his mind this climb. There is no curry on any of the landings as he trudges upward. Too cold for the children, he assumes. His keys are in his right pocket, believe it or not. The apartment, as he enters, is dark and stale. He turns on a lamp and sits down on the white couch as air escapes from the cushion under his weight. There is a strong odor of onions from the couch. He is staring out the window thinking what little snow they have received this year. That does not bother him. It is colder than the back of his head, however, in this part of the country in winter if the sky is clear.

PING.

Edward: Baby?

Edward has never called him baby before.

Man: Hi Edward. How are you? How is your grandma?

Edward: She better now i think. I stay with her. She did not sleep well. I just woke up.

Man: I am happy that she will be ok. It sounds like it. How old is she?

Edward: 87

Man: Oh my.

Edward: Jes

Man: It is getting close to Christmas. Do you have shopping to do? Do you buy something for everyone in your family?

Edward: No I no shopping I have no money.

This statement throws the man off. No money. Is he being literal or just dramatic or what? The man just realized Edward is not working. Why is he not working while he is in Colombia? It seems odd to him.

Man: I am sorry. Will you get presents from any of your family?

Edward: No. I will not get present.

This seems strange to the man as well. He assumes it may be a cultural difference. Something seems strange there, however. The man does not address it further.

Man: How would you feel if I sent you Christmas present? We would have to hurry. I imagine it will take some time for a present to reach you.

Edward: OMG 🙊

Edward: That is kind. I love.

Man: Everyone should have at least one present on Christmas to open.

Edward: Jes

Man: I will think on it today and see what I can come up with.

Edward: I love it. Anything that came from jou I will love.

Man: Thank you Edward. What will you do? Now? It is late there. Yes?

Edward: Jes. I will find something to eat. My grandmother does not have very much in her house. I make me somethin to eat now. I send jou some video I made for jou today. When I eat then we talk more.

Man: Ok, eat lots and lots of food Edward. We will talk in a bit.

The man forgot to tell Edward he made a video of the tree with the Christmas lights on it for him. *I will send it to him after he sends me his video,* he decides. He wonders what video Edward has made for him. If he is correct, they will be exciting. He feels a familiar tingle.

The man is sitting, staring out the apartment window, thinking about Christmas. The extended family who used to come up north for the holidays. Some members of the extended family came two, three times a year. Most of them came only at Christmas time.

There was one family member who came mostly in the summertime to help with the harvest and make a little money.

The man as a child was targeted by this family member. As has been mentioned before, the young boy did not use his voice. This visitor quickly discovered this.

"Will you go and gather the eggs from the chicken coop?" the man's mother asked of him as a boy of eleven.

This memory for the old man has been under the blankets in a forgotten linen closet in the back of his brain.

The boy became tense. He needed to pee suddenly. He knew there was a man visiting from the city. An uncle or an older cousin.

The chicken coop was in the backyard twenty or thirty feet from the back door to the house. It was early in the day when his mother made her request to the boy.

The man can remember a stuffy heat that summer. There were dust bunnies prancing about the dappled sunlight everywhere. They always held false promises.

The boy had on his brown faux velvet robe with the blue wide piping around the neck area and down both of the sides. Only in the seventies would a designer have that surreptitious moment on the designing table and think, *Faux velvet, brown, blue. Delightful!*

The man is now ill at the image of his skinny self in that robe and what happened underneath it.

The boy did as his mother asked. He passed by her working at the kitchen counter cooking something. She smelled of Jovan musk. Soft and feminine. When he exited the back door, he was very leery. As he stood on the crumbling concrete stairs at the back door to the house, he searched the property with his eyes. He could feel the presence of sin close by. He could smell his uncle. He could smell his crotch from the back door. The boy was forced to wear that smell on himself for two summers.

The boy stood on the back step, worried about his mother and her wishes. He peed himself. He had to go and get the eggs. He knew where the predator was. The boy walked the green mile to the coop. He could hear the hens clucking in anticipation of the biological material they would soon be picking at on this summer morning.

The boy lifted the rusty wire latch connecting to a very large rusted nail. He couldn't see inside. He was sun blind. He could, however, hear the man's breathing in the darkness. He could hear him masturbating. It was too late to turn around. This family member had been waiting in this poop infested hen house of picky women who laughed at every move he made.

The voice said one word:

"TEN!"

The boy peed himself again. A lot of pee. It was hot and shameful. The boy knew what was expected of him. This was the second of these summer games.

The boy said one word:

"NINE!"

The voice in partial darkness now said, "Odd number. You lose! He then allowed himself the choice of which act the boy would perform on him.

"EIGHT!"

The boy was silent. Mortified, ashamed, dirty.

It stunk in the coop. The chickens were laughing at the boy. He was lost inside his head.

"COUNT!"

The boy whispered, "Seven."

Again, there were tasks to perform. The chickens had reached a fever pitch as they talk and peck at each other's neck.

The adult in the coop. The man who could go to prison for the rest of his life then said, "SIX!"

The boy knew what happened below the number five. He is silent.

The man sitting at home on the white couch, reliving this moment has just had an epiphany. A paradigm shift he has not had in relation to this childhood trauma before. The man remembers these events very clearly now in his head. The smell of coop and crotch. He recalls the hens chortling at him in recognition at the numbers being said out loud and what they may receive after such numerical rape event transpired.

Fucking birds!

Stupid!

Laughing together as many of the adults did when the boy was in church. Gossiping as they pecked at each other's necks. The same way women did in most theological societies. The only difference was the hens in the coop would peck without malice aforethought! These women's forked tongues came out at the post office. The black slick was spewed out at ball games. The human beings these tongues were directed at, hide in the bathrooms, in the dark corners of the public eye. They hide under the bleachers at the ball games they must attend. These targets of ridicule would sneak out of the building all together if they could without God as a guide. They ran!

Fast!

Far!

The man knows he cannot run from himself now, but his younger self did not.

The last number in the coop game to be spoken aloud was barely audible.

"One," the boy said, and then he peed.

Blood!

The epiphany the man has just had as he thinks about the coop is that he, himself, has never been touched. He cannot remember a kindness of any kind from these men who used him. Even when they were in orgasm. At least during an orgasm, most of those having it will be in such narcissistic nirvana they will offer a term of endearment or touch you in a way that makes you feel you are wanted. That never happened!

The boy could not understand why he was so disposable. Sure, he was a skinny holocaustic, some said. Very young. Not able to speak for himself. He was always unclear as to why he was never shown affection.

The man has spent the rest of his life searching for the ghost in the chicken coop. The ghost of human touch. The ghost that stole his security.

The boy left the chicken coop with his head down and his brown robe secured at his waist. He was in deep shame. It was dirty. He was dirty. He was terrified. Down his leg, it was hot. He could do nothing now about his piss.

He entered the back of the house that led to the kitchen where his mother was expecting the eggs. The boy forgot the eggs! More piss. She was cooking something on the stove top. The boy tried to walk past her without her seeing his shame.

It was then, for the first time, the boy intuitively sensed a very disturbing, unsettling feeling in the very corners of his soul.

She knows what is happening to me. The boy couldn't say why. There was an unspoken truth. A glance between mother and child. Almost a challenge the boy felt from his mother as he struggled to hold his bladder.

She made eye contact. The boy looked at her. She did not say a word. The boy walked to a corner of the house where he could converse with the gods of injustice and self-loathing. There was no response. The boy inspected his battle wounds. He then changed his clothing and exited the family home to wander the foothills in search of magic and glitter.

The man has not thought about this for many years. It is yet another dark memory that has reintroduced itself in the last few months. Why? He does not yet know.

No word from Edward yet. No videos either. He wonders what it might be like to physically be there right now with Edward. Would his breath stink? Would they be uncomfortable? Is their culture and world so different that it would pose a problem? Just daydreams and useless thoughts. He is happy to have thoughts of pleasure at this very second. The chicken coop gives him chills.

Christmas time used to be so pleasant. He remembers, most of the time anyway. His mother was brilliant at creating magic for him. He thought she was not quite human. As the years passed, he discovered how human she was.

Early on as a child, the man discovered his parents had many secrets regarding their own siblings. There was an understanding the young boy couldn't explain. Nor did he ever try to. Such a thing was not done with his parents. But then, the boy was so young, why would they share secrets with him? He would not understand them. So, he felt them. Sensed them. He was uncomfortable with the people his parents became when they were around their own siblings.

The boy knew from first memory he was not of these people. Those around him who had mundane thoughts. Those who saw no spark in anything around them. Those adults who took things from children. Took things that were not theirs. They never had them in the first place. Maybe that was why they took parts of the boy.

There were other aunts and uncles who would see it as a novelty to come to the Podunk town in North America to visit the family. As mentioned before, reader, it was not such a long distance from the big city south. Zion, some called it.

They came on holidays. They came on long weekends occasionally. The boy looked forward to their visit at first. Mostly because they brought candy. Always candy, licorice. The great big bag of red and black licorice.

The boy thought these people were rich. To have the "big bag." They also brought bags of candy bars. Full size, and soda! Holy hell. Never ever was money spent on soda in the boy's house. What a treat! The boy had white bread with butter and sugar sprinkled on it just the other night to satiate his need for sweets and comfort. Lots of sugar. When there was sugar!

They came.

The adults did what adults do.

They reunited.

They pretended they loved, or even liked, each other.

The man now remembers knowing dark, bitter ugliness from his mother when these members of his father visited. He was never told anything, but he could hear acid on his mother's tongue in pretense when these visitors came.

There was an aunt and uncle who disturbed the boy above all other family members that came for the holidays. Actually, there were others who were troublesome as well. However, these two pieces of work are whom the man is now remembering.

The man becomes ill at the thought of how they singled him out when he was just a child. The wife of the uncle was "uptight" is the only word the man can think of now to describe her. Actually, that is a boldface lie. The man can think of many words to describe his aunt. His father's youngest sister. However, none of these adjectives in his head compare to the thoughts he has of her husband.

As a young boy, he assumed the adults would take care of him. He also assumed these people of his father's blood were safe. They were not, nor was his father.

The boy was always excited at the idea of visitors. Primarily because there was nothing in this town to excite or expect other than work, heat, or no heat. Food or no food. Self-acceptance or not. When there was a family visit made known to the boy, he was excited. A sense of breaking with the routine. A sort of, *Get me the hell out of this trogg-like existence that is this town with too many apricot trees and not enough pickers* was the boy's thought.

The boy learned quickly those who escaped to the country also felt free to sew their frickin weird ass familial crap on the boy.

On one such occasion, these family members of his fathers, and by the way, his mother did not want them there, the boy could sense, although she pretended well enough.

The boy could see as well as sense the tension in the house between these adults who were all pretending! The boy's mother had perfected the art of pretense. The boy could never figure out what was missing in her touch.

It took many years and truths spoken to him as a man that he began to place the pieces together of his mother. The boy was afraid of her. He was afraid of her dominance over him.

Years later in Spain, walking along a cobbled path, the man discovered the power he had given her his entire life. The man, then in Spain, had to stop along la caille presidente and take a breather when that epiphany hit him.

When he was a child, his mother had a way about her the boy did not trust. He did not know it then, but has since discovered what it was.

Ignorance.

Pretense.

Showing face.

Any cost.

At son's cost.

Repeatedly.

You, the reader, may now be saying to yourself, "Really? Could he whine just a little more? Perhaps a little cheese?" Yes, it is true. We human children go through whatever we go through. Many stories are much more horrific than this one.

The boy, nor the man, wish to taint the memory of their mother. It is already tainted. She will never admit it, ever. She has placed herself in Zion with, and chosen to be sealed to, her husband forever and ever. I'd bet money the man's father would take another card. *Bit of a digress there, reader. Sorry.*

The aunt and uncle would come to visit. They had young children of their own. All of them were much younger than the boy and his siblings. Still, they came.

The man remembers the aunt very well. She terrified him as a child. She condescended to him to his face. She smirked. For reasons unknown to the boy at the time, she had an axe to grind. She chose a child to grind it upon. She could not tell the boy's father all the hurt he had caused her as his younger sister. She took some of that out on the boy, who is now the old man of this tale.

That was nothing compared to her husband and his perverse need to wake the boy up in the middle of the night when they were visiting and whisper in the child's ear. "I know what you do with Chaise. I have seen it. You little fuck, you're filthy. You will go to hell. You like it too, don't you?"

The boy, of course, was once again alone and had no way to tell his uncle what a sick fuck really was... Him!

The boy could not talk to anyone about these incidents. He would wake from his night terrors of uncles whispering in his ear or aunts in the kitchen acting Christian with the boy's mother. That night, the boy saw two black forked tongues. One in the kitchen in pretense. The other the boy felt swab his inner ear.

The boy went about business as normal at the family house in North America while the visitors were there. Well, business as usual was now hiding from the psychotic aunt and her licorice stained and bloat faced husband. Apparently, he only showed his forked tongue to the boy after dark. No one else seemed to sense the danger around him, or they did not care. Most likely, he did not show his tongue to anyone other than the boy of this story.

The old man thinks to himself now on the white couch in between tears and memory. Those two probably saw each other's forked tongues often as they argued at home when one or the other insisted on being right. Around the dark corners of their home, the tongues were fighting for dominance. Apparently neither of them was able to leave their snake-like mouths home prior to traveling north to terrorize a child over the years of seven to sixteen.

The strange thing, the old man once again thinks as he reminisces, is why could he not stand up for himself?

You see, reader, there is a theme presented more and more to you about the boy's thinking. The adult boy still does not stand up for himself.

The fall came. The boy started another year in school. This year was different. He was in real trouble. He had to attend a school of rednecks where you physically had to castrate a sheep for a final grade.

This was a very short time before the tragic, unspeakable thing happened to another like himself in another rural town not far from the boy.

The young man, Matthew Shepard, was so brutally murdered. The man is crying again. Matthew was bound to a fence post, pistol whipped, beaten about the head and face in a field and left for dead by two other young men.

Matthew was homosexual. The murderers were not. The man needs to vomit. There were many forked tongues up north. As Matthew discovered…

The old man as a teenager had a clear understanding of the danger he was in minute by minute when in public in this small, neurotic, fanatical, Mormon town.

The trouble was the boy could not get away from himself. He became dysmorphic. He stopped looking at himself in the mirror, in his face, in his eyes. He did not recognize the reflection. He was painfully tall and skinny. He was bullied daily. It was not called "bullying" in those days. It was called shame guilt. No one to talk to about it. Loathing.

Many years spent alone in the foothills.

Wandering.

Searching.

For glass.

For god.

For the sun.

There never were any answers for this boy. No *ah-ha* moment. No help. Just black forked tongues. The boy had descended into a very dark place where he would not know another peaceful night's sleep again. It became a foe for the rest of his life.

A bolt of lightning and a crash of thunder breaks the man's reverie. *Holy hell! How long have I been daydreaming?* he wonders. He looks at his phone. His vision is blurry. He is struggling to put the image of Matthew out of his mind.

It is now past ten in Colombia. He decides to send the video he just took of the Christmas tree. There are two videos. The man can be seen walking around the obnoxious, bright tree smiling and pointing and basically acting uncomfortable. He sends them anyway and captions them.

Merry Christmas, Mr. Arias. Christmas 2018.

There is a response from Colombia five minutes later.

Edward: 🧑🏿

Video attachment (2)

He opens the first video attachment. Edward is in his grandmother's green bathroom. He is naked. The water is running fast from the shower head behind him. He is erect. He is filming himself using a vegetable as a toy. The video is very graphic. Up close and very personal. Edwards androgyny is terribly sensual. Being Latino helps. Edward completes his mission in the bathroom as was just witnessed by the man.

The second attachment is Edward cleaning himself in the shower.

Man: You are so sexy Edward. You have no body hair. Do you shave your entire body? I miss you.

Edward: all for jou my sexy

Edward: completely for jou.

Edward: I miss jou to. Do jou want to see us naked now?

Man: Call me.

The two of them spent the next hour on the phone together. Edward was whispering so as not to allow his grandmother to hear his conversation.

Man: May I ask you a question Edward?

Edward: jes of course

Man: You use a vegetable to play with. Is that what you prefer or…...?

Edward: Prefer? Wait please.

Edward: Ah I google word prefer. Ja Ja Ja. It's all I have. I have no money. I never have own toys before.

Man: Ok. Now it is Christmas. Would you like a few personal items for yourself?

Edward: I no understand.

Man: Sex toys, lubrication. That kind of thing.

Edward: OMG. 😊

Edward: Jes. I like very much.

Man: Ok. Tomorrow I will go to scandal and pick out a few things for you and I will send them for your Christmas gift. Will you give me your address? I can mail it.

Edward: Jou sure? I'm excited but I can't buy anything for you.

Man: That is not important. I would love it for you to have some real items of your own. You will love the way it feels.

Edward: OMG. 😊

Man: Tomorrow I will go to the store.

Edward: Can I see?

Man: See what?

Edward: What will you get at this store?

Man: I do not know yet. I can call you on video when I am at the store and show you all the items and we can decide together. Secretly of course. What do you think?

Edward: My sexy. You are so hot. Jes I want.

Man: Ok it is a plan. I will get it in the mail quickly. How long does mail take to get to Colombia from the USA.

Edward: A couple weeks I tink. I'm no sure.

Man: What do you have to do tomorrow?

Edward: No ting. I stay with you all day.

Man: Awesome that makes me happy. Goodnight. Call me in the night if you need me.

Edward: Ok my sexy. Goodnight.

The man's brain is racing at warp speed. So much to think about. The video of Edward is marvelous, not to mention their conversation. It is very sexual this thing they have, even though they are nearly five thousand miles away from each other.

What kind of gift should I buy for him? he wonders. *Guess I will make some suggestions and let him decide. We will do it all live so he will see everything I see.*

The man has a smile on his face as he lies down in bed. His sleeping medication is starting to work. He is pulled further and further into the bliss of unconsciousness.

Edward: sleep well babe

The Chicken Coop

Chapter Twenty

The man wakes from another restless night of tossing and turning. His feet and knees will no longer be ignored. They have alternate plans for the man, apparently. They seem to laugh at sleep. At rest. At peace. Almost like birds do, he thinks.

Shit! What an ugly way to wake, today. Thinking of birds, feet, and knees. If it was not so hideous it would be laughable. He must shake it off. Get coffee. Keep moving.

He instinctively reaches for his phone which is always turned off at night. There are no lights anywhere in the bedroom. The fire alarm has been disarmed. That little frickin light on the thing glows and lights up the whole room at night. Absolutely not. *I'd rather burn*, the man thinks. The blinds have been secured to the sides of the window frame with huge oversized, overstuffed pillows.

There can be no light nor sound in the man's bed chamber. As it is now, he will sleep, at most, four hours a night. He will wake at the whisper of the day's trouble. He will hear his mother's voice and wake. He may hear a toilet flush next door and he'll not sleep the rest of the night.

There is something otherworldly that visits when you have gone several days without sleep. The man has had this problem since childhood. It has reached dark proportions.

He can now see he has missed a message from Edward. As he reads Edward's well-wishing of slumber, the man smiles. *What a joy to smile naturally again,* thinks he.

Today he will work half a day. He will drive into the city where he can purchase some Christmas items for Edward. These cannot be found in the suburbs. He must go over the river and through the woods to the naughty shop.

After the morning rituals are performed, he sends Edward a message before he heads off to work.

> Man: Good Morning Edward. I'm going to work. I hope you slept well. I missed your text last
> night, but it is nice to see it this morning. Eat some breakfast and I will talk to you later.

The man really has an easy day today. A few clients to see then he is free. It is frigid cold as he opens the garage. The car will take a few minutes to warm up even in the garage. It's one of those days where an inversion has laid its ugly blanket over the entire valley. The cold is locked into place until another storm rolls in. It could be weeks.

He is at work a bit early. So, he wanders to the breakroom to make another coffee. The room is empty. That's always a bonus. He still has a bit of a cheesy smile on his face. Surely those around him notice a change in him. A lightheartedness. He thinks about Spain fairly regularly. He has always wanted to visit Spain. He has told no one of his intention to go there. It's just kicking around in the back of his head like lotto balls in a wind bowl.

The man finishes his clients, cleans up a bit. Then he locks up and heads to his car as he has done several thousand times before.

Still no word from Edward. He has decided Edward sleeps most of the morning away. Sometimes into afternoon. The man can remember sleeping long into the morning when he was not able to sleep at night. Still, the man finds it annoying. He decides he will grab some lunch and head into town to do his shopping regardless. He will just buy what he wants to give Edward and it will be more of a surprise.

The drive to the city would normally take twenty minutes or so in light traffic. The weather conditions have made it difficult to see. There is a dense fog tackling the highway. The man arrives at Scandal Novelty and Adult store forty-five minutes later.

He is frazzled. He could see the tension in the faces of every driver on the road. Sending it bouncing back and forth from car to car as if they were all in a pinball machine. Scandal is located in a bit of a low scale business district. The building itself is pink and looks a bit rough. The man has not been here in a very long time. Only when an occasion suggests some sexy underwear and a novelty or two. He would come more frequently were it closer to his apartment.

Ping.

There he is! the man thinks. *Yes!* There is a message from Edward.

Edward: Good Morning. As you wake?

The man can't help but smile every time Edward asks that question.

Man: I slept ok thank you. How are you today Edward?

Edward: I good. I stay at grandmother's last night. I will go to my dad's tonight.

Edward: What are you doing right now?

Edward has a way of communicating that has endeared him to the man as no one has before. Is it the language barrier? Edward has asked the man on several occasions what he is doing right now. It always leaves the man with an anticipation that drives him loco.

Man: I am shopping for your Christmas present Edward.

Edward: OMG, 🙈 Noooo! Really? Right now?

Man: Yes. I am at the store now. Do you want to see?

Edward: Jes. Of course. I so excited babe.

Man: I will call you and turn the camera on. So, you can see what I am seeing.

Edward: OMG. I can't talk. 😩

Man: Why?

Man: It does not matter. I don't want to talk in the store about what we choose either. It's embarrassing.

Edward: Jess. We text. As we look. 🖤 🖤

The man is inside the store. He has first opted to choose a pair of underwear for Edward. He has called Edward and can see him on half of his phone screen. He looks tired. He is not fully awake, it seems to the man. That irritates him. Why this? Why that? The man suddenly has a million questions about Edward's behavior. Now is not the time, clearly.

He texts Edward and asks him what style of underwear he would like.

Edward texts him in reply: Show me something that you would like to see me in!!

That's easy for the man. He has a very specific type that turns him on. (THE READER WILL BE SPARED THE DESCRIPTION.) Suffice it to say, a pair was chosen between the two of them.

The next bit of shopping was to happen in the back of the shop. The adult novelties. (AGAIN, READER, YOU WILL BE SPARED THE INTIMACIES OF THIS SPREE.) The man chooses several items he does not show Edward. He seems to be well-educated in this department which actually surprises the man. It also pleases him.

A large shopping bag in hand, the man leaves the store with Edward in cyber tow. This is going to cost a fortune to mail to Colombia, the man is sure of it.

Man: I still need your address. I'm going to mail it now.

Edward: I can't wait to get the package. We will have fun together. Here is address 4414 Violetta caille, Medellin Colombia 050001

Man: You will love the items. There are a few surprises in the box also.

Edward: OMG! 🙆🏽 You drive now?

Man: Yes, I'm driving to the shipping co. now. I will mail it express. So, you will get it quickly.

Edward: My sexy.

The man is correct. The cost to ship the box express, which is seven to ten days delivery, is close to four hundred dollars. There is no guarantee of a delivery date or even if the package will make it all the way to the final destination, the very helpful and overly cheery woman at the UPS counter informs him. "Once it leaves America, we really have no control over the delivery.. You will get a tracking number that should help. Even in Colombia."

Well, at least that is some assurance. A tracking number.

Man: I've just sent the package Edward. I hope you love it. Merry Christmas beautiful man.

Edward: My sexy. Thank you so much. I am very excited to see it. I love you.

As he reads the "I love you," from Edward, he about drives off the road. Normally, the always awkward "I love you" stage in dating someone this short of time is a turn off to the man. Not so with Edward. The man has always known the moment he meets a man whether he will love them or not. He has known for some time he is in love with Edward.

Man: You are welcome Edward. Let's hope it arrives safely and quickly. I'm driving back home now. So, Let's talk in a bit ok.

Edward: Jes. No text and drive. Be careful. Talk soon. 🖤

There is a light snow falling as the man drives towards home. Traffic is heavy. It's the beginning of rush hour on the freeway. He chooses alternate routes all the way home.

Once inside, he drops himself on the white couch and begins the recovery process of the climb. Outside the window is a bleak scene. Gray. A mere shadow of snow. Not enough to be annoying. *These winter evenings do not end*, he thinks. It's nay on to six, and he feels as if it's midnight.

PING.

Edward: You home now my sexy?

Man: Yes, I just arrived.

Edward: I'm so happy. I horny now.

Man: Oh really?

Edward: Jes. I have a question?

Man: What is your question?

Edward: On the app, do you meet many men?

Man: Well, over time I have met some. Why?

Edward: I mean to have sex?

Man: I have before, yes.

Edward: Do you know the app well?

Man: No, I don't really know what I'm doing most of the time.

Edward: We can share the app. There is an option to link accounts. So, we can decide together.

Man: Decide what? I am not sure what you mean.

The man has some idea what Edward means, and he is very uncomfortable, and a bit saddened.

Edward: Maybe you could meet someone and we can turn camera on. So, we see it.

Edward: You can see my account too and everyone that leaves me messages? You can see they profile?

Edward: and I will see the guys there on you account and I help you pick ones.

Man: If I choose to do this, that means that you will have access to everyone I have spoken with. You can also then pull up all conversations and read everything? Is that right?

Edward: Yes. It's true. You can also see all of my conversations.

The man has taken twenty minutes or so to respond to Edward's request. He is extremely uncomfortable with the idea. *What I say and to whom I say it is private. It's mine alone. Well, and the individual to whom I am saying it,* the man thinks. He is not ready for that level of honesty with the twenty-three-year-old he has recently met. Not even met. Cyber romance is all it is really. No matter how much he cares for or loves Edward.

It then occurs to the man that Edward can tell if he is "active" on the site anytime he chooses to look at his profile. This has never been an issue before simply because he has never dated anyone on the site. He has "hooked up" but not exchanged information. Never talked about love or family. He has never cared before now.

Man: Edward I am uncomfortable with you having access to my sexual life with others. Most of its fantasy talk, but its mine. It seems like an invasion of privacy to me. I'm sorry. 😔

Edward: "Invasion of privacy" What this is?

Edward: Never mind I use translator again. You will see my talking too! It does not bother me. I have nothing to hide. What are you afraid of?

Wow. The man has not yet experienced this side of Edward. He seems angry suddenly. He is being very aggressive about this whole issue. The man can see Edward is attempting to manipulate him.

Man: I am not sure that I'm afraid of anything on this site. I simply am not willing to let you in my head that far just yet.

Edward: I no understand you.

Edward: Do you have WhatsApp?

Man: Yes.

Edward: Let us move to WhatsApp. I am bored with this site. What is your full name and your phone number?

The man is all too happy to move this relationship, or whatever it is, to a site that is not a dating site. Or hook up site. Whatever the hell it is. Edward has suddenly taken the aggressive role. The dominant one. Today has been slightly annoying. Edward has been annoying. The old man will let it be for now.

Man: Here is my number Edward. I have given you my full name several days ago. Look for it back on your texts from me. 521-661-9638

Edward: I can't find you.

Edward: What is your county code?

Man: oh yes, I'm sorry. There is a 1 before the 521. 1-521-661-9638

The man truly does not have a clue about WhatsApp either. It has been years since he set up the account and many months since he used it. Let alone had another person contact him.

Edward: I just send a message to you in WhatsApp.

Where is the WhatsApp icon? The man does not recall ever noticing it among the other apps he has downloaded. Holy hell! It is nowhere to be found. He doesn't want to seem uninterested, but he does not have WhatsApp downloaded anywhere. He googles it. Google takes him to his app page. WhatsApp is apparently locked up in the anonymous cloud that holds all hopes and dreams and apps as well. Who knew? The man clicks on the cloud icon next to the app he has just found.

Presto. The man's WhatsApp has been restored to him. With all the information saved quietly away next to a cumulus or a cirrus or even out near the stratus. Holy hell, it is too much for the man to think about. He really does not care. Give him a book any day over a computer or a bloody phone.

The app takes about fifty-five seconds to download the information it has been keeping watch over. The moment it is downloaded, there is a mechanical sound coming from his phone. It's the message notification alert. He must have chosen that ringtone for this site at some point. He questions his judgement on that decision immediately upon hearing it. It is a sort of high-pitched purring sound. There is a number that indicates how many messages he has. Forty-seven total messages. Holy hell! Why did I close this app? He will investigate later. Now he must respond. He opens Edward's message and his picture is there with his phone number and date and the number of messages he has left. In this case, it is one.

He pushes the message icon and Edward's message is visible.

> Edward: Hello my sexy. Send me a message WhatsApp now. We use this. I will delete the other app since you don't want me to help you.

Another bit of passive aggression the man notices.

> Man: I received your message. I'm using WhatsApp Edward. We will use this mostly to communicate with each other?

> Edward: Yes, it is more secure. I am going delete the other app. We can also talk on messenger. Do you have Facebook? Instagram? Pinterest? Zoosk? Tinder? or be naughty?

He has not heard of any of these, other than Facebook. Holy hell. These are the very moments when he must seem old to a twenty-three-year-old.

> Man: I like using WhatsApp. I like the format better than shadow. I have a Facebook page but I never use it. I have not been on it for years. I have no Instagram, because I do not really care to see photos of myself. I do not know the others.

> Edward: Well you can use your photos to get yourself noticed. I can help you organize your photos and it will make a new page for you that will make people attracted to you.

Does Edward want to help, or does Edward want access to all his photos so he can see what is there? Hmmm.

> Man: I am not really interested in all of that Edward. I really am a bit shy believe it or not. It seems silly to me to be so serious about my outward self.

> Edward: I find you Facebook page. It is ok. You have two accounts. One for work and personal one. Give me access to your photos and I will start tonight to organize and post them.

> Man: I am nervous about it all. I am going to shower now. I am tired. Where are you?

> Edward: I join you in shower. I at grandmas. Then I must go home to my father's house.

> Man: Can we see each other on this app when we want? When we shower? May we see each other?

> Edward: Jes, you see. I call in 10 min. I will be sexy too jou.

> Man: yay!

He gets his things together. Clothing, shaving gear, toothbrush. It is all placed on the shelf in the shower. *Holy hell. I need clean towels,* he discovers. Racing to the linen closet, the man returns to the shower where the water is running hot and fast.

While he is holding his phone, there is an incoming video call from Edward. The man nearly has a heart attack. The call was so quick. He did not expect Edward to respond so fast. The man pushes the accept call icon. Immediately upon accepting, Edward's naked body is on the screen.

Edward: Hi my sexy.

Man: Hi Edward! You are Beautiful!

Edward: Turn on your camera. Turn it around so I can see you.

It took several seconds to figure that one out for the old man.

Edward: There you are! Your sexy.

Man: I do not feel sexy. I am cold and naked. I cannot figure out where to put the phone so you can see me and not get my phone wet.

Edward: Do what I do. Put your phone in a large glass and stand it up. So, we can see.

Man: Genius! Like we did before.

The man runs to the kitchen to retrieve a large mouth Kerr jar. He places the phone inside the jar and makes sure the camera is on, then places it on one of the very small shelves in his shower stall. The jar teeters a bit but finally rights itself. They can see each other perfectly.

Edward is standing in the green tiled bathroom again. He is naked and fully erect. Every time the man sees Edward's erection, he is a bit shocked. Holy hell it is huge. Edward is soaping his body while fully hard. The man is also erect! Neither of them has a small member.

The man suddenly remembers one evening on a video call with Edward, they both became curious about the size of each other's penis. Both men wanted to know which of the two had the larger penis. They measured. Both members were the same size.

(THE MEASUREMENT WILL NOT BE MENTIONED HERE. SORRY, READER. IT IS A NATURAL THING TO BE CURIOUS ABOUT IT EVEN IF YOU PRETEND IT IS NOT. JUST KNOW THIS READER, THEY WERE BOTH HUNG LIKE A HORSE, AS WAS SO OFTEN SAID ON THE FARMS WHERE THE MAN GREW UP.)

Enough debauchery. The rest of the shower went as you would expect. Touching. Looking. Questions about this or that on each other's body. After the climax, the two were tired.

Edward: You beautiful babe.

Edward: All for jou.

Man: I feel the same way Edward. I think I am falling for you.

Edward: Falling? What is this?

Man: Never mind, Edward. I must lie down. My feet and knees are in much pain.

Edward: I want message you. Take care of jou. Please come to Cartagena for us.

Man: I have tried. I cannot make it happen. It is too soon. I am sorry.

Edward: Maybe Spain? See us in Spain?

Man: Yes. That would give me time to put it all together. It could actually work.

Edward: 🐙

Man: I'll do some research and we will talk more.

Edward: Ok my love. I go to my fathers now. I text you when in bed.

Man: Ok Edward. Take care and eat something.

Edward: JA JA JA JA

The man never did give Edward access to his photos for Facebook and Instagram. He knows Edward will surely ask again. The man has the feeling that Edward is bored at home. He has never mentioned a friend. He does not seem to leave the house. Perhaps it is a money issue. If he is not working, there would not be income, most likely. Surely his father would offer a stipend while Edward is in Colombia on break or holiday. The man does not know why Edward is even in Colombia. Why spend the airfare to go home if you cannot afford to buy yourself some food?

Every time he has asked Edward what he will do today, he replies he is doing nothing. He is home all day and night at twenty-three years old. Something is strange about it, the man thinks. He will leave it be for now.

It is now after midnight. It has been a crazy day full of emotions the man reflects as he chews on his sleeping pill. He is too lazy to get water from the kitchen. Twenty minutes later, he is out for the count.

Chapter Twenty-One

Holy hell! The man has woken up in the middle of the night in a cold sweat. An Ambien induced night terror. His heart is pounding as he lies on his bed. He is wide awake now. His head is throbbing.

Birds! There are always birds in his dreams. They are never gentle fluffy creatures. Often, they talk. They always mock. *I must get out of bed and shake this off. Get some water, a snack. Anything to stop these thoughts of birds*, the man thinks.

The man has fragments of his dream flash back to his head as he walks to the kitchen. There was a Karmann Ghia in the dream. Yellow. What is that about? There are pieces of the dream slowly moving together in his head like the answer to a riddle that takes all day to grasp.

It was David's Karmann Ghia. Holy hell. David's Volkswagen. It was the very first willing sexual encounter of his life. In the backseat of a Volkswagen Karmann Ghia. David was a high school flame. He was so cool and sexy. The man's memory shifts in between David's face and his car in his foggy waking state. There was not a backseat in the car he now remembers. An empty space. There was not even a cushion to sit on.

He cannot tell now if it is the dream he is confusing with reality.

It was his senior year of high school. He had just moved from the tiny community he grew up in to the big city south with his younger brother *(WHOM YOU KNOW, READER)*. His parents moved them to the big city because there was not enough work available for the man's father. No more farming. No more of that small town that almost killed the man when he was a boy.

He was very excited at the prospect of moving away from the thinking that many employed in that small community.

Maybe, the boy lay awake at night thinking, *there will be others like me.* That thought so fascinated him it was very difficult to remain calm as the move became closer.

He was also saddened for his younger brother whom he loved very much. As you know, they shared a room together as children. They peed off the roof and giggled all night. They cuddled when they were too cold. The boy inside the man was loved in a way that probably saved his life.

The man returns to his memories of the Karmann Ghia before his brother popped into his head.

The back

Of a car

With another

They were parked in someone's driveway. He cannot remember other events or places around that moment. But he relived it not thirty minutes ago in a dream.

The touch

Exploration without pain

Natural

God given

No face

No expectation

No counting

No master

Another living soul wanted him. This was a new sensation for him. David was touching him. He could talk if he wanted. No pee.

The young boy in David's arms in the back of a Karmann Ghia began to cry softly.

The old man sitting on the edge of his bed in the dark begins to sob.

David became upset and began to cry as well. David was concerned. He asked if he had done something wrong? Had he hurt him? Did he want him to stop? Never was this said to him in the past.

He never did tell David what he was experiencing emotionally in the back of that Volkswagen. They held each other without talking for some time. For the first time, these two young men were free to express their affection in the back of a car. No fear of getting shot in the head. No fear of being pulled behind a pickup truck in chains until dead. No fear of God. No fear of parents. Real-ness for the first time. Ever.

The boys were so moved by the intensity of this moment. They began to kiss. Chills vibrated up and down the body of the young man. David clearly was responding in another way. Never in his life had the boy kissed anyone. It was extravagant. It was wet. There were tongues. This was so new and so real for them both.

The old man now smiles on the edge of his bed.

They performed sexual acts on each other. There was no turning back. Neither wanted to turn back. This was the moment it was first understood. *I can be wanted. Desired. Loved without force! Every human!*

This understanding began a lifetime obsession for human touch. Sexual touch. Not always the physical act itself. The feeling the man has when he knows someone finds him sexually desirable. Sexy! Nothing was the same after that moment for the boy, or the old man.

Chapter Twenty-Two

The night is very long. The man's head is foggy. The memories of David have him feeling haunted. He also feels joy in seeing David again all these years later. Even if it is in a dream.

Christmas is two days away. He is not terribly excited at the prospect of gift purchasing and last-minute shopping. He can put it off no longer. He must get up and get moving.

After work the ghost of Christmas present will ensure all on his list will have something to open from him. It is a short list. "Thank you, deities!" the man says aloud.

It is another bitterly cold foggy morning. The man descends the mountain to his vehicle. It is particularly thick, this fog today. Dangerously so. He must drive very slow along with all the other fools working this close to Christmas. Even those not working this the week of Christmas who are full of cheer and simply have to get out of their homes and have a coffee or breakfast merely to socialize.

He eventually arrives at work where there is not a creature stirring. Not even Sister Strouse. She prefers to be called "Sister." She comes into the workspace very early every morning to clean all the common areas.

"Good morning, Sister," the man offers.

She smiles and moves on.

Two clients later, which is about three hours, there is an unfamiliar sound on the man's phone. It must be a WhatsApp notification. He knows by now it is Edward. Edward is rarely awake before noon.

> Edward: Good morning my sexy.

> Man: Hello Edward. How are you today? I had strange dreams all night. I am a bit tired.

> Edward: Ooh noooo. I'm sorry. You are working today?

> Man: Yes for a few more hours. Then I must go and buy a few things.

> Edward: It's Christmas coming. Jes I forgot. I still have no package you send. I am worried about it. I need to know exactly the day it will arrive so I can receive it.

Man: Yes, it has been longer than they said it would be.

Edward: Do you have a tracking number.

Man: Yes, I do somewhere. I will see what I can find today and let you know. What are you doing today?

Edward: I will go with friends to the beach soon.

Man: Oh, that sounds nice. How warm will it be?

Edward: 21 C today, I think.

Man: That is 70 degrees here, I think. Wonderful.

Edward: Jes my sexy.

Man: Ok I must get back to work for a bit. Talk soon.

Edward: Talk soon my man.

Well, that was a sexy enough thing to say, "Talk soon my man." Wow. Heart pounding, the man gets back to work. He has made a mental note to find the receipt from the shipment company for any additional information they may have. Perhaps that overzealous happy girl will assist him if she is there.

He does find the receipt and tracking number printed on it. A few hours later, back home now, he can tackle this without distraction. He enters the tracking number for the package.

No information is available. He then locates the number for the shipping outlet and talks with a very helpful shipping agent who informs him the package is not in the United States. It is due to arrive in Bogota, Colombia for customs, and then on to the final destination. There is no information if or when it will arrive in Bogota.

Well. Holy hell. This is going to prove to be difficult, the man is thinking. It is a third world country. The government could do whatever they wanted with the box. It is out of his control he now realizes.

Something has been bothering the man. Edward said he was going to the beach. Edward has never mentioned friends before now or left the house, as far as the man knows. It is none of his business; the man knows this. The way Edward acted in his last few texts was somehow off from his usual mood.

The man decides to open the app they met on. The dating app. He is curious to see if Edward deleted his profile as he said he was going to. Not only has he not deleted it, Edward is active right now. Which means he is using the app now.

Again, none of my business, thinks the man. *We have no commitment to each other.* It does seem Edward would intuitively know it would not be okay with the man for him to be actively talking with others. If he is talking with other men the way he talked to the old man, then he is less than genuine.

The man assumes he is going to the beach with someone he has met on the site. Edward has no money. Someone will have to pay for him.

Try as hard as he may, the man is irritated. *A bit sad, and a titch jealous if you must know reader.*

The man leaves the site open and browses the application. He discovers many options he was not aware of. There are a small handful of messages left for him on the site from other members. Nothing interesting.

He is bored with it. There are things that must be done today. Gifts to buy. It will be a small Christmas for everyone who may find themselves on his list this year.

The traffic is hell. The crowds are too cheery. It's moments like these, when he sees heterosexuals en masse that he really feels like an alien. He has always felt a bit discombobulated to be in the middle of it.

One stop done. He crosses off three people from his list. There is just one more stop and he will be finished with his Christmas shopping.

All is accomplished without the man totally losing it. Although there were several moments, triggers. Irritants that could have easily produced an adult beverage. Not today, however. He is off to the white couch.

He has become used to texting back and forth with Edward in the evenings. He looks forward to the distraction that talking to Edward brings. It allows him a bit of an escape from this dark winter and the holidays. Edward must still be at the beach. Now sitting on the white couch, the man is bored with the television. Bored with the book he is reading. It's twenty-three degrees outside. It's far too bitter to go out again into the holiday mess happening everywhere.

Maybe I should meet or talk to someone on the app. It would at least entertain the thoughts that this down time brings.

The app is still open on his phone. Coincidentally, so is Edward. *(YES, HE LOOKED, READER.)*

He has several messages that interest him. Clearly, this site is for one thing only. How has he missed the obviousness of it? The man chats back and forth for an hour or so with a particularly interested party.

Finally, it is decided the man will host this fellow. Michael is his name. He is very handsome and also at home alone bored and looking for some companionship.

The man lets Michael in and directs him to have a seat on the white couch.

Michael sits, a bit nervously. "I like this couch very much."

The man is getting two glasses of water and has to stifle a smile when Michael makes the remark about liking the couch. "Oh, thank you," the man says. "It's fairly new. This small apartment really does not have much going for it."

"I think it's awesome," Michael says.

The man sits on the couch next to Michael. He really is beautiful. He is mulatto. Very large, full lips. Beautiful caramel skin. Black curly hair, and that butt! What the hell? Why did all the white men get into the back of the line when butts were dispensed?

They chatted. They got to know one another a little bit, all of which led to one thing. Not hard to figure out. It was amazing. It was hot! Temperature wise. Sweaty. They kissed each other! That does not happen generally. *Mount me if you must, but not a kiss.* It is a silly line the man picked up from a movie somewhere and has, since hearing it, kept it rolling around in his endless mind chatter. He would love to say it to Michael, but he just giggles to himself instead.

It was a very pleasant evening with Michael. He seems to feel mutual. The two of them part company after a few more gropes and tickles.

"I would love to see you again," Michael says.

"It's a deal. I enjoyed it very much. You are a very sexy human being, Michael. You know how to find me. The same way we did tonight," the man says as Michael begins his descent to the parking lot.

It's after ten p.m. here. It's after midnight in Colombia.

Why have I not had a text from Edward?

As he gets ready for bed, the man realizes he is in trouble. He misses Edward. His emotions are all over the place. This makes him very uncomfortable.

Edward sends a text to the man the next morning. It is very short and very impersonal. Edward says he had a great time at the beach. That it is cold, and he is tired and hungry. He then ends the text by saying, "Talk later."

Hmmm, the man can't decide what to do with the text. Where to place it, in the mass of jumbled emotions and thoughts skating around in his head.

Christmas morning. The man is having his coffee as he stares out the window. It's gray and cold. The only creatures that can be seen moving about are the winter birds that flit about as if they are all late for a very important meeting. Mocking someone, somewhere. He knows the mocking of birds. It starts a sweat bead at the base of his neck that will reach its final destination at his lower back.

The man gets a cheesy little growing smile on the corner of his mouth remembering what happened on the white couch the night before. He wonders if Michael could smell the curry on the couch while he was lying on it. He did not say so. *I hope not,* the man thinks.

It's nine in the morning; too early to make his few house calls for Christmas. Edward will surely be sleeping still.

Happy Christmas! Merry Christmas! Love you! Happy New Year! Happy Hanukkah! These words start to pop up on the man's phone from Christmas well-wishers.

The last message is announced with a familiar chime. Edward has sent a text. The man opens it.

Edward: Merry Christmas babe.

Man: Merry Christmas. You are up very early on Christmas morning.

Edward: Jes. My stepbrother is very excited. So, we watch him open his gifts.

Man: You must be tired.

Edward: Jes I'm tired. Have you found out anything about the package?

Man: Just that it is no longer in the United States. It is headed for Bogota for processing. I'll leave you the tracking number. As soon as the postal service is open again, would you call them and see what they can tell you.

Edward: Of course. I call Monday morning.

Edward: I see that you were on the app last night did you have fun.

How does Edward know he was on the app last night? Then he realizes he can see when Edward is on it too. He must investigate said app for security options.

Man: It was a quiet evening here. I thought I might hear from you.

Edward: I have no phone service at the beach. No wi-fi.

Edward: Did you have sex?

The man does not know how to navigate these waters. His first and natural instinct is to tell the truth. It almost sounds as though Edward wanted this to happen. Too much thinking for the man.

Man: I had someone come over to my apartment we had a nice talk and he had some wine.

Edward: May I see?

Man: See what?

Edward: Your pics from last night and videos.

Man: I didn't take pictures or videos.

Edward: Oh. Show him to me on shadow.

Either Edward is voyeuristically turned on or jealous! The man does not know what to think. He has never been in this kind of situation before. He feels as though he should intuitively lie to Edward. But then there is a sexual element to Edward's curiosity that is a huge turn on to the man. *Holy hell! This is uncomfortable.* The man is wondering why he's verklempt. He knows, inside himself, that he is in love with another man who lives in South America, who is moving to Europe very soon, and he does not have the means nor the ability to give the man what he needs. No, that is too simple actually. It's not about needs really. It's about what he will accept and what he will give. Is it an equal dividend? It should be. It does not seem likely.

Edward: Let's switch profiles on shadow.

Man: I'm very nervous. I am uncomfortable as I told you before.

Edward: Why? I don't understand what you are hiding from me?

Man: I'm not hiding anything from you. We have only recently met. I don't understand why you should think I'm hiding? You don't really even know me Edward.

Edward: Jes, I know you very well.

The man is beginning to sense an annoyance, as well as an arrogance, in this boy of twenty-three. Holy hell.

Man: What is involved in exchanging profiles?

Edward: You must give me your account name, your password and your email that you used to set up your account.

The deed is now done. Edward has access to the man's account. Full access. He later learns that not only did Edward have access to his account, but there is no way to know when he is looking at it. The old man also gains full access to Edward's account. Edward provides all the necessary information so he can do so.

The man has a sense this was not a great idea. He also wants to please this twenty-three-year-old. The man has begun day-dreaming about taking care of him as he has always done with others. Put them first.

The man chooses to stop fretting about it. It's done, what may come, may come. *Edward will now see who Michael is and read our conversations and the after talk. He will see it all. It doesn't really matter*, thinks the man. *Edward and I have had no discussion about being with other people.* It's just a month into this thing, and the man is not up for that conversation quite yet.

He must get himself put together. He needs a shave. To style his hair. To find an outfit to go out into the tundra to do his calling. Actually, just a few stops. His mother and father and a brother all live together close by. So that's three birds with one stone.

He has a sister who lives in the city. But he won't go and see her this year. The skeletons have begun selling their bones for space in the closets in this family.

The man's senses are accosted as he opens the apartment door. The drop in elevation. The necessary action to get to the garage. Completely detached. (As you know, reader.)

The sun is at its brightest white. The reflection off the light snow that covers the ground makes the man tingle. Almost high. (almost)

His mother's house is first. Easy enough. His dad and brother are there, so this is a fruitful trip. All the pretense is stuffed into the bottom of the Christmas stockings. Situated beside the Christmas crackers. If the two of them should choose to cause a commotion of truth, in the dark of that stocking, tt would be worth seeing.

Two hours later, there is some yummy food in his belly. The man departs for the stairs and the white couch.

It's three in the afternoon, Christmas day. There is literally no one parked at the complex. *Where have all the Indians gone?* There is not one to be found. This complex really is nothing more than a short stay for most who live here. They have dreams of home ownership. Some may be temporarily working in the area and are being housed by their companies. He certainly does not plan on another year on Everest.

It is getting darker by the second. It is 27°. The man remembers a line of poetry he once read.

"What is the value of time if locked in a season of death?"

What, indeed? he thinks. Holy hell! "That was an uplifting bit of scribe," he says sarcastically aloud.

Eureka! The top of the stairs. He is intact. Now to crack open the door. Will it be onions? Garlic? Masala? Jasmine? Basmati? He pensively opens the door. He walks in the apartment, there are no smells. All throughout the apartment there is no odor. There is not a smell to be had.

"Holy Helen Keller!" he says aloud. Delightful. *There will be no nasal annihilation tonight!*

Man: Merry Christmas Edward!

Nothing. No response from Edward. He is most likely spending time with his family.

The man settles in for the holiday. It's been relatively quiet. It is bedtime for him when he hears from Edward.

Edward: Merry Christmas.

Edward: My sexy.

Edward: How are you?

Man: My day was very nice. A little family time and then just relaxed at home.

Edward: Jes. me too. Family all day.

Edward: I want to see us tonight but I am at my father's house.

Man: Its ok Edward. I'm going to bed. I'm tired now. Good night baby.

Edward: 😳

Edward: 🖤

As he lies in bed waiting for the sleep gods to take him, the man wonders about Edward's family. How different they are from his own. His father seems strict, from how Edward has described him. The man is tired. He is tired of trying to figure out this South American way of life. At least Edward's life. It's time to shut this day down.

It sounds like the pathetic excuse of someone who did not grow up in a cyber age. No computers. No cell phones. The man can barely navigate his own technological activity. Young he is not. He knows this. He is thinking the very thought as he begins to breathe deeper and deeper to a false state of sleep. He wants to talk to Edward again. He does not even know what he wants to say. Nevertheless, he wants to see him. To hear his voice. Edward rarely will do a video call for reasons that remain unclear to the man.

> Man: I'm in bed now trying to sleep but you are on my mind Edward. How are you? What are you doing?
>
> Edward: I playing with my phone. How are you?
>
> Man: I'm ok. Feet hurt. 🙁
>
> Edward: So sorry babe.
>
> Man: I want to see you and talk to you. Can you take a video? call now?
>
> Edward: No now. There are people here. Maybe later when they sleep.
>
> Man: Why does it matter if others are around?
>
> Edward: Because I can't talk very loud if they are home.

Again, it seems peculiar to the man the way Edward explains everything as if it were obvious. The man leaves it alone again for now. Along with all the other tidbits Edward shares with him that do not quite compute.

> Edward: I looking at shadow. I see Michael's pics.
>
> Man: Oh?
>
> Edward" Jes my sexy. He is very hot.
>
> Edward: Can we meet him in a trio?
>
> Edward: You like him?
>
> Edward: I read what you say to him. I want to watch you have pleasure wit Michael.

The man has forgotten Edward can get onto his account anytime and see all the activity the man has engaged in these last few days. He has accessed Edward's account one time. Days ago. There were many older men who had left messages for Edward and pictures of themselves in various, shall we say, stages of undress. Of course, everything was in Spanish. The man could not read any of it. He lost interest quickly. It seems so wrong to look in on Edward's private life. Sexual life. The man logged off Edward's account and has never returned.

He has no idea how many times or how often Edward is on the app using his account. Apparently, there is no way on the system to notify an account holder when someone else other than themselves is actively viewing or accessing the account. For shame!

Chapter Twenty-Three

The old man and Edward continue to text each other daily. Many times a day. They share more and more of each other's lives. The man begins to see a kind young man in Edward. He has shared information about his childhood, about his parents' divorce and how difficult it was for him. In particular, the way it affected his mother. Edward spoke of another brother; an older brother not far in age from Edward.

There is a sort of peace that settles over the man during this time of discovery with Edward. They laugh. They share mutual interests. Edward tells him of his love of whales.

The new year comes and goes. Edward has not received the gifts that were mailed to him. The man can sense a sort of urgency about the imminent delivery from Edward. He asks the man every day if he will call the postal carrier he used for the delivery and ask them where the package is. Many calls were made both here and in North America by the old man, and in South America by Edward. The package is stuck in Bogota. That is the only information available to either party.

Edward asks the man more and more about profiles he has read on the app that are leaving messages for the man. (That Edward has access to)

"Do you like this?"

"Do you like that?"

"This would be hot."

"He is hot."

"What will you do?"

He then asks questions about Michael. Edward has mentioned Michael once prior, but the old man swept over it in the hope that the matter was closed. The man and Michael have chatted briefly on two or three occasions about that night they spent together. They speak on the app. Edward has access to the entire conversation. Edward brings the subject up daily.

On one particular day in January, Edward sends a message to the man announcing:

I have a question my sexy

Man: What is your question?

Edward: Do you like trios?

Man: Trios? You mean a three way? As in sex?

Edward: Jes. 🙈

Man: Well I don't know honestly. Generally, I think I prefer to give my attention to one.

Edward: JA JA JA

Edward: I want to do a 3-way call. I know someone that is your type.

Edward: I have sent him your picture. He wants to meet.

Edward: To call us.

The man is a bit saddened Edward wants to include another person in the relationship. A relationship that is entirely online. These characters have not met. Yet the man feels something toward Edward he now questions.

Edward: What do you think?

Man: I'm not sure. What is he like? What did you say to him? He has seen me?

Edward: Jes. I have shown him many pic of you. He wants you.

The truth here is simply what it is. The man did not want to do this. The man wants Edward alone. The man wants Edward to want him alone.

Man: Ok if you want to try it then, I will too.

Edward: My sexy. I have him on the call already.

Edward: I will add you to the trio and you accept the phone call. We see all of us at once.

Holy hell. Edward is already talking to this man. For how long? What in the hell has he told this guy?

Man: ok.

The phone then rings and on the screen is Edward waiting for his call to be accepted. The old man accepts the video call. Instantly on the man's screen is Edward, another man, and in the upper right corner the man's image. Live. Edward types on the screen.

Edward: Hi sexy. How are you tonight?

The man is honestly stunned.

Edward: This is my friend Camillo.

Camillo: Hola. You very sexy.

Edward can also send text messages to the man Camillo cannot see. How? The man has no clue. What the man is clear on at this point is that he does not like this.

Edward (to the man, private): You no talk?

Edward: You like him?

Man: I'm uncomfortable.

Edward: Try. He sexy.

Edward (texting now to both men): What do you like for sex? Camillo?

Edward: Show us you now.

The man has exited the phone call. He is on the verge of tears and fury. How dare Edward do this. He is jealous and quite literally flabbergasted at Edward's insensitivity. Edward calls the man on the phone. A very rare occasion. Edward can rarely talk out loud on his phone to the man (as you have discovered, reader). The man does not answer Edward's call. Edward calls again. And again. The man accepts the fourth call.

Edward immediately wants to know what happened. He asks the man if he did not like Camillo? "He no sexy?"

"I tell him about Jou."

"He very interested in phone sex."

"He is still on video wait for you."

The man informs Edward, not only is he not interested in Camillo, but he is in fact very saddened Edward wants to involve him in a third person video chat/sex or whatever he intended.

"Why would you not speak with me before doing this?" The man wants Edward to explain. "Why do you want another man involved? I don't understand what you are doing," the man tells Edward. "I do not want to hear or read what you say to another man. Especially when I'm there with you live! I'm sorry, Edward. This was a very big turn off for me. Tell Camillo that I'm sorry, but I'm not interested."

Edward: OMG 🙈

Edward: Give me one moment please.

Edward: I explain to jou.

Edward: I so sorry.

Edward's explanation of the event was an attempt by him to give the man pleasure. Edward met Camillo on shadow. He told him he had a friend he wanted to do a trio on video with. Edward tells the man he wanted to see him live on video talking and sexting with another man.

"It makes me sad to hear you talk to another man, Edward. I am not interested in all of this. I'm sorry."

Edward placated the man. The whole situation was brushed off quickly and without responsibility or acknowledgment of Edwards intentions.

Edward: Is ok babe. We try again with someone else.

It is not long before Edward brings it up again. Two days in fact. The two days prior consist mostly of trying to find the missing Christmas package. The only thing they can determine is the package did indeed arrive in Bogotá several days ago. No information is given as to when it might leave Bogotá and advent in Medellin. Edward's father's house, some four hundred miles to the east, is where the package should be by now. Edward is becoming very impatient about it. He seems almost nervous somehow to the man.

Edward: Hello my sexy.

Man: Hi Edward. What are you doing?

Edward: Noting. Sitting at my grandmother's house.

Man: You love your grandmother so much don't you?

Edward: JA JA JA Its true.

Edward: Let's try a trio again.

Edward: This time you invite Michael over to your house.

Edward: You will have your camera on so, I can see.

Man: I'm at work now. But I am about finished. I'll text you when I get home ok?

Edward: Ok babe.

As he wraps up his day and locks the doors, the man is again a bit heartbroken Edward wants others to be involved in this thing.

Obviously, Edward is bored, and I am not enough apparently, the man decides as he is getting into his car to head home. It is a simple truth. The man cannot understand how someone so young puts these things together for himself. He has done it many times. He must have. He is not shy when he describes what he wants to the man. It's a different world for the man. Yet he cannot seem to deny Edward's wants and desires. This definitely makes the man uncomfortable. However, he somehow wants to please Edward. Over and over again. The man continues to feel a need to please others before himself.

Man: Ok. We can try it. What do we do?

Edward: Invite him over to your house again. Have sex with him.

Edward: We will set up the phone so I can watch.

Edward: You will have to put the phone somewhere that I can see and hear all.

Man: Will we tell Michael that you will be watching us?

Edward: What do you think about it? Will he agree or no?

Man: I don't know. I really don't have any idea.

Edward: Will you ask him? Or you think he shall not know.

Man: I don't think he will agree to film it.

Edward: So, we won't tell.

Edward: You can set your phone on the table by the white couch.

Edward: Let's try now and see how you will do it.

Edward: I call you on video. I can't talk but I will text you how to do.

Man: ok.

Edward calls. His face is on the man's screen and there is no sound.

Edward: Hi my sexy.

Man: Hi babe.

Edward: I can see you very good. Are you holding the phone?

Edward: Put your phone on a table or somewhere that I can see your whole body.

Man: There is a table next to the couch. I'll try that.

The man places his phone on the table under the window at the end of the white couch. They go back and forth with the camera angles and Edward dictating what should be done and where on the couch and how it should be done.

The decision is made. The man will appease Edward's needs. Edward claims, as always, he is only doing it to please the man. The conversation ends with the newly used phrase "I love you" from Edward.

The man feels like shit. He has agreed to what he instinctually wish to do but does anyway.

The man sends a message to Michael. He texts of his desire to see him tomorrow if he is interested. He does not mention Edward's name, nor the intention to film the activity. Michael responds shortly in the affirmative. He is interested in coming over tomorrow to see the man.

The man knows he will not tell Michael what is really going on. Michael may be on a sex site, but in the little time Michael and the old man have spent together talking, the man has learned Michael is a man who would not allow himself to be filmed. He would think it very odd the third person is on the phone in Colombia. He has a moral compunction to this deceit. The man is sure of it. And rightfully so.

The old man sits on his white couch in ponderance of his choices. He knows he has fallen for a child. He knows this child does not feel the same as he. He cannot sleep.

The man does eventually fall asleep many hours later in a state of dishonor and loathing.

Chapter Twenty-Four

It is a very strange time for the man. This point in his life. What he is accepting. What he decides is validation. How he feels about his age. He is acting as if he were twenty years old again, like Edward is doing. The man listens to himself every time he and Edward communicate. *Communicating* is a stretch of the imagination. The man has become a puppet of sorts. He is fully aware of this.

The deed on the white couch involving the man, Edward, and Michael takes place the next day. The afternoon actually. Still winter. Still freezing. Still gray and ugly.

It is a total disaster. The man cannot achieve an erection. Edward texts the man every few seconds demanding the camera angle is wrong. He cannot see. The lamp is in the way. The pillows are obstructing his view.

The man is sick inside. He only wants to be away from this moment. He wants Edward to want only him.

Not ten minutes into the debaucherous white couch incident, the man puts an end to the transmission. He apologizes to Michael for his lack of performance. Michael asks him for money. The man declines and Michael leaves the apartment.

Edward has called the man every few seconds. Edward has texted many times.

The man is devoid of feeling. He is crying now silently in denial of truth.

Edward; Please answer me.

Man: Hi 😫

Edward: What happened?

Man: I could not do it.

Edward: Why?

Man: Because I want you and you are far away. I don't want to do this ever again. I'm sorry.

Edward: Ok. No problem we no again.

Man: No, we won't. I won't.

Edward: You did not get hard?

Man: No, I could not.

Edward: I know you. I saw. You only were excited when you saw my face on camera.

Man: yes.

Edward: Ok. We no talk about it again. We will move on ok?

Man: Yes.

There is a new coldness in Edward the man feels but cannot acknowledge.

The conversation ends that night with Edward expressing an urging for the Christmas package that has yet to make its way from Bogota to Medellin.

Things change yet again the next day.

Chapter Twenty-Five

Edward has only two weeks before leaving his family home in Medellin, Colombia forever.

The man has told Edward of his intention to come to Spain in the spring. Edward has told him of his desire for him to do so.

"Jou stay at my apartment," Edward said. "I show you Spain."

Of course, the man would never allow himself at his age to be dependent on Edward for housing or anything that may cause him financial struggle. It was simply another contradiction from Edward's mouth the man discovers.

The man is at work. It is mid-morning. There is a text notification chiming from his phone. He knows it is Edward texting him. He is always a bit twitter pated at the sound of Edward reaching out to him.

The text is from Edward. However, it is a picture message only. The man is with a client and yet he cannot resist the urge to open the attachment.

On his screen is a picture of a box resting on what looks like the front entry of a home. It is the Christmas package. It has finally arrived. Edward must have just received it.

Edward must be so excited. Santa Claus finally found his house. The man can imagine the smile on Edward's face as he opens it. These are items the man has held in his hands and now they are in Edward's hands. It makes Edward feel more real to the man. It's almost proof of life. That is how the man sees it. Holy hell. How exciting. The man can hardly contain his excitement. Edward has asked about the package more than once a day in the last few weeks. Edward and the man have discussed what will happen when it arrives. Edward will make a video call to him and he will wear the underwear and model it for the man. There are several pairs of sexy underwear. And, as discussed, he will use the toys on live video.

(NOTE TO READER: YOU CAN USE YOUR IMAGINATION REGARDING THE TOYS. SUFFICE IT TO SAY THAT EDWARD PICKED OUT THREE OF THEM WHEN THE MAN WAS AT THE STORE, SCANDAL. HE THEN CHOSE FOUR MORE ITEMS FOR EDWARD. EXCITING, THIS BOX!)

The man is finding it very difficult to concentrate at work now. He has envisioned every item in the box and what Edward will show him. It is most uncomfortable having these sexual fantasies when your aggressive Russian client is seemingly aware your mind is on something other than her.

It has been over two hours with no word from Edward. The man is a bit impatient as he anticipates the action. Maybe Edward is using it all now. Making videos for the man. Yes, that must be why he has not texted him about the box and its contents, the man has decided. His thoughts return to the steaming, fuming, eye bulging client. She is by now a Christmas cracker about ready to pop her top.

A familiar *ping* sounds from across the room where the man is charging his phone. It has now been close to three hours since the picture of the box arrived. He can wait no longer. He excuses himself from the room with phone in hand as he finds the restroom where he can have some privacy for a few minutes.

There is a video of Edward modeling a white thong. He looks great. He said he had always wanted to wear a thong. Now, on video, he is. It is a very short video. The man cannot see any other items other than Edward, the thong, and the green bathroom.

The video ends with. OMG! 🙊

That was a bit odd, he thought. *Edward loves to show videos of himself. Where are the rest?* The man waits five minutes more. Nothing else comes from Edward. Holy hell. The man puzzles as he goes back to work.

There will be more videos and after work they will see each other live, the man is sure of it.

Four hours later, the man has completed his workday. The Russian woman he was working with became satisfied with the old man eventually. The sun is actually shining bright today and it's above forty degrees. The days are getting longer which lifts the man's mood instantly; he notices the subtle difference every day now.

Nothing from Edward. The man is a little concerned now. It just feels wrong somehow.

Man: Edward? How are you? Are you happy with your Christmas presents?

No response.

It is most strange. The man cannot understand.

Home now and sitting on the white couch. He does not really know what to do. To text again? Maybe just call? Video call? Try to reach Edward on Shadow?

The man opens the Shadow app. The notifications on his app are in Spanish which means Edward is still watching what he is doing here. The man clicks on Edward's profile he said he deleted. There it is. It shows Edward was active this morning.

The man is sad. He simply sits and stares out the window. Tears are forming. He feels betrayed.

Man: Edward Where are you? What do you think about the box?

Edward: Yes, I here. How are you?

Man: You're there? That's all you say. You have not even mentioned the Christmas box.

Edward: I made a video for jou. Did you see it? The underwear is very sexy. I like.

Man: Yes, I saw it you look great. Where are you? Show me everything we can play with them later in bed.

Edward: Jes. I want. I'm at my fathers house. I text you soon.

Man: Ok. I'm excited. We have waited so long for this moment.

Edward: JA JA JA

Holy hell, is the only thing the man thinks about it all. Edward is being unsure and non-committed. He is actually acting nonplussed and a bit mean. Perhaps a bad day. "Who knows," the man says to himself. "Later perhaps it will all make sense to me."

It is 10:30 p.m. Mountain time, 12:30 a.m. South American when Edward texts the man.

Edward: Hi. How you?

Edward: What are you doing?

Man: I'm lying on my bed relaxing. I looked at shadow for a little now I'm getting tired.

Edward: Jes its late. I deleted the Shadow app already.

Obviously, Edward is lying, but why? The man plays along. There is an awkward several minutes pause before either party sends the next text. This also had never happened before.

Man: What are you doing?

Edward: I went out for a bit now home. My dad and stepmom are here.

Man: So, I guess that means we cannot play together with your Christmas presents?

Edward: I sorry. 😖

Man: Well, won't you just show me each item and tell me what you think? You will have questions about how to use two of the items I chose for you.

Edward: I scared. I tell truth to jou

Man: Yes, please do.

Edward: Jou mad?

Man: Should I be mad Edward? Do you think that your behavior toward me today should have made me mad? You did not respond all day. You have waited and talked about this damn package for so many weeks. I guess I thought you would be so excited and want to share it with me.

Edward: I so sorry.

Man: That's it? No more explanation? Did you even look at everything I sent? There are other gifts. Nonsexual gifts. You have not said you have seen it. Nor have you acknowledged me for all I have gone through to get it to you.

Edward: I tell. I very scared wit my father. I tell you before he machismo. He no know I gay. I have told no one.

Edward: I gave you grandmas address for the package to be delivered. I did not want to have package come to father's house.

Edward: My father would demand to see what it was. My stepmother would open it herself if I was not there.

Edward: If they know I received a package, they will search for it when I'm not here.

Man: That's a lot to digest right now. I don't know what to say.

Edward: My brother is very mad at me.

Man: Why would your brother care? How does he even know that you received a package or what its contents are?

Edward: I tell him about package. I tell him about you. I need to hide it. He wants me to take it all to trash somewhere. I don't drive. I have no car. My brother, he very very angry with me for making risk for both of us.

Man: I don't remember you telling me much about your older brother. I don't even know his name. Where is your brother now? Why does he want you to throw it all away? It sounds like paranoia to me. I want to know if you have looked at everything in the box.

Edward: My brother move to Spain two years ago to marry a man from Spain. He can work legally and live freely in Spain now. He divorced now. He just needed papers to live in Spain.

Man: You did not tell me your older brother is gay.

Edward: He live with his ex-still in Madrid. He mad at me for taking this kind of package inside my father's house. No family no that we are both gay

Man: Do you really plan to destroy it all? Or threw it all away? Do you have any idea how much money all those items in the box cost? What about express shipping? Do you know how much I spent on that? It was a lot of money Edward. Close to a thousand dollars all together.

Edward: I don't know what to do all day I am nervous. My stepmom is here all day wit me.

Man: If you are going to destroy the package, I insist that you mail it back to me. I will keep it since you don't want it. I can't believe this. You chose some of the items. We talked about them in detail. You talked about them. You were so excited for your present. Or so you said to me. Now I wonder if you just lied about it all.

Edward: I no lie. Don't be dramatic.

Man: What did you just say to me?

Edward: I figure out a plan.

Man: I am not being dramatic Edward. It seems to me it's the other way around.

Edward: Other way round? What this mean?

Man: Never mind.

Man: Did you even look at everything in the box? The card, the things inside the card. Any of it? You keep avoiding that question.

Edward: No, I so sorry.

Edward: I very scared of my father.

Man: What would your father do if he found the box or what is inside the box? Would he assume that you are gay?

Edward: Jes. He would kick me out of house and out of this family.

Man: I'm sorry that you are having such an uncomfortable time with what was supposed to be a Christmas gift. One that you wanted and asked me to mail to you. Do whatever you want. Burn it. Throw it away. Do whatever. Such a waste of money and time. I'm going to go now. Take care Edward.

Edward: Nooooo

Edward: 💔 💔 💔 💔 💔 💔 💔 💔 💔

Edward: Please talk wit me.

Edward: I soooo sorry. I need you.

Edward: I very sad.

Man: I'm still here Edward. I'm sad too. and confused. What will you do?

Edward: I tink I will wrap it all in tape to cover it and then tape it to the inside of my suitcase.

Man: It is not illegal contraband Edward. You need not tape it all up.

Edward: I hide it from stepmother. I have see her look through my bags before.

Man: Edward you are 23 years old. You have completed a college degree. She cannot go through your things. Put a lock on your suitcase. Lock your door when you are not there.

Edward: It is different here in Colombia than is in America. People are different. I cannot lock anything in my father's house. Anything inside his house is his he says.

Man: Yes. That is certainly frustrating.

Edward: I'm such a loser.

The man can tell Edward has begun to cry now as he texts the man.

Edward: I can't see to come out. I very afraid.

Edward: You have been through it already. You were strong. You tell you family and friends long time ago. I have shame. I feel, guilty. Full of sin. I worry about god.

Man: My beautiful Edward! I have been through it. It was very difficult and took several years to come to terms with it. It is different for every gay person. When the time is right for you, you will tell the world. But it's your experience and yours alone. I cannot help with that. But I can be there for you in the aftermath I can reassure you that you are made in god's image. He did not make a mistake with you Edward.

Edward: What is aftermath? Means what please?

Man: It just means that during the period of time. Just after you "come out" you will need to talk and feel loved and supported.

Edward: I need to get to Spain. It will be good. I'm not ready now to tell. I leave in a few weeks' time.

Man: Yes, I know Edward.

Edward: You will come to see me?

Man: Yes. I am coming in the spring.

Edward: OMG. My sexy!

Man: So, what about the box? You have it figured out? Do you feel safe?

Edward: I tink I call my brother again and he tell me what to do.

Man: May I ask you a question Edward?

Edward: Of course.

Man: Did you already throw away the box? When your brother became angry and he told you to get rid of it? Did you get rid of it already?

Edward: No, I have all still. It is all covered in tape now. I show you in Spain.

Man: Thank you for sharing more of your personal life with me Edward. I 🖤 you.

Edward: 🖤

That was it. After weeks of anticipation and discussion about the Christmas box, the man receives nothing more than a heart emoji. No mention of the money the man placed in the card for Edward. No mention of the other usable nonsexual items that Edward needed.

It's true, reader, the man did get to know Edward a bit more. Very personal, very emotional things Edward was willing to share with the man. Maybe the Christmas box brought Edward closer to his own truth.

The man is still pissed about the box, however!

Chapter Twenty-Six

Edward never brought up the box in conversation. The card, the money inside the card, the chocolates. None of these items were acknowledged.

The man never asks about them. He feels he knows the answer, and Edward's silence about the contents of the box was enough evidence for the man. The box was gone.

Over the next few weeks, Edward rarely texts the man. Edward is preparing to move to Spain, saying goodbye to childhood friends at long dinners Edward does not share with the man.

There are two events that take place between these two men that change the way the younger of the two feels about the older. The white couch and the Christmas box.

The man continues to feel the same love for Edward. He knows Edward has lost the affection he may have felt in the beginning. It is lost in a few short months. (Oh, to be young again, eh, reader?)

The day of the move comes for Edward. The man hears nothing from him most of the day.

Edward: Hello.

Man: Hi. You must be busy. You leave in an hour? Correct?

Edward: SI. We drive to Bogota to airport. Will be long drive 5 hours or so.

Man: How long of flight from Bogota to Madrid?

Edward: 12 hours.

Man: It will be fine. You can listen to music and watch movies and rest.

Edward: Jes. My father calls at me know. I text you when in Bogota.

With a heavy heart. The man visualizes Edward leaving Colombia and leaving it for good. It is never spoken of again. Edward texts the man from the Bogota airport.

Edward: We are about to leave airport now. I let you know when I in Spain. Take care.

That was it the whole day from Edward. He has a lot on his mind, there is no doubt. Clearly the man is not one of them.

> Man: Have a safe flight Edward.

The man has provided a few items in the Christmas box for Edward to use on his long flight to Europe. A prepaid music card. Some whale music to download. Prepaid, of course. A Netflix prepaid account card for movies. Edward does not mention these items. Ever.

The days now are long and semi sad for the man. He half-heartedly completes his job requirements. It has been two days since he heard from Edward.

The man has not been able to stop obsessing about seeing Spain. He is sleeping less and less. Always a problem. He cannot drink nor eat well. He is too excited at the prospect of seeing this amazing country and, of course, Edward.

The man becomes a bit giddy when he imagines leaving everything behind as he runs away to Spain. Never before has he attempted such a thing. He realizes this is the only way in which these things happen. He must actually book the trip and then everything will fall in to place. He ups and goes.

He is not sure if he can make this trip ever happen for himself. He really has very little money. He is involved with three family members in a business that recently closed. It was given away actually. The man has been held responsible for some debts left behind by other family members. (It is not important that you know how this happened, reader.) This is no diatribe on why you should not do business with family. That is perhaps another book to be written. An entirely different scribe. It's a bit like a scab. It cannot be peeled off; it must heal a bit first.

The man has been to many banking institutions asking for a personal loan. Eventually, it happened. He is approved for enough money to finance his trip and to take care of a few of Edward's needs as well.

The man really does not know if he can repay the loan.

(AS HAS BEEN MENTIONED HERE BEFORE, READER, "WHAT DO YOU REGRET IN YOUR LIFE? WHAT YOU HAVE DONE? OR WHAT YOU DID NOT DO?")

The man will not live the remainder of his life without meeting Edward in person. He cannot. He *will* not. Whatever the cost, he will pay. Even in blood.

The man can sense Edward is no longer interested in him. He remembers a time when Edward begged him to come visit him in Colombia. A time Edward wanted him to come to Spain. "I will show you the best of Spain," he said.

The man dreams of dinners out with Edward. He daydreams of walking through the magic city called Madrid. He plays out the nights of sex together with Edward in his arms. Most of all, the man dreams of Edward falling asleep in his arms.

He purchases many new clothes for this trip. The man wants to look amazing with Edward out in public. He is not yet aware that he is a foolish old man.

The man sets aside a large cache of money to give to Edward. He purchases many gifts for him. Everything is in vain (as you will soon see, reader).

He has made his choice weeks ago, mentally. Now, with the money deposited in his bank, it's a done deal. The man will leave April the eighteenth at eight p.m., arriving in Madrid fifteen hours later. The long flight has him very concerned about his knees and his feet. He will take this adventure. This is a once in a lifetime trip. The man has taken hold with both hands and will not let go now!

The man decides he wants to do some charity work while he is there. He has emailed several organizations and chooses to work with two of them: the homeless and a facility that houses terminal aids patients. Both organizations respond via email that they will love to have some help while he is visiting.

That will give me something to give to the city of Madrid and to its people. Three days, three hours a day of serving others during this ten-day trip. Sounds perfect to him.

The man has not told Edward the trip has been purchased. He has told him he is coming but has not made it a reality for himself until now. After many searches on his computer, looking at hotels and B&Bs, the man decides he wants to stay in more of a boutique style hotel. He wants it to be very fancy. Modern. A room that has a lot of glass and straight lines in the architecture and particularly large. He decides on the hotel, Regina. The Regina is located in the city centre.

The Regina has it all. It looks like a beautiful room on the hotel's website. The room has a balcony which helps the man make his choice. He books the hotel and flight together. The carrier is Delta. The man books comfort class for his flight to Spain, as well as the return flight home. Comfort class is really nothing more than a few more inches of leg room and seat space. The airline suggests that meals are booked, as well as the seat reservation to ensure the most comfortable flight experience possible for the dollar amount.

(WHAT DO THOSE WHO DO NOT WISH TO SPEND THE ADDITIONAL ONE HUNDRED AND FIFTY DOLLARS DO, READER? DO THEY STARVE? ARE THEY PARCHED THE ENTIRE DURATION OF THE FLIGHT? DO THE SKY MATTRESSES EVEN ACKNOWLEDGE THEIR PRESENCE?)

The man would normally balk at such an injustice. He would, under other circumstances, leave an email for the director of flight affairs informing he or she of the caste being played out on this flight. Not today. The man is far too excited to leave his mundane life in North America to jeopardize his flight plans due to the ignorance of most American conglomerates. He decides he must have an additional level of comfort due to his feet and knee problems. Not to mention sitting hour after hour in an encasement of metal and wires entirely dependent upon the captain and crew to deliver him safely to Spain.

There is an hour and forty minutes layover in Atlanta. "That's not so bad," the man says aloud. A fifteen-hour trip total. When he thinks of the entire duration it will take to arrive in Spain, he feels a bit nervous. He is also ecstatic it is booked.

Well, that's that! It's going to happen in less than two months. That will give him time to work in more clients he surmises to help with the expense of it all.

Driving home from work is a breeze. No more holiday traffic. Marvelous. He has been practically high all day knowing he has booked his trip to Spain. As the man drives homeward, he wonders if he will hear from Edward tonight. He should be in Madrid by now if all went well.

Walking up the stairs, the man sees a beautiful little Indian girl. She hides behind corners and stairwells. She sticks out her head far enough to flirt a little with the man. He walks over to her and retrieves some gum from his pocket. He offers it to the girl. Her eyes become huge. She puts out a very delicate, reluctant hand and accepts his treat. She then turns and runs as fast as a cat being chased by a neighbor's dog.

That beautiful creature is the greatest part of my day, the man thinks.

As he enters his apartment, he is suddenly aware of how alone he is. How lonely he is. Helen Keller! Talk about a buzz kill. The man puts some leftovers of some sort in the oven for dinner. He honestly does not remember cooking them nor what the food actually is. He cannot tell from the looks of the tinfoil wrapped glutenous concoction.

He then grabs his laptop and plops down on the white couch. He types the word "Madrid" in the search engine. Image after image pops up. Architecture. Tours. Shopping. So many things to see. The man tries to imagine which building Edward lives in as he looks at all the amazing buildings in the city centre. They are very expensive properties. Surely, he can't live in one of these. He is imagining Edward living in one of these amazing buildings like a king with servants and young men fanning him with palm fronds when his phone chimes and forces him back to reality.

Edward: Hello my sexy.

Man: Edward, are you safe? Are you in Madrid?

Edward: Jes, I here. I so tired.

Man: Oh good. I'm happy you made it there safely.

Edward: Ja Ja how jou?

Man: I'm fine. Just arrived home. I'm relaxing.

Edward: I'm going to sleep now. We talk when I wake.

Man: Ok goodnight.

The man had hoped Edward wanted to tell him about his trip. The man wants Edward to tell him how he feels about leaving Colombia. Clearly, he wasn't interested in conversation. He is tired after his long journey.

The man is dejected after the brief texts with Edward. The leftovers he reheated for himself no longer appeal to him or his stomach. He decides to have a bowl of cold cereal instead and crawl in his bed. He wants to talk to Edward about the hotel he chose and ask him if he knows of it. The man knows he will not speak with Edward for many hours. Frustrated and a little sad, he reluctantly turns on the television in hopes he will think about anything other than Edward.

Another workday lies ahead for the man. He must see an important client tomorrow. She may hire him to design her California home. It is very appealing to get out of this February weather to the sunny state of California. It would be a dream, even for a few days. Even with all these thoughts tumbling around his head like the gentle cycle on his washing machines, the man does eventually sleep for four hours.

The morning is uneventful as he eats some hot oatmeal with heavy cream and a pinch of sugar. He showers and dresses and is on his way out of the apartment. He checks once again to see if he missed a text from Edward. There are no messages.

On an impulse, the man pulls up Edward's profile page on Shadow. Just as the man suspects, Edward is online now. The man is angry. Angry at himself for his transparency. *Edward is stringing me along. Period!*

He closes the app and fumes the rest of the drive to work.

The next six weeks are difficult times for Edward and the man. Their communication becomes ridiculous. Edward is using a translating app regularly now. The man is also using one. Oftentimes in Edward's texts, the whole text is in Spanish. The man tells him so, and Edward becomes a bit snippy. So, he no longer tells Edward when he writes in Spanish.

Edward is apparently not interested in the man understanding what he is saying. So, the man downloads an app to translate the texts for himself. There are many translation errors. Many things Edward says in Spanish translate to mean, ugly, spiteful sentences. In one such text, the message translates to "Your mother is a whore!"

When the man reads it, he becomes sick. He wonders how many of the texts Edward had written in Spanish were spiteful, and he is getting a perverse pleasure in knowing the man does not understand what it says.

The text that reads in Spanish, "Your mother is a whore," so upset the man, he asks a Spanish friend to translate it for him in the event he made a mistake. The friend says the message is calling his mother a whore. The man becomes sick and furious.

The man brings it up to Edward. His reaction is that the man overreacts.

"There is something lost in translation. You always assume the worst thing with us."

"That is not true," said the man. "It's written in a language I don't understand. I took time to have it translated by a Spanish speaking friend of mine. All those involved say that what you texted me is just what the translating app says."

Edward boldly ignores what the man tells him, simply changing the subject completely. Sweeps it under the white couch, so to speak.

There are several of these "translation incidents" with Edward and the old man on the app. This is the cause of much frustration and anger for the man. He asks Edward specifically if he means to write these words. Edward always denies it and says the app is mistranslating it.

The man cannot understand why Edward would want to write anything hateful to him, period! There was never a misread or misunderstood text from Edward prior to him arriving in Spain.

At least the man has Spain in the near future. This makes him smile. Edward will be the kind, loving young man in Spain he was in Medellin, Colombia.

Man: So, what will you do for work then? Are you eating? What about your brother? How is that going?

Edward: I look for work every day. My brother knows a man that helps immigrants find work wherever they are qualified. He tries to find work every day for me. My brother is very stressed about all three in same house. I want help my brother but I can't find good work.

Man: You are young and strong. If it is your dream to live in Spain, you will make it happen eventually.

Edward: Its true what you say.

Man: I'm going to change the subject Edward. There are some things I need to say to you. Please don't interrupt and just read what I send you. Ok?

Edward: Of course.

Man: Things have changed with you and your attitude towards me. At first, I thought moving to Spain was the only reason. I realize now that you began to change immediately after the Christmas box incident. I do not understand the reason for your change of attitude. There are times you are downright meanspirited. You have so much on your mind. I can only imagine the distress you must feel leaving your old life for a brand new one. You tell me that you have taken the items from the box with you to Spain. You have not mentioned anything about the contents in it. I placed items in a card for your journey to Spain. There were nonsexual items in your present for Christmas that, to me, anyone, stressed or not, would be happy and uplifted at the sight of such items. You have not mentioned one of these so I can only assume you disregarded the box in Colombia at the insistence of your brother. I cannot interpret what your brother is so concerned about. Nor why he seems it necessary to tell you to get rid of it. Obviously, there are familial roles preset, dictated by tradition. I understand that you are young. 23 years old. You do not present an image of timidity in any situation that I have become aware of. I find it hard to believe that you suddenly have become shy regarding your sexual adventures. You were extremely blunt and most sexual from the beginning. High pressure and rapacious right from our first texts. You presented a video of yourself in your grandmother's bathroom utilizing a rather large vegetable on yourself to me within a few days of meeting me. You chose what personal items you wanted to pleasure yourself with when we had our video call together in the novelty store. You were so excited and aroused. That was a great deal of our conversation for weeks.

"The frickin box." My point in bringing it up again is that you will not give me the courtesy I deserve by telling me what you really did with the box. You have not mentioned one item specifically. That is why I believe you tossed it. The whole thing is curious to me. It has left me feeling like an idiot. I am saddened by the knowledge that you will not speak about the matter.

The man's eyes have welled up and become red and swollen. He re-reads his elongated text again and then hits the *send* button.

Several minutes pass. The old man has finally learned that when there are long pauses in between texts, Edward is using a translating app. It takes him much longer to respond to a particularly long text.

The man's phone rings. It is a video call from Edward. The man accepts the call.

Man: Hello Edward.

Edward: Jou crying. I can see it.

Edward then instantly breaks down and begins to sob. Edward then ends the transmission. Either his brother has walked into the room or his brother's ex-husband. *Whatever that means,* the man wonders.

The man knows very well Edward will not answer his phone if he calls him. He does not even try.

Ping.

Edward: I so sorry. I want jou to be happy. You sad alway now.

Man: No. I'm not always sad. I only become sad when you play games with the truth.

Edward: I no play games. Jou always think the worst. You think this thing about the box and jou no know. I'm tired of talking about box. It bores me. It gives me more stress.

Man: Ok, Edward. Whatever you say. You are incorrect in your assumption of me. I feel that you have taken advantage of me and used me.

Edward: OMG.

Man: I'm sorry if I hurt your feelings. It needed to be said. I am coming to Spain on April 18th Edward. It is booked.

The conversation ends when Edward hangs up. He does not return a text. He does not call back. Trouble in paradise, it seems.

The man lies in his bed rather angry at Edward and himself. The man sleeps for two hours.

Chapter Twenty-Seven

April 18th is approaching rapidly. Edward contacts the man by WhatsApp only these days. He rarely speaks of Spain, his life there, or the man's upcoming visit. The conversations are short and clipped on Edward's end. In fact, he seems to be assuaging some of his guilt for his actions by not texting at all for longer and longer periods of time. On the occasions Edward and the man do speak or text before the trip to Spain, Edward seems to have forgotten prior conversations. Such as when exactly the man is coming.

Edward would text: Where are you staying?

The answers to all of Edward's questions have been answered by the man several times. All the details. Edward simply does not care to remember them. Edward is too stressed to deal with the old man's feelings. He says so in many of these texts.

The old man prepares his clients for his absence over the next few weeks. All is taken care of there. The apartment is taken care of. (There really is nothing to do to prepare the apartment for his trip, dear reader. Just walk out the door.)

The old man and Edward text back and forth a bit the day before the man's trip to Spain. Edward asks, what time he arrives in Spain, what he planned to do while in Spain, and did he need transport from the airport to the hotel. Without waiting for a response, Edward asks what hotel he is staying in.

The man has given him his itinerary (as has been told to you, reader) weeks ago. This itinerary has never been mentioned by Edward.

The man is going on an adventure, regardless of Edward's attitude, tomorrow evening to Madrid, Spain. It is surreal to the man. It is actually happening. This trip means more than a chance to meet Edward. It is an opportunity to finally see the country that has captivated his imagination. The queen! Isabela the first. Isabela the second. Ferdinand, the queen's husband, the palaces. The man is sure this is a now or never situation. He shall never have the chance to do something like this again. He is, however, concerned about his feet and knees. Surely there will be much walking in Spain. Pain is always the juggernaut waiting to pounce and deflate the man's future plans. His decision is made, and he has come to peace with it.

He is packed. Everything is ready. It is April 18th. A spring day in the Wasatch Mountains is as unpredictable as the water that rushes down from atop this mountain range bringing with it life-giving water for all. It is raining hard. The rain is coming down in sheets of a very high thread count. Swift clouds race over the mountains like an angry god, climbing and rolling with territorial conviction. The man does not care. To him, this will always be the 18th of April that he went on a journey. The last 18th of April.

Chapter Twenty-Eight

The Delta airplane finally lands in Madrid. It is 8:50 a.m. in Spain. The man has arranged for transport from the airport to the Regina Hotel on April 19th Madrid, Centro City.

The Regina! The man is exhausted upon arrival. He has had a painful travel day. He is actually beyond any natural response to exhaustion. The thoughts the man has of meeting Edward in person are now obsessive. The man does not admit that even to himself quite yet.

The man is riding a natural high. There is no question of sleep or rest now. The time for sleeping has passed. Due to the excitement of the trip building, the flight and travel time, the man last slept thirty hours ago.

The man knows the demon that steals his sleep. He has known it since the day he was taken to the "doctor" as a child. Somehow, he has not been given the gift of slumber. Not in his memory.

The taxi drops him off a full block before the hotel. He is not aware of this yet, but there is a huge construction project going on directly in front of the Regina.

The taxi driver spews out many words the man does not understand. His finger pointing and gesturing is clear, however.

"Get out!" Thirty-five euros the driver demands, approximately forty-seven dollars in America. Holy hell! The hotel said it was a complimentary shuttle ride.

The man exits the taxi with his luggage the driver half-heartedly extricated from the trunk. The driver points in the direction of the hotel. The man hopes that is what he is pointing at. The man does not retrieve money from his pocket for a tip. He may be in Europe, in Spain, but he is not stupid. The driver did not take him to his destination.

The man says under his breath, "Fuck you too, amigo!"

He walks around the construction barricades haphazardly placed everywhere. He walks in the direction of the taxi's finger. He wanders. He is uncomfortable with his bags. The crowds of people walking don't exactly stare at him, there is an absence of staring that unnerves the man. Perhaps it is a regular occurrence that a 6'5, 260lb American with white hair and blue eyes should be wandering toward El Sol Plaza carrying luggage.

The man realizes he has passed the hotel. He turns around. Follow the breadcrumbs. AHH. The Regina. Construction work is loud and active all around the hotel. *Holy hell! Just get to your room and chill for a bit. There is nothing to be done about the construction at this moment,* he decides.

As he enters the hotel, he smiles. It's small. Boutique like. Just as he wanted. It is clean. The restaurant/bar is directly to his right as he enters. The hotel concierge is snappily dressed and wearing a smile to match his suit. The staff busily attend to the needs of all who desire it. There are huge banana fronds in oversized Spanish thrown pots every six feet or so. The ambiance is charming.

The man stands at the dark, hand carved wood counter and gives his name. Computer entries are made. Pleasantries are made. The woman helping him clearly is not of the European Spanish. The man notices the nap to her hair. *Brazilian,* he thinks. She is beautiful, of course, in her tailored pantsuit.

He asks the Brazilian woman about the hotel amenities he has paid in advance for: a daily breakfast, a soundproof room, spa services (two massages and two facials), and most importantly, the fitness center at the hotel.

Hotel Regina has none of these amenities to offer him, she informs the man. His mouth is agape in disbelief. He shows the lovely girl his itinerary. The receipt for all these extras has been processed and charged to his credit card.

"I'm sorry, sir, we have none of those things. You are certainly welcome to have breakfast in the restaurant each morning."

"Can you not bring it to my room in the mornings?" the man asks.

"I'm sorry, we do not offer room service at the Regina," she responds in a very thick accent.

The man is quickly realizing he is not in America and has no choice but to deal with the situation later with the booking company.

The porter is waiting to take the man to his room. As the porter takes the luggage toward the elevator, the man turns around and asks to have a bucket of ice delivered to his room. He may as well have asked for the woman's first-born child by the look on her face at the request.

"Ice? Why?"

The woman actually said "why" to him.

The man has reached the end of his kindness rope. "I'm not sure you need to know why," he says. "Please bring me some ice, por favor."

"The problem is, we don't actually have ice," says the young, beautiful Brazilian girl.

The man is… What? Dumbfounded? Is he naïve? No ice? Impossible!

"But," says the beauty from Brazil, "we will see what we can do to accommodate you."

With no other desire at the moment than to hear from the person he has traveled some four thousand two hundred miles to Spain on his mind, the man acquiesced. He follows the porter to Room 301. The room is beautiful. It is smaller than it looked in the photographs online. But beautiful, nonetheless. Honestly, the room was chosen by the man initially for two reasons: the bathroom, and the large windows that opened on to a balcony.

The bathroom is wall to wall glass. Ceiling to floor. The glass can be made to change from clear glass to an opaque glass with the flip of a switch. Very handy if someone is in the bedroom while you are on the toilet. The assumption is that Edward will be staying with him over the next eight days.

The windows are the full length of the room from the ceiling to the floor. The ceiling is twenty feet from the floor. Actually, the windows are French doors that open onto a very small, but lovely, gilded iron balcony.

The man unpacks everything he brought with him for the trip. He is smiling contagiously. Spain! He can't believe he is actually here. He is on such a high, he paces the rooms in anticipation of what he will do first.

He is sure Edward will contact him any moment. After all, he did come here to meet him.

The man freshens himself up: brushes his teeth, changes his attire in to something more fashionable as opposed to comfortable.

Earbuds in. Music is playing at full volume.

> MUSIC DOWNLOAD
> "ADAGIO" IN G MINOR
> B-TRIBE
> SPIRITUAL SPIRITUAL ALBUM

Listen and walk with the old man. He is alone. He feels his loneliness here, in Spain, more than ever. The music gives him the autonomy he needs.

He leaves the Regina and walks. He has no clue where he is walking or why. He just wanders. The city of Madrid is holding him hostage within thirty seconds of leaving the Hotel Regina. The man is acting very cool. He is trying to look as if he has done this a million times. Those around him will assume he resides here in Madrid and is on his way to work or an important meeting by the briskness in which he walks. The man does not look like a tourist. He doesn't act like a tourist. In truth, the man is so excited at all he sees around him that he is trying his hardest not to poo poo a wee bit in his manties. Therefore, he requires a moist towelette which he does not have with him. (He is certainly not going to ask about where one might find a moist towelette, dear reader.)

The architecture all around him is surprisingly varied. Some deco. Some French design. A great deal of baroque design as well, and, of course, Spanish architecture. The buildings are very congested. Practically on top of each other in some areas. The roads are cobbled and shiny. He assumes the shine is due to all walking and the cleaning happening here. The sound his Ferragamos make as he walks on this cobblestone makes his mouth and his heart smile. It is early in the day in Spain for the natives to be out and about. This, the man does not yet know.

It is now 11:00 a.m. in Madrid. The man walks in the direction of the very small crowd that is moving downhill slightly. To where? He does not know nor care. He is inspired. He is awestruck. He is emotional. He is waiting for one thing.

As the sidewalk levels out the man's knees and feet allow him to think of other things. He has reached El Sol Plaza. In this short three-and-a-half-minute walk or so from his hotel, the music on his earbuds has changed.

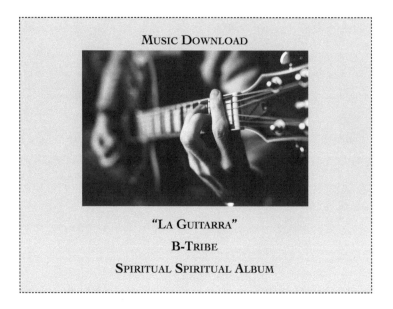

MUSIC DOWNLOAD

"LA GUITARRA"

B-TRIBE

SPIRITUAL SPIRITUAL ALBUM

The sensitivity of the guitar in the music in this pitch brings him to tears. It is unbelievable. He is in Spain. The country that ruled the world for so many years. It shows. Everywhere. In the architecture. In the pavement. In the air. On the wind. The man can feel the energy of all that was gained and all that was lost here over the thousands of years fighting to appease the queens and kings of the past.

There is still no word from Edward. This first day in Spain is shockingly beautiful, and yet a sadness is creeping inside his soul. It is a slow progression familiar to the man, yet he will not face it.

The exploration of Madrid for the man is inside his every fiber. He has been walking on the streets of this amazing city for four hours now and feels as if he has just come home.

There are no chickens. No parakeets. He simply feels a part of, rather than separate from, for the first time in his life.

The man is very thirsty. He is hungry. He cannot eat or drink. His stomach will not allow such mundane pleasures of food or liquids. He is far too excited in his current state of mind. Overwhelmed by this magical city, the man's personal playlist of music continues to resonate from the tips of his earbuds to the bottom of his exhausted feet as he investigates each nook and cranny that presents itself to him.

MUSIC DOWNLOAD
"LOS SALINAS"
B-TRIBE
SPIRITUAL SPIRITUAL ALBUM

The man is looking for a few things to buy for Edward. While he is fascinated with all he sees as he wanders the city, he feels a little less like a tourist when he is on a specific mission. He wants to purchase items he knows Edward wants but cannot afford himself. Music, clothing. Jewelry?

It is four in the afternoon when Edward finally initiates conversation.

Edward: Hi! You are here?

The man is both excited and saddened. Edward knows he has been here all day yet he has not texted until now. It is another enigma to the man how Edward behaves. Perhaps Edward wanted to give the man some time to himself this first day in Spain. Maybe he has slept all day. The man gently stores these thoughts in his memory. Truth telling, he just wants to talk to and see Edward in the flesh.

Man: Hello Edward. Yes, I am in Spain.

Edward: What hotel?

Holy hell! The man cannot believe Edward asks this again. The man remains in denial.

Man: Regina

Edward: Where is it?

Again, the man is crestfallen at Edward's lack of care in remembering the basic information the man has told him before about his trip to Spain.

Man: Acai in Madrid Centro Center.

Edward: I come.

Man: Do you need money for the ride?

Edward: Jes

Man: How can I do that? Uber or cab? Shall I pay your driver? When you arrive?

Edward: I take uber. No worry now.

Man: Ok Edward. I can't wait to meet you for real.

Edward: I am equal!

The man will not have time to shower and style his hair before he meets Edward. That is bothersome to him. He has had this moment planned for months in his head. He knows exactly what he wants to wear when they meet. He has purchased one specific outfit. He has planned on a specific style for his unruly, wiry grey hair right down to the underwear and shoes. The man has had this moment mentally written in stone. *Oh well,* the man thinks, *there is nothing to be done for it now.*

He returns his earbuds to their rightful spot in his ears and selects "Bolero" by Maurice Ravel. A favorite of his. It always reminds him of Edward. Why? He does not know. This composition stirs something in him that seems related to Edward somehow. The entire reason he is here is about to become reality. He will hear Edward's voice in person. He will touch Edward. No more virtual reality. He is so hungry and thirsty, yet he cannot satiate nor imbibe.

There are now many hundreds of people milling about. Some are the obvious American tourists. A fair number of Japanese tourists with neck cameras and an obnoxious tour bus always within eyeshot for this group. The crowd has become so thick he cannot walk forward. His shoulders are too much for Spain's natural flow of pedestrian traffic. He must walk almost sideways. It is raining. It is cold. He is wet. He couldn't care less. He is heading for the Regina to meet Edward.

Edward: I almost there.

Man: I am walking there now. I am close, I think.

Edward: I see you soon.

As he walks, he can recognize certain landmarks. He is close to his hotel. Very close. He can now see the ATM machine that sits on the front sidewalk just outside the Hotel Regina. Ten feet away from the glass doors that allow entrance to the Hotel Regina, the man can see Edward getting out of the back seat of a car. As the man reaches the glass doors, he cannot breathe. He is dizzy. The lack of sleep and nourishment, combined with the anticipation that has been building inside of him since that first cold day in December is now releasing from his body. His legs are weaker than usual. His back is sweating. Edward is directly behind him. He can feel it, sense it! The man turns around and their eyes meet for the first time.

There is no smile for the man. There is a look of boredom on Edward's face. His eyes are much brighter and greener than they appear on camera. The man smiles from ear to ear. He cannot hide his excitement.

"Hello, Edward!"

Edward replies with a softly spoken, "Hello." He makes no attempt of touch with the man.

The man is uncomfortable so he does the only thing he can think of at the moment. He reaches out and offers his hand in a handshake. They touch for the first time. Edward's hand is delicate. His fingernails are either painted with a clear gloss or buffed to an unnatural sheen, the man notices. He also cannot decide if the handshake turns him off or on.

The two of them enter the hotel lobby. The man asks Edward if he would like to stay down here at the bar. "I do not want to make you feel uncomfortable."

"We go to room. Is no problem," Edward replies.

As they enter the elevator, the man notices Edward's shoes. They are boat shoes. Cheap looking. They are made of a light brown canvas material. Edward is very petite. The man feels like a giant next to Edward in the small elevator space. Edward has on a pair of very tight khakis. A sensible dress shirt buttoned all the way up tight to his neck with a dark blue sweater looped around his neck. Edward has a cough. There is the pungent odor about his person of cigarette smoke and cheap cologne.

The man pushes the button marking the third floor. It is just the two of them in the elevator. Edward seems almost…cold. Unfamiliar. Not the person who sent all those messages. All the sexting. Many loving and kind messages as well as the naughty ones sent months ago.

The conversation is stiff and formal between the two of them. The man is wearing a smile he cannot hide. He inquires of Edward's health, how his day has been, if he slept well the night before. All of Edward's responses are quipped and lacking in emotion.

The elevator indicates the journey to the third floor has been successfully executed and the doors open for them. The man shows Edward to Room 301.

The French doors have been left open for some fresh air. The thin sheer draperies are moving about restlessly against the doors as if they have been laundered in itching powder. He makes himself a mental note that the only thing missing from the view as one enters this beautiful room is flowers. *Damn, I forgot to pick up flower*s, he chastises himself mentally.

Edward walks in and comments on the loud construction just outside the open doors. "A train under the street is coming," Edward announces. Edward has on a heavy pea coat.

The man asks him to get comfortable. "Something to drink, Edward? Are you hungry?"

Edward replies in the negative.

(*Note to reader: You must understand that, in these first initial moments, the man can think only of a first kiss. A touch. Any sign of affection. He is staring at Edward's ample lips. He is having impure thoughts. Yet what came so easy on the phone these last several months with Edward seems lost now.*)

Edward initiates zero conversation. The man takes a stronger approach and invites Edward to dine with him tonight.

"I have only one hour now," is the response from Edward.

"One hour? You can only stay one hour with me?" The man is honestly gob smacked.

"Jes, my brother, he come in an hour for me. I work today."

This was new. Edward did not mention he was working prior to now.

"Oh…" the man stammers. "How about after you finish work? You can come back and we could eat late. I don't mind."

"I no off till four in the morning," he said.

"Four a.m.? What kind of work are you doing?" the man asks.

Edward tells the man he works illegally, and he is very nervous about it. He distributes handbills. (*Although that was not the word Edward used clearly, reader.*) Handbills to tourists.

(*Note to reader: Okay, strange, yes? He is handing out some sort of tourist information until four a.m. Do you buy it? Reader? The man does not.*)

The man came to Spain to find proof of life. Edward is finally sitting just in front of him, but he is about to ghost him. The man feels a sense of gloom coming over him.

Edward stands from his chair and moves over to the side of the bed where the man is sitting. The man is nervous suddenly. The smell of cigarette smoke is making his eyes water. The man assumes Edward smokes and he has never known. The smell of cigarette smoke is unpleasant to the man as he smoked himself for thirty years. He put the last cigarette down over ten years ago.

They are both sitting on the edge of the bed. Thighs touching, hearts pounding (at least the man's is). The man puts his right hand on Edward's left thigh. Electricity pulses in the man's veins. Edward's response is to initiate sex. He attempts to take the man's pants down but cannot succeed in the procedure of lowering the man's zipper on his own.

The man is uncomfortable. He is not prepared for sex. He has not cleaned his undercarriage since morning, and he can smell travel on himself. There are so many ways the man envisioned this first sexual encounter with Edward. At least the first one that was not cyber. This is not how it is supposed to happen. He cannot stop himself. He tries to kiss Edward.

Edward is not interested in any sort of tenderness. He moves his lips away from the man. Edward then attempts felatio in a way that becomes clear quickly to the man that he has not done this before. Edward has an orgasm touching himself in very few minutes. He silently pulls up his pants. The awkward silence. Practically pea soup in the air.

The man is truly shocked at the whole event. It is over. He has spent hours at a time with Edward sexting. The first time for real, it is over in three minutes, and Edward's only interest seems to be in himself.

Edward apparently receives a text message of some kind as he looks at his phone nervously. There is no sound or vibration coming from his phone the man discerns. Somehow, Edward knows or is expecting a message at this precise time, the man deduces from his behavior. He announces his brother is outside to pick him up.

The man is incredulous. Speechless. He cannot believe this is the extent of Edward's interest after all these months.

"I go now." This is all Edward has to offer the man.

"Okay, goodbye," says the man. He has tears in his eyes.

Edward quickly retrieves his pea coat from the chair where he left it and tells the man he will see him tomorrow.

After the man closes the door behind Edward, he is at a loss. It is seven p.m. in Spain. His first day here and he is alone. He decides he cannot sit in the hotel room another second. The sound of thunder is his only companion now. Earbuds in their rightful place, the volume is at its peak.

MUSIC DOWNLOAD
"INTRO"
B-TRIBE
SPIRITUAL SPIRITUAL ALBUM

It is dark outside as the man joins the foot traffic on Calle de Alcala 19. The traffic is marching toward El Sol Plaza. The man follows. There are many hundreds of people walking about. There is a feeling of jubilee the man senses among these beautiful Spanish people. They all seem to be celebrating something. As he reaches El Sol Plaza, a short few minutes' walk from Hotel Regina, he is bombarded with women dressed in all black offering rosemary sprigs to anyone willing to pay what they ask. The man does not speak the language of these women. He has no clue what they ask for, nor what they represent.

It is cold. There is a light rain falling. The man has no jacket or coat to warm him. The crowd has gathered along the streets that encroach the plaza. Many are taking pictures of a huge bronze sculpture of a bear standing tall on his hind legs. Tourists, he assumes. The man can hear a clamming raucous of some kind even over his earbuds. As he removes them, he hears what sounds like a band. A live, loud, brass band. On the other side of the square, he sees bright lights. Artificially bright. Then he realizes it's a parade coming closer and closer to the heart of Sol Plaza. From where, he has no idea.

Walking across the small square, the man is once again walking sideways to lessen the blow his shoulders seem to make on the lovely Spanish people. There are barricades along the small cobbled road as well as security and police with weapons every few feet. The parade is in view now. There are many people, men and women, dressed in some sort of peasant attire walking the parade route. There are no children watching the discombobulated moving mass, he notices. It occurs to him now as he scans the crowd of onlookers that there are not many children anywhere. Odd, he thinks. He half-expects to see the children catcher with his top hat and snare to be circling the crowd. He chortles at himself.

A short distance behind these peasant clad actors is a float, or a large object. He cannot make out exactly what it is even at this short distance. The darkness and the rain allow him terrible depth perception, even with his glasses on.

Waiting with the hundreds of others for this object to come closer, the man finds himself lost in thought. Edward is continually in the back of his mind. Like an earworm, it simply will not leave or change position in the order of his thoughts. He realizes, again, how sad he is over the meeting with Edward. Maybe not sad; that word does not cover it. More dejected than sad. Any one of the people around him now, should they choose to look him in the eye, would see a man who is cold. Who is wet. They would see this man crying. They would see he is alone. They cannot see how thirsty he is nor know his hunger. Both for food and for a Colombian living in Spain. None seem to notice nor care. It is a parade after all.

There seems to be a statue bobbing along this cobbled street held up on a platform by several men. Holy hell! It is Mother Mary. It is Passover today. April 19, Friday. The man has totally forgotten. Passover was not celebrated in the small town he grew up in. In fact, it really was a bit of a mystery to the man all together. Something about the slaves of Israel being freed and the last supper as a celebration of this enormous accomplishment. Easter is Sunday, this is one of those years where the two events coincide in a calendar year.

The people all around him are screaming and cheering. Some of the onlookers, particularly the older women, are wailing as the float goes by. Some try to touch the figure. This is the reason for the armed police, the man now understands.

When the statue of Mary passes directly in front of him, he notices it is clearly made of paper mâché. She has been added to and re-touched and repainted many times, he can see. *She looks like a drag queen,* he thinks with a stifled chuckle to himself. The platform she is placed upon is not level. The men carrying this fifteen-foot gal struggle to keep her upright. She bobs to and fro as they proceed past the man. It is the most surreal thing he has seen. It makes him giggle.

The procession comes to a halt. Everyone, including Mother Mary, stand in confused anticipation.

There is a kafuffle now behind the man on the street opposite him. Lights, music, screaming. It appears to be happening again on the adjacent street. The man cannot imagine. Another Mary? In her coronation crown? A bigger gown? The man simply cannot be reverent. He smiles large enough for his chicklets to glow. He can't resist the temptation to see.

He crosses the square to the curbside along with many others. The same thing is presenting itself to him. Men and women peasants walking by. The band is very loud and somewhat tinny sounding. As the float comes within earshot for the man, he realizes it is not Mary, but Jesus Christ in drag on this side of Sol Plaza.

(NOTE TO READER: IT IS NOT THE INTENTION HERE TO OFFEND ANYONE. THE COMICAL SIDE DE-SCRIBED HERE IS IN NO WAY MAKING LIGHT OF THE SUBJECT DEPICTED IN THE PARADE. PHEW!)

Jesus is lit up like a marquee at a red-carpet event. He is adorned with flowers pasted to his huge form. He stands fifteen feet tall on the top of his wobbly platform. Jesus has on a newly purchased synthetic black wig from CVS or Big Lots. It is placed very low on the figure's head and above the new eyebrows that looked as if one of the nuns of our perpetual sorrow had just freshened up with a sharpie.

As interesting as this scene is, the man has had enough. The noise on the plaza is giving him a headache. Getting away from this many people crammed into a small square becomes difficult. The side streets that lead away from Sol Plaza are blocked with police barricades, armed policemen and police-women. Many of these officers are mounted on beautiful lean, black, and uber shiny stallions. The man is forced to follow the procession behind the statue of Christ with all the other spectators. Flowers often pelt his person as the holy and righteous attempt to have their flower land on Christ as they throw them from every direction.

The man cannot help but smile as a carnation is hurtled to the side of his neck.

This walk of redemption to the church of El Cristo De Medinaceli is proving to be cumbersome. He is thirsty. His mouth seems to have stopped producing the natural wetness it needs. His uvula feels like the bells atop many of the churches he is passing. Hanging there. Stuck. His lips have begun to crack slightly in the corners. He is sweating on this cold wet night. He wants to drink. He knows that will soften the reality of this day. A quick shot. Vodka. Warm or cold. It used to be that it had to be ice cold, the vodka or, at the minimum, shaken gently over ice. The insidious urge is so strong! He is aware even now he would take a warm vodka. It would be just the ticket! Screw the consequence.

Once again, he cannot remember why he stopped drinking. You drink liquor. You begin slowly to feel better. Then you feel worse. Yet you don't stop the madness. So dramatic and stupid is this shit.

Yet you are not in control. Your heart and your brain are on two different continents. The old man knows all this. And yet, all these years later he begins to feel a slip. A shift in the planet's atmosphere. A newness pulsing in his crotch. The feeling of losing control is coming over him completely now.

Due to jetlag, the sorrow of Edward's response to meeting him, this parade, being utterly alone in a foreign country, the man begins to cry again. On his lower back he feels a cold sensation like animated angry ice cubes racing to get to his shoulders before they melt and lose their power over him. The feeling moves to his middle back not five steps farther. Then he sweats again. Then chills. He then feels hot as Hades. He is burning up. The man needs to drink. He can feel the old sensation of opiate infection in his back now too. The sensation travels almost circular around his entire back. He needs relief. He is soaking wet from the rain, the ice cubes melting, and the sweat traveling down his back to his butt where it pools. He needs to smoke something. He is having thoughts of self-harm. A feeling of sadness and the recognition of his old compadre called depression is visiting him on this holy trek. The man knows these thoughts stem from his childhood. All those times he was not loved in the way he needed. Intellectually, he knows this. His heart has taken a U-turn, however. He has learned he must ride out the sadness if he is to survive.

The first opportunity to separate himself from the other pilgrims, the man takes it. He veers left off the parade route.

Not half a block away from Jesus and Mary, and now the man is alone on the street. It seems everyone in Spain is on Sol Plaza. There are shops open as he walks but there are no shoppers. It is very quiet.

He needs to rest. His feet are barking. His hips have left his body for another healthier man to carry. He stops in a semi dark alley to take some medication.

No water. Holy hell. He pops four Advil and an oxycodone in his mouth and chews them just enough so he can swallow them. He then stretches his feet and heels. This moment, alone in Spain in a dark corner, he finally lets it all out. He sobs. He lets himself feel the day at last. Minutes pass. He has decided he will walk farther rather than go back to Regina. It is close to ten. Surely, he will hear from Edward soon. He wanders on back toward El Sol Plaza, although he is walking on a street adjacent to Acaila 19. He knows not where or why he continues. Shortly after the block of Sol Plaza, there is an incline in the terrain. He is in great pain now, and he has the chills. Still, he walks on.

The architecture of many of the buildings he is walking past are beautiful. Most are made of thick stone that have been plastered. Over hundreds of years the sun has bleached these beautiful structures to a sort of burned white. There is gold gilding on several of the balconies, doorways, and window frames. There are also Spanish rod iron gates surrounding many of the entrances to these magnificent properties. What goes on inside most of these architectural marvels, the man does not know. Whoever the artist was that created the ornate, complicated patterns in iron that adorn these gates was truly inspired. What has the man so captivated by the buildings is that most of them are lit with a soft, yellow-white artificial light source. Along the roofline, turrets, alcoves and windows. A great deal of thought and euro has been produced to light these manmade wonders, the man assumes.

He has reached an apex of some sort in his walking. His feet indicate this by his level of pain. He is no longer walking on an incline.

The man can see a church ahead of him. It is white. It is boldly glowing in the dark. The church is illuminated by artificial lighting all around the landscaping. Again, there are lights tucked into turrets on the roof line as most of Madrid seems to be. It is a beautiful sight to see as he walks around this place of worship. The man has meandered over a mile outside of the city center of Madrid. The sky continues to weep upon him. The temperature has dropped significantly.

> MUSIC DOWNLOAD
> "SUMMONING THE MUSE"
> DEAD CAN DANCE
> WAKE ALBUM

The man is becoming very tired. The events of the day, in particular the lack of sleep, are giving him poor judgement.

He now is walking a decline in the topography. The terrain is no longer buildings stacked upon each other. It has become darker and colder. There are no people around this area. He is lost. There are no longer street lamps. Apparently, the money funded for the lighting of Madrid City Centre ran dry some three hundred yards ago. The tourists that visit this stunning city clearly do not wander this far outside the city limit. He has no idea which direction he walks. He now is two miles outside the city centre. There are no cars. No people.

The man wants only to hear from Edward. A familiar false comfort. Someone he knows in this country. He decides to text Edward.

Man: Edward, I think I need some help. I'm cold and wet. I'm walking and I've gone too far outside the city. I'm SOOO tired Edward.

Edward: Where are you?

Man: I don't know.

Edward: Take a picture and send.

The man takes several photos in the darkness. The church he passed some time ago can be seen in one photo. But only just. The other pictures have no landmarks. He sends them to Edward.

Edward: I can't know where it is. I have to go my boss is watching everything I do.

That is it. That is all Edward is capable of. Once again, the man is gob smacked. He begins to well up. It is incomprehensible to him how Edward doesn't seem to give a shit at all.

He cannot walk any further. He has become a bit delirious. Dehydration and the lack of food intake has made him weak. He searches for a place to rest his head. Just for one minute. He must close his eyes. Up ahead about fifty yards, he can see a tree. It's large. He moves toward it. As he gets closer, he recognizes the tree as a juniper. He knows this from the 4-H club he belonged to as a child. The tree is ancient, twisted and knotted with the trouble it has seen. The man must get on his knees to get to the trunk. He is hidden from view of anyone or anything. He lies his body down and pillows his head on the wet earth. The smell is heady under the bows. Somewhere nearby, the man hears a bird cry. Along with the echo of birdsong, in the dark of the night, the man becomes ill.

Dry heave

Birds

Rape

Thirsty

Spain

Alone

Insomnia

Back sweat

Cold sweat

MUSIC DOWNLOAD
"SONG TO THE SIREN"
DEAD CAN DANCE
LIVE CUTS

The man dozes off listening to "Dead Can Dance." He sleeps for forty-nine minutes. He does not dream.

He wakes sweating and disoriented. For several seconds, he has no memory of himself or where he lies. It then comes to him hard. The force of his brain letting him in on his situation at hand is like Hiroshima. At knowing who and what he is, he sobs a deep guttural cry. *Holy hell! I'm in trouble,* he says to himself. *I must get safe.*

The man crawls out from under the juniper and truly has no clue how to find his hotel. *A cab! Call a cab. An Uber. What is the address of the hotel? What is my hotel called? Holy hell.* He has no memory of his hotel name.

The man finds his hotel, The Regina, two hours later. It is 2:45 a.m. as he takes off his filthy wet clothes. His body is numb. He is wide awake again. He drinks a gulp of water too fast and wretches it up.

Despondent

Awake

Asleep

Ice

Fetal position

Chills

Back sweat

Feet

Knees

Pain

The man decides to try Edward one last time tonight. He sends a text message.

> Man: Edward, if you like you may come here after work and sleep.

Edward does not reply. The man does not sleep more that night. Most of the remaining hours of the night he thinks about Edward's attitude. He also is visiting the place called the Whatszits in memory, along with the juniper tree he has recently left.

The old man is a boy of twelve or thirteen perhaps. This is one of those memories of childhood that remain so pleasant and happy that fear of disillusionment has always posed a very real threat to the man, and to the boy.

He was at the home of Virginia Whatszit. Truly! Virginia Whatszit! Virginia was in charge of the 4-H Club in the boy's small town. It was a wonderful program initiated by the United States Department of Agriculture. At least that was all the boy knew of her credentials.

She was a small woman. She had very coarse gray hair, shoulder length, layered, frizzy, unkept, wild, and free was she. She wore polyester pants. She wore polyester blouses that presented an unsolvable mathematical pattern to them that would make even hawking spittle her way.

Mrs. Whatszit had two children, as far as the old man remembers. A boy a year or two older than the man in this story. A girl a year or two older than her brother. The girl had a head of hair the color of a sunset. A flame that was said to match her cootch. At least that is what he heard coming from his older brothers as a child.

The truth was the boy knew not what a cootch was for some time. He always thought it was Agnes, reader; you know, as in *Gootch*.

The Whatszits were not popular in this little backwards, often uneducated, town. They were frequently ridiculed behind their backs. For some reason unknown to the boy, many inhabitants of this small town often seemed to feel better about themselves when making others feel worse.

This family were simple Christians that had an aversion to dusting. The boy absolutely loved going there for the 4H Club. He would enter the home that smelled of several dust layers covered in a layer of sebum and topped off with a layer of the family's epidermis.

This sounds utterly horrifying. It was not. The boy found magic around every corner. Books were stacked up to the ceiling in every crevice. The windows were bare on the inside. It was not an option to see out of them from the inside. The boy was sure there must have been several years of grease and happiness that smeared the panes. The walls were gray. Not intentionally, the boy noticed. There was just enough space to move from room to room via a carved-out walkway between the rubble and debris. The boy imagined using a magic map to navigate this sorcerous, legerdemain. There were no pictures on the walls.

The old man walks again in this place in his head.

The boy wanted deeply to explore this magic cave but, alas, never was he given the opportunity. The boy often wondered after leaving the Whatszits, *Where did they eat? Where indeed? Where did they talk? Was there running water there? Where did the children sleep? Did the children sleep? Did anyone sleep here?* The boy loved it.

The matriarch of this house was teaching the 4-H Club members how to take care of and manage local flora and fauna. Yet every plant in her home was as dead as the color of her hair. She was also teaching the children how to recognize many different indigenous plants in the area. The children often, in these 4-H Club meetings, went hiking in the smoldering hills that surrounded her home. Off they went. Backpacks on, magnifying glass at the ready! Serviceable shoes! Mrs. Whatszits always wore serviceable shoes. Blocky heels maybe one and half inches thick. Square toe. Always brown and a bow on top of the toe area.

The bow was always dusty around the knot area and inside the loops. The boy loved the sounds her shoes made when she walked, even on soft surfaces. Her marvelous serviceable matronly shoes announced her presence. She had a very soft voice. She was constantly repeating herself in most conversations, particularly group conversations.

Mostly what was heard was:

"What?"

"I beg your pardon?"

"Huh?"

"What did you say?"

"Say that again please?"

You get the picture.

The boy reached a point in their time together where he did not even try to hear her. Her soft tone and slightly nasal delivery made the boy relaxed and content.

The old man wonders now if he even completed the requirements of that club to earn the badge necessary to move onto the next badge of interest.

The boy did not care about completing the assignments, per se. He was just thrilled enough to spend an hour every Wednesday at the Whatszits' home.

Mrs. Whatzits' houseplants bored her. The boy could tell. There was not a green plant in the entire residence. In fact, many of these plants were placed in positions around the house that actually prohibited care. Too high on the macramé knot to reach for water. Too low and under a side table. Behind rows of books. These plants, dead as they were, seemed to enjoy providing the all-important nutrients their demise created for the sludge that grew very well on top of the dead Ficus or creeping Charlie. Bacteria forms carving out their own existence, grew their own life. Bacteria and fungus. They made the house smell earthly. The boy always wanted to stay in this magical house where he could express himself in any way he chose without being forced to go to therapy over it, or to be raped for his behavior. Just to listen to the silence in the Whatzits' home made the boy feel at peace. Silence to the boy, at his own home, made him want to run.

When the old man recounts his days at the Whatszits' farm, a smile instantly forms at the corners of his mouth. What is behind that smile is magic; scads of magic. There are some particular magical memories that stand out to the man when he thinks about Virginia Whatszit. The first being the gingerbread house that rested atop the Frigidaire.

The style of the gingerbread house was traditional enough. Sort of castle-ish, sort of cottage-like. Sort of grand in an understated way. It was clear to the boy the entire project was handcrafted. There were gaps at the seams where these sections were cemented together with icing. Most usually the makers of the gingerbread house used hard tack candy to support the lack of architectural measurements, or the oven that baked the outer shell of the house shrunk the panels more than was intended. Which suggested to the boy that the mixing of the gingerbread walls was eyed rather than measured. A simple amateurish mistake when baking, the boy always thought. The royal icing used to create icicles on the roof line was now the color of yellow ochre. Furthermore, all the icicles lay on the tin foil covered cardboard. Askew, as if the abominable snowman had hacked them off in hopes of replacing one of his own missing teeth. Much of the candy that would normally adorn the house had been picked off. As evidenced by fingerprints left behind in the icing. Most likely on a fast Sunday where the good and faithful children find their stomachs unable to resist food, glorious food!

There was mold covering the darker corners of the gingerbread house. There was a pale layer of dust on top of everything that must have been from a recent kitchen incident the gingerbread house surely witnessed.

The boy wanted more than anything to touch the ramshackle abode. To put his finger inside the missing front door. To feel the only remaining curtain made of a red licorice roll hanging. All the furniture, the windows, the candy, all was strewn about the floor. The boy wondered if tornadoes hit gingerbread homes the same as they terrorize a perfectly fine single wide.

The home of these humble people was a total mystery. The boy was not afraid for once. He did not worry about pissing himself. There was nothing but love and absolute genius in every corner of that home. Early in the morning on Wednesdays, the boy began to anticipate his visit to the Whatszits.

Oddly, now thinks the man, *I do not remember any other children with me on those 4-H forestry visits to Mrs. Whatzits.* Hmm?

There were two pieces of magic, as mentioned, at the Whatzits. The other magic bit resided in the farmyard of the odd family. The property was askew with many rusted ancient farm implements.

Like dinosaurs lying dead in their tracks this equipment must have heaved one last heavy sigh and thought, *I cannot sow nor reap another thing.*

These iron monstrosities lay scattered about the property here and there in deep repose. They seem to say, "I dare you to make me move." There was a time when the boy would take his magic bag of glitter and glue and off and wander alone through the hillsides and farmlands in search of these hidden gems, lying down amongst the very thing they spent their lives cutting down with gusto and bravo.

The boy could not help but apply a layer of glue to these iron oddities. There were many favorite kinds. The trick was how and what to use on a rusted dinosaur's back.

Then he would apply glitter of different colors and hues. There was a mathematical equation to the placement of glitter. We shall return to the Whatszits, however.

The farmyard of the Whatszits was similar to their home. Items strewn everywhere. Feeding troughs. Bailing twine. Rocks. Fencing material. Utter chaos the boy could sense an equation of a higher power at work here.

A two-hundred-year-old barn. One only had the opportunity to see a barn such as this when traveling north through this part of the country. The barn was swaybacked. Massive, even in this state of disrepair. The barn looked as if it had just exhaled a deep breath from the depths of its lungs. The boy could not tell if the barn was safe to enter. Other than a fat cat with one eye and a limp the boy had never seen anyone, or anything enter or exit the exhausted heap of amazing architecture. The barn seemed to be happy in its state of hibernation. So, the boy left temptation alone.

There were many animals about the farmyard. A small herd of sheep. They had huge bodies and small heads. They were Shropshire and Suffolk varieties. They roamed about the farmyard visiting one another and always had much to say.

There were five or six goats in a constant state of hunger and dishevelment. A swayback mare that clearly loved the barn as she was always found hanging out with some part of her body leaning against the swayback barn. When the boy wanted to give her some sugar or carrot. Mostly carrots. The boy was not likely to give away sugar. Even if it was the wondrous swayback mare herself. She had not been shod in many years from the look of her feet. But she was happy.

There was also a bull. A huge black bull that had nuggets in between its legs that always made the boy ponder.

There was also a very gentle heifer. A guernsey. Soft to the touch and a look in her eye that always welcomed the boy on each visit. She often came up to the back door of the Whatzits' home when the boy arrived on Wednesday afternoon to get a peek at him. Otherwise, she hung very close to the feeding trough. She was always peckish, the boy noticed.

The boy would visit with the animals weekly. There was something different about these animals and the place they inhabited.

The whole of the property was different somehow. The boy felt different when he was anywhere on the Whatzits' property. The boy loved Virginia Whatszit. He thought she looked odd and quirky. That she was a bit off in her head. He loved everything about her.

As the old man lies awake in Spain, he has just now put the mystery together. The mystery of the Whatszits. The reason for the animals' peace, for that's exactly what the boy felt there. Peace!

The man is suddenly taken aback by this memory. How did the animals show him peace? It was the family. The family that had no pretense. No judgement. No attitude. They just were. The animals had nothing to fear from their captors. They were left alone. To just be!

The Architcture of Spain

The Juniper

The Watzits

Mother Mary on a Float

Chapter Twenty-Nine

The sound of jackhammers and the constant beeping of construction vehicles in reverse gear began at seven outside the man's balcony. He has slept forty-nine minutes under a juniper tree in close to three days now. He lay in bed last night cold and lonely in that space of half sleep.

That hateful strange space where you are so exhausted, but your brain will not shut down. You twitch in your bed. You change positions continually. You're hot then you're cold. Just as you feel your body falling, drifting into the loss of sleep, your brain shoots you a thought, a memory. Reality and anxiety force you wide awake again. Like pulling a bucket of water up from a deep well. When it reaches the top, you must deal with it.

The man gets out of bed, opens the drapes, and pulls open the doors to the patio as far as is available. There is a slight breeze. It's a very cold breeze but it feels good. Cleansing almost. The sky, as the man pokes his swollen face toward it, is a dark gray. The clouds are clearly pregnant. There is no sign of the sun.

He now is anxious and decides he must get moving. There are many things to do today. As he slips into the shower, he makes a mental list of his errands and activities of the day.

Flowers

iTunes card

Whale bracelet

Cash

The leather journal

He has no idea where to find some of these items here in Spain. Some of the items he has brought with him.

As he continues a luxurious shower, he is excited about exploring the city more and finding what he is looking for.

(NOTE TO READER: YOU SIMPLY MUST KNOW MORE ABOUT THE SHOWER ITSELF. THERE ARE SIX SEP-ARATE KNOBS TO ADJUST. IN THE CENTER OF THE GLASS ENCASED MARVEL RAIN FALLS IN HALF OF THE SPACE. OKAY, IT'S NOT REALLY RAINING, OBVIOUSLY. IT DOES, HOWEVER, FEEL LIKE RAIN. ON EI-THER END OF THE SHOWER SPACE, HUGE AMOUNTS OF WATER DUMP OUT FROM A LONG HORIZONTAL SLIT ABOUT EIGHTEEN INCHES LONG. IT'S MUCH LIKE A WATERFALL AT BOTH OF THE ENDS OF THE SHOWER STALL. FROM GADGETS HALFWAY DOWN THE WALLS COME A ROTATING, PULSATING BLAST OF WATER. ALL THESE ELEMENTS CAN BE USED TOGETHER OR DIALED SEPARATELY. TRULY A MARVEL, READER. YOU MUST MAKE THIS PURCHASE FOR YOUR OWN SHOWER!)

Showered, lotioned, and dressed, the man is excited for his activities of the day. The first thing is to find an Apple store for an iTunes card for Edward. *Is there even such a thing here in Spain?* Surely there must be. Apple products must be all over the globe. He answers his own doubts. *Google!* He rarely has a need to google anything. It's not a natural choice for him. Google informs him there is an Apple store on El Sol Plaza. *Holy hell! Right on.* The man is on it.

Over the first months of texting and sexting with Edward, the man wanted to share music with him. Most of the music the man has an interest in has become something of an obsession.

He must try to eat something. He feels weak as he exits Regina. Directly across the street from the hotel is a McDonald's. (It's true, reader.) Simply because it's so close and it's early for the Spaniards, he chooses the McDonald's. Nothing else will be open at nine a.m. (You may think it's four a.m. right, reader?) NO. It is mentioned before. The Spanish are not early risers. Or at least that is what the foot traffic tells the man.

There is practically no one out on the street other than the construction activity. The man orders an egg biscuit with sausage and cheese. On the menu the man notices many items that Americans would find odd. Sliced tomato with fresh basil and soft cheese and vinegar. Truly this is on the menu. The man giggles. He orders a shot of espresso which is water to the Spanish apparently. The man can only stomach half of his biscuit. It makes him feel nauseous. He is pensive about downing the shot of espresso now that his stomach is upset. He leaves the espresso on the tray and vacates the McDonald's.

He is headed for El Sol Plaza. A short walk from Regina. As he reaches the square, there is vir-tually no one around. Most of the boutique shops and specialty stores are closed. The signs in most win-dows inform the man that 11:00 a.m. is the respectable time to start business. The man giggles. Holy hell. After walking past the Apple store twice, the man eventually makes his way back to it. Closed. *Cer-cado!* There was no indication of when the store would open today.

Clearly, I'm not in America, thinks the man.

What is next on his list? The whale bracelet he brought with him. Edward loves wales, (as you know, reader). The man found the exact one Edward sent him a picture of months ago and he ordered it to give to Edward. He also has brought with him a leather-bound journal so Edward can write his thoughts down, or use it for anything he wanted; it's just a handsome book. He has the cash in his pocket he intends to give Edward as a way of helping him get a few things he may need.

Mainly groceries are what the man will suggest. Flowers! He needs flowers for the room and some for Edward.

The man decides to explore more of the city. Most shops are closed, but what the hell. Edward has not responded to the invitation to spend the night last night, nor has he yet this morning. He is surely sleeping. It seems odd to the man Edward is not with him now sleeping in at the Regina. *If I had a man that I loved come to North America from as far away as Europe to see only me, I would be there every possible moment. Holy hell, even if it was just a friend, I would stay with them,* thinks the man.

Somewhere in the back of his mind, the man is aware of the possibility that Edward does not love him anymore. He is very young. The young fall in and out of love almost daily. *Surely, I will hear from him soon*, he optimistically assumes.

He chooses to walk some of the many smaller streets entirely made of cobblestones. It is cold and gray again today. There is no break in the clouds as he looks upward to the sky that he can see. It is mid-April; he had so hoped the weather would be sunny and there would be flowers blooming everywhere. He did not pack for a wet, cold spring.

The man continues on. It is sprinkling very lightly now. A very narrow steep on his left displays a six-foot model of Christ on the cross in the window. From what he can see, it looks like a Christian store. Through the window, he can see many books. Crucifixes adorn much of the wall space inside. The model of Jesus Christ at crucifixion in the window is very haunting. The man is not likely to forget this image anytime soon.

He walks on and on and then circles back toward the semi-familiar territory of El Sol Plaza. He has no desire to get lost again. At least so soon after last night anyway.

There are so many stunning things around every corner it gives the man the giggles. The architecture in Madrid is, of course, hundreds and hundreds of years old. There are new buildings thrown in here and there. Some are from that dreadful period. The seventies! These particular structures are an eyesore to the man. "What do I know?" he says to himself when passing one of those structures.

It is 12:30 p.m. in the city of Madrid. The clouds are moving by as if late for a date with cirrus or cumulus. Every few minutes these travelers in the sky drop a little wet reminder they are in charge. The city is very clean, as far as the man can tell thus far. No graffiti on darkened buildings. No trash collecting itself in corners due to the gales of April. Homeless, yes there are plenty of the homeless sleeping it off in some of the darker areas. The man will locate the shelter for these homeless Spaniards later this afternoon and check in with his contact there to see how he can help. For now, he heads toward the Apple store.

There are many on the streets now. It is almost as if everyone knows you do not go out until 11:45, at minimum. That would be a.m. The crazy thing is, they all seem to come out at the same time. It is the strangest thing the man has seen in any city.

The Apple store is in sight and is clearly open now. Like every other Apple store on the planet, it is standing room only. It is an uneventful purchase. The staff are very helpful. Everyone he speaks with use near perfect English. Amazingly, the man thinks to himself, he has had no issues with not speaking the native tongue here. It certainly makes things easier for him. It also allows him to feel even more at home here. He truly is amazed at the freedom he feels here. Nobody gives a bull pucky who you are or what you wear or who you date.

There are many gay men in the city of Madrid. Everyone is free to express themselves. All are free to show affection for their chosen one. Men hold hands in public. The man would be shot between his eyes if he did such a thing where he grew up. The man hopes he will be able to express his feelings with a gesture toward Edward with a simple hand hold as they walk together. Maybe a little kiss at dinner. Holy hell, the man is amazed at the possibilities in Spain.

iTunes card in pocket, the man exits the two-story Apple box and heads up in elevation toward his hotel. He is looking for flowers. He has not explored farther than his hotel in the direction he is now headed. Whichever direction that is. He has no idea. It is simply "up that way" to him.

Despite the cold, dark weather the crowds continue to grow. The man notices in the crowds walking hither and thither there are many older couples out shopping. Older than the general population. Madrid city is largely congested with the young generation. The man observed that upon arrival here. It occurs to him now that he has not seen many children in the city. There are many now. Running about acting as children do. He had not really noticed them before now. *Ahh! It's Saturday. Most people go shopping and run errands on the weekends. It is Easter tomorrow. That explains the diversity of the crowd,* he assumes.

It is nearly two o'clock in the afternoon as the man walks past his hotel in search of flowers. There has been no word from Edward. Despite the joyous atmosphere around him, his mood is darkening. He is hungry and thirsty. The barking has returned with a vergence in his lower extremities. It is time for Advil and oxy. The man chews all five pills. The bitterness in his mouth somehow feels deserved. He gags and throws up in his mouth. He walks on.

Tired

Lethargic

Cold

Wet

Dizzy

Hungry

Thirsty

Flowers

Holy hell. I must eat something. Now! He finds a small store. Much like a 7-11 in America. Nothing looks good to him. Most of the products he cannot tell what they are. He buys a Snickers, although that is not what it is called in Spain. The wrapping is the same as it is in America. He also purchases a Coke to settle his stomach. Leaving the store, he opens the candy and takes a bite. It is stale and very hard.

He has difficulty swallowing it. A long pull on the Coke will help him think. It is warm and does not taste the same as he remembers Coke tasting. At the first trash receptacle he finds, he tosses both items into the garbage. He knows that even that little amount of sugar will help him push on.

The man is wet again. The rain is very light. Almost a mist really. It might be refreshing if it were not so cold out. He needs to find a jacket of some sort if the weather is going to argue with him every day like an ornery friend.

As he walks, block after block looking for a flower vendor, he sees a barber shop and decides to see if someone there will clean up his hairline and clean his face and trim his shadow. There are two young men in the shop visiting when the man opens the door. Barbers, he assumes, due to the identical smocks they are wearing. The man asks them for help with what he requires.

One of the men says, "Yes, my friend here can do all of that. Please sit down here." He directs the man to the barber chair in front of the other fellow. They both appear to be in their early thirties and, of course, are very handsome to the man. They are Spanish after all. As the gentleman is putting on a Sani neck strip and then a lightweight cape, the other young man speaks to the man's barber in Spanish.

The man can make out much of what they are saying due to his gestures, and he speaks slowly. This is a very important week for the man. So, he reiterated the exact length he wants his beard. Faded slightly around the perimeters, left full on the interior. The neckline is to be left natural but clean of any rogue hair.

The two barbers converse a bit more. The gentleman who spoke English well told the old man he was in very capable hands and to relax. He then left the shop.

The man does relax. He is in the hands of a professional. He can tell by the confidence in which this man holds himself as well as his implements.

The man turns the volume up to max and listens to the next song cued on his playlist.

> MUSIC DOWNLOAD
> "THE PASSION OF THE CHRIST"
> PETER GABRIEL
> PASSION

The man closes his eyes and thinks of his friend who was crucified. Also, the spiritual part of himself that was taken as a child and young adult. The man's lips quiver as he lies in the barber's chair. Tears silently and slowly exit the corners of his closed lids and find their way to the soft compassionate barber. He gently wipes them away without a word. He rests his hand on the top of the old man's hand and simply lets him be. He lets him rest. The man's breath deepens. He feels safe. The touch of this stranger has given him respite.

The man falls asleep. He dreams of human touch. Of Jesus Christ and of Mary Magdalene. A strange dream indeed. He dreams of Judas' kiss. He wakes in a cold sweat with the barber sitting on a stool next to him, observing him. His hand is still on top of the old man. The man feels panicky. He tries to sit up. The barber gently holds his neck and shoulder in place in the supine position. The music has ended in the man's earbuds.

The barber removes the devices himself from the man's ears. He places them in one of the man's hands. The barber leans slightly forward toward the man's ear and he speaks Spanish. "Eres Amado por machos."

The man does not understand. He can make out "por machos" but that is it.

The barber pulls a lever on the chair and the man is again upright. Despite the redness in his eyes, his face looks great. The beard is exactly what he wanted. He smells great, so he thinks. This man, this barber just smiles at him. Something has happened between the two men. It is a moment the old man will never forget.

The man gets euros out of his pocket for payment. The barber pushes the money along with the man's hands back toward his sides. He is refusing payment. The man is reluctant. The barber shows the man to the front door of the shop. The man turns around and looks him directly in his bronze eyes. No words are spoken. The man has a fifty-euro bill wadded in his hand. He reaches towards the pen pocket on the barber's smock and quickly shoves it in and leaves before the barber has a chance to stop him.

Well, that was quite the experience! The man ponders how amazing humans can be. The man will never forget this stranger and his love of mankind.

Still no word from Edward. Unbelievable. The man is walking in a different direction from where he came. He wants flowers for his room, and for the Colombian whose heart seems to be leaden.

Ah, finally a flower shop. It is a beautiful little corner shop with a black awning that bears a fleur-de-lis in white. The shop is small but has many beautiful fresh flowers to choose from. He chooses white. A monochromatic arrangement. Roses, Large. White hydrangeas. Chartreuse Gerber. Fern prawns. White lilies and a pale-yellow variety of tulip. The store attendant, or florist actually has been watching what the man has selected. She has a smile of great approval on her cheeks and mouth.

The man clearly looks American because she immediately asks him in English if he would like her to arrange them. The man declines her offer. (Can you imagine reader? Someone arranging your flowers? Not this man!) The very kind woman does, however, throw in a very large bunch of lemon leaves. Just the green touch it needed. She knew! She wraps them all in brown parcel paper and tied it up with a brown string. The man giggles. Brown paper tied up with strings. Is there anything better? The man nearly has another cerebral vascular accident when she totals the bundle up. *Holy hell. Ninety-five dollars equated*, the man realizes. *Oh well, it will do nicely*, he decides. He chooses a blank white card with a beige envelope and fills it out there in the shop with a black pen. It reads: *Edward, I am very happy to meet you, Hermosa. XO*

The card is sealed in the envelope. On the front of the envelope, the man writes a simple *E*. It will never be opened.

Upon returning to his hotel, the man realizes he has forgotten to find a jacket and an umbrella. His hair is wet. As well as his clothes. Again! He is looking forward to the marvelous shower. A very long one. He stops at the front door to inquire about a large vase. He is informed the porter will bring it right up and they will bring up some ice with it. The man smiles and says "gracias" to the girl. Another beautiful woman who is clearly local. The man offers his hand and his name and then turns to head to the elevator.

The third floor is a bit stuffy and humid today, he notices. He has yet to see any other guests in the hallway. His room is clean and fresh. The doors are open to the balcony and once again the sheer curtains are dancing against each other as if competing in *Spain's Got Talent* program. He undresses. He is wetter than he thought. His body feels as if it were someone else's. He is almost numb.

The shower feels unbelievable. All knobs are turned to max capacity. The man gingerly lies down on the shower floor in a fetal position and rests. Dozing off here and there. His shower is forty minutes long. His skin is flaming pink and is as wrinkled as a peach pit. Shaking with chills, he wraps a towel around himself and puts on his shoes. He can no longer walk even two feet without his shoes on. The pain is too great without the support of a shoe.

On the table near the French doors, he sees a huge vase has been placed there. A bit disconcerting since the porter brought it in without permission while the man showered. How did he not feel an energy change in the room when the porter entered? *Strange,* he thinks.

The vase is perfect. Large. Square and clear glass. Over a foot tall and wide. Someone at the desk noticed how large the flower bundle is that the man was carrying. The porter is such a lovely and gentle man. He must remember to tip and thank him when he sees him next.

The man is thrilled to have flowers in the room. Even if they are for Edward. The man then creates a state fair blue-ribbon arrangement. The variety of flowers and soft leaves make it look very professional and polished. The man centers it on the table. The card for Edward is attached to one of the tall calla lilies.

The man sits down in a chair next to the open doors and looks out upon the street. No construction today. Saturday. There are many people coming and going. Mostly a blur of black hair to the man without his glasses on.

His phone chimes to indicate he has received a text message. It must be Edward. He looks at the time. It is 4:46 p.m.

Man: Hello Edward. How are you today?

Edward says he is fine. He asks the man how he slept. He asks how he spent his day. The man provided minimal details for Edward. He realizes he is acting cold and formal in his responses to Edward's questions. He cannot help it.

"I come to see you," Edward says.

"Yes, that will be nice. I am in the hotel now," the man responds. "How will you arrive? Will you take a train or bus or what?"

Edward tells him he can take a train or bus, but it will take him two hours to arrive.

The man asks Edward if he would rather take an Uber at his expense, of course.

"Jes," Edward replies.

The man gives Edward his credit card information and allows him to use it.

Edward says he will see the man soon.

Sometimes, the man understands, a little too late perhaps, he has no ability to recognize what is directly in front of him.

In time, the man will recognize the undercurrents at work in this thing with Edward. The one-sidedness. The deceit. As he stares out the doors waiting for Edward, he has begun to see the truth, and it makes him sad.

Leaving the Apple store earlier put to mind the old apple orchard that lay next to the first family home he and his family lived in as a very young boy. Sitting here in Madrid, waiting for a twenty-three-year-old Latino from Colombia, his thoughts travel nearly five thousand miles away to his childhood.

It is the first home the man can clearly remember. Playing kick the can with his brothers. The smell of cinnamon rolls hot from the oven. The earthy smell of the land that surrounded the house. The chicken coop and the green mile he walked to get there. There are many pleasant and joyful memories here as well as the ugly ones.

The man can sense a change; a shift in his atmosphere. His world. Spain has released many memories and the man has yet to know what and why this is happening.

He snaps back to the present time as fast as he left it in his thoughts. Edward will be here soon.

He has placed the items he has purchased, as well as the ones he brought with him for Edward on the table under the flowers. He feels like a silly child with a first crush, yet he cannot control his emotions. He knows better than to even try anymore. He feels what he feels. His head does not match his heart nor his soul.

There is a soft knock on the room door marked number 301 at Hotel Regina. The man has that tingling sensation between his legs at the sound of Edward at the door. He takes a quick glance in the mirror in the bathroom before he opens the door. This is as good as the man can look with no sleep, little food, and a few drops of water in three days.

His breath is stolen from him the second he opens the door to Edward standing there. Those green eyes and black hair haunt him hourly now.

"Hi, Edward, come in. You need not have knocked."

Edward smiles and says simply, "Jes." He walks into the room and sits on the edge of the bed. There is no evidence he feels at home here. He is stiff in posture. He does not remove his pea coat. It is buttoned to the utmost possibility. He is wearing the same shoes as yesterday. The same pants. A different sweater covers a different button up collared shirt underneath. It is the sort of attire the man called "preppy" in the eighties. Edward was not born yet then, so this choice of clothing is proof that fashion repeats itself.

Ugh! The man feels old suddenly.

"Take your coat off please. Would you like something to drink? I have Coke or Gatorade or water. Actually, it's all there in the fridge. You can look and choose whatever you want."

Edward removes his coat and lays it on the bed. He chooses a lime Gatorade from the mini fridge and sits back down on the edge of the bed.

The man sits down at the table next to the open doors and the cold breeze. It is raining again, and the sun is finding its way to another country. The man can tell Edward is cold. He shuts the French doors much to his own dismay. "Is that better? You are cold?"

"Jes, I am cold," Edward replies.

"Come over here and sit next to me at the table and I will warm your hands for you."

Edward moves over to the table. The man takes Edward's hands into his own. Edward's hands look like a thirteen-year-old girl's hands inside of the man's massive phalanges. Edward's hands have never seen work; it is clear to the man. His nails are again polished or buffed. His hands are ice cold. Surprise!

The man rubs them vigorously to warm them. Edward seems to wince at the vigor with which the man uses. He can sense Edward does not like it, so he stops rubbing them and leans back in his chair and sighs with a little tear in the corner of his eye.

The rain is coming down in sheets outside the doors. The surface of the glass on the doors has enough rain on it to make the man's vision blur as he stares outside.

"I have some things for you, Edward," he says with new excitement. "A few gifts."

"Really? For me? Jou no have to bring me anything. I have nothing for jou!"

"Don't worry about that. There are just a few things that remind me of you. Some things from our conversations in the beginning. Would you like to see?"

"Jes, of course," Edward replies.

The man cannot tell if Edward's demeanor is naturally stoic or if he is actually bored. He does not smile. He acts as if he is forcing himself to get through this. As if he were a child enduring a church sermon that won't end.

The man takes the leather-bound journal off the table where all the gifts are positioned. The journal fastens with a long leather tie that wraps around the journal several times.

"This is for you to record your thoughts and hopes and dreams. You see it is small enough so you can carry it with you wherever you go if you choose."

Edward unties the journal and briefly thumbs the empty sheets. "Thank you very much. I love it."

The man hands Edward the iTunes gift account. "This will give you an iTunes account for two years, Edward, so you can download your favorite music or videos. I remember when we first met, I wanted to share music with you. But you didn't have a way to download what I sent you. Do you remember?"

"I remember *everything*," says Edward

The man did not like Edward's emphasis.

"The item that I enjoyed finding for you most is this." He hands Edward a midnight blue box.

Edward is curious as he stares at the box. He opens it. There is a cobalt silk bag inside. He opens it and pulls out the whale bracelet. It is the exact bracelet Edward sent him a picture of months ago when he informed the man of his love for everything whale. The bracelet is made of fine braided leather that connects together with the tail of a whale made of platinum. Edward is genuinely thrilled with this gift. He is grinning from ear to ear. The man puts it on Edward's wrist. It fits perfectly.

"This is too much. All of this gift. I thank you so much," replies Edward.

"The flowers are for you as well, Edward. Have you ever received flowers before?"

"Never," Edward replies. He is totally disinterested in the flowers. He does not look at them really. The card is right on a top stem, clearly visible to him. He makes no attempt to open it.

The man takes out three hundred American dollars folded so the amount cannot be seen, and reaches over to Edward and stuffs it in the frequently overlooked fifth pocket in his pants. He tells Edward this is just a little money for him to do whatever he needs with it. "I worry that you do not have enough food," he tells Edward. "Maybe you need some personal items that we never seem to get when money is tight. I hope this will give you a little relief and help your brother to see you are helping in the household."

"No, I cannot accept this." Edward attempts to remove the money from his pocket, but his efforts are unsuccessful. His pants are too tight. He stands to get at the pocket from another angle.

The man takes Edward's hand and pulls him to the edge of the bed and gently nudges him to sit next to him. "Please take it. It makes me happy and gives me some comfort to know you have a little money in your pocket. You can eat on work breaks or buy a coffee or anything. Just for you."

"I will keep, but I no spend it," Edward says.

"Okay good." The man then leans in toward those green eyes and kisses Edward on the mouth.

Edward does not respond once again. The man just does not get it. Edward then undoes the man's pants and motions for him to pull down the pants and underwear. Edward then pulls his own pants down. Just far enough so he can service himself. He performs oral sex on the man. The man cannot concentrate. He feels as if Edward is simply attempting to repay his gifts. Edward completes his own orgasm in less than three minutes again. He then excuses himself to the bathroom. The man takes the opportunity to pull up his pants and re-group his thoughts. The whole experience feels so cold to the man. His lip quivers a familiar dance followed by a single tear drop to his chest.

When Edward comes back from cleaning himself. The man asks him if he would like to get something to eat. Edward tells him he has to go now.

"Let me walk you to the car or train or whatever you take."

"Is no problem, I will do it," Edward says. He then informs the man his work is very close to the hotel. That he will walk.

"Let's walk together. I would love to walk in Spain with you."

Edward replies he prefers to go alone to work.

The man gives in. "Okay, Edward. Take care." He shows Edward to the door.

Edward attempts a half-hearted hug and then leaves.

An hour and half. That's how long Edward stays with the man this time.

There really are no words to describe what or how the man is feeling after Edward leaves. Suffice it to say, it is very low.

He must try to eat something. He feels the body and the brain fighting each other, as if they were enemies. His body is exhausted. His brain is in charge.

The rest of the evening the man wanders the streets of Madrid. He does not hear from Edward. The man eventually lies his head to rest on his pillow at 11:30 p.m. He manages to gag down some fruit and cheese today. He lies awake in bed wired and lonely until 9 a.m. It is then his brain allows him to sleep for thirty-five minutes.

.

Jesus Christ

Sanhedrin temple police

Judas Kiss

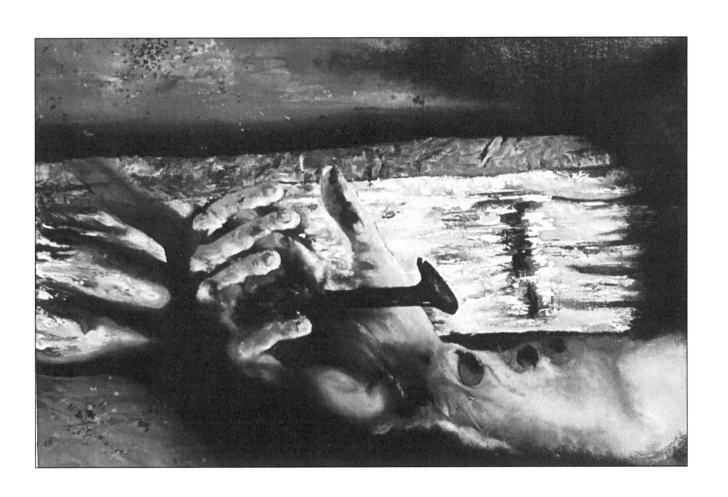

Crucification

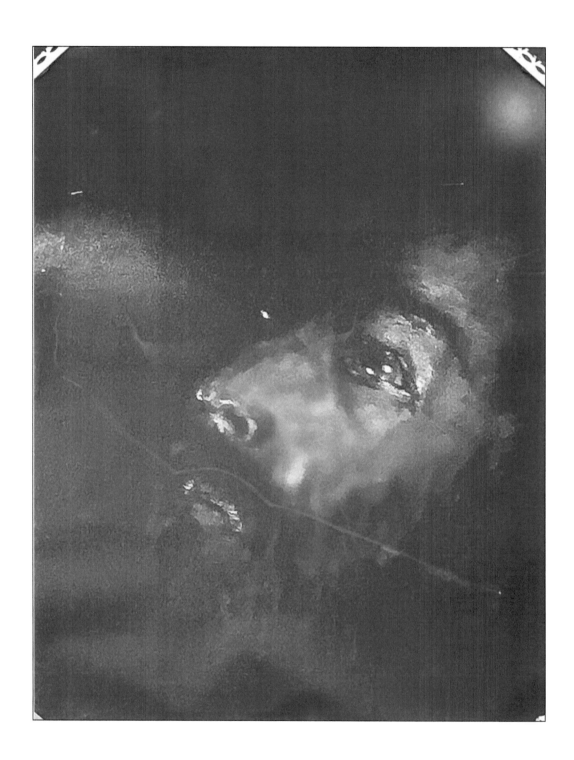

Resurrection

Mary of Magdala

Searching for flowers

Chapter Thirty

The sun eventually rises above the horizon. There is a soft golden hue to the room. Then it is gone as fast as it came. The clouds are moving across the sky in slow motion. The sky is beautiful this Easter Sunday morning. Purples and blacks, deep blue, orange, and yellow. The clouds may appear to be in slow motion, but they are shifting quickly about. Rain again today is very likely from what the man sees outside his French doors.

The man has no reason to believe he will see or hear from Edward any time soon. Disappointment is his morning guest today.

The man performs his morning rituals A little less enthusiastically than he would normally. He is moving a bit slow this morning. His hair styled. He chooses the warmest of clothes he has brought with him. He heads out, for what? He has no idea. At least tomorrow he is working with the homeless center. He is looking forward to some structure to his day. He thinks too much when he is bone idle.

Sitting downstairs at the bar, he asks for some orange juice and some fruit. The bar maid is very kind and the two of them chat for twenty minutes or so. The bar is empty. It's 11:00 a.m. Within forty-five minutes, the bar and restaurant will be crowded with Easter brunchers. He inquires of the barmaid what she might suggest he do today.

"Are the stores open here on Easter Sunday? Museums? Galleries?"

She informs him happily that everything will be open today. She gives him a few suggestions for the museums she has visited. She does not have any interest in galleries. She seems almost embarrassed to admit. She cannot help him there.

Google, the man remembers. Google will take you anywhere.

The fruit is cold and refreshing. He eats the whole bowl for a change. The orange juice does not go down so easily.

The man googles "museums near me." There are several that are walkable. The first one is very close to the Hotel Regina. He remembers passing it several times. It should be out the doors and to the right some 200 feet. As he exits the hotel lobby, Old Man Winter accosts his senses. *Holy hell! I will get a jacket today if nothing else.* His nipples are at full attention as indicated by the stares of other men walking past him. No rain yet. However, it is clearly cueing up to do so.

Museo de La Real Academia de Bella's Artes de san Fernando is the name of the museum of which the man is standing in front. It truly is close to Regina. The ticket price is very reasonable. He chose to mill about rather than join a tour. Earbuds in, playlist going. He enters the museum. The crowds are thickening slowly like a Thanksgiving gravy. There is beautiful art everywhere. Many Goya's. The architecture of the building is very old indeed. The museum academia was created in 1744. The man is easily lost in his head among this spectacular art.

Two hours later, he walks down the front steps to the street level.

The man locates two more museums and spends the better part of the day enjoying art. He is emotional after viewing such beauty. He is also very thirsty. As he walks back toward El Sol Plaza, his touchstone, he finds a little shop selling rain ponchos and various light jackets. He finds a jacket that fits him, almost!

Feeling warmer, he has a new energy. He approaches El Sol Plaza from the east side of the plaza. He is standing against a stone railing that encircles a train entrance. The train is underground. There are what appear to be very old stone stairs leading down to the underground of Madrid. As he rests his feet and knees, he is considering the art and sculpture he has just seen in the museums.

A young man carrying a snare drum at his waist comes up the stairs from the train, the man assumes. What catches his eye is that the drum is in play position, as are the sticks in his hands. A bit odd, the man thinks, as the young man walks past him. He then stops some fifteen feet from where the old man is resting.

He begins to softly play his snare. Some of the people in the plaza stare. Most walk past him without thinking about it, it appears. From the man's vantage point, he can see virtually the whole plaza as well as the streets that funnel down into it. From Calle de Preciado's another snare is coming carried by a young woman this time. The man removes his earbuds. Something is about to happen. He can feel something riding the cold breeze. The sky above is a solid gray now. This young woman, snare and sticks in position as she walks, soon reaches the other drummer and immediately begins to play the same tap in rhythm.

From across the plaza on Calle De Carvao walks a woman carrying a flute in her hand. No case, just the bare flute. She joins the other two drummers and begins playing.

The old man is literally fascinated at the scene before him. He knows the composition well. He listened to it just yesterday on his earbuds. He asked Edward to listen to it months ago, but it seemed above his ability to focus on it.

There are now musicians coming from every possible entrance to the plaza. From Calle De Carretas, a cellist! From Calle Elle la montera a violista. The orchestra is building, not only in numbers, but also in sound. Harps are wheeled in from heaven, it seems to the man. Oboe, piccolos, violins, bass clarinet, bassoon, trumpets, trombones, viola, saxophone. All reed instruments. All horn instruments and percussion. The entire orchestra entered El Sol Plaza from different directions without acknowledgment of each other. There are trumpet players and French horn players and trombone players situated on the upper floors of several of the buildings that encircle the plaza. The windows are fully open as the musicians lean out to play their part of the score. This is a flash mob. The music is Maurice Ravels, Bolero.

(Note to reader: Maurice Ravel grew up in France, eleven miles from the border of Spain. His mother was Basque and grew up in Madrid. When you listen to this, you will surely notice a Spanish influence. It was written for a Russian actor/dancer as a ballet. The piece was not recognized as a masterclass composition in the beginning performances. Ravel was virtually snubbed by other composers of that time. In 1928, Ravel was flamboyant in dress as well as personality. Many claim to know he was a homosexual. How can it be proved now that he is gone, and at what point? Don't you agree? Reader? Bolero was his last full composition. He died in 1937.

Bolero is considered his masterpiece and played by many orchestras around the world. The music download here is also a video of the London philharmonic performing the piece. It is important to see the individual musicians playing to truly feel the piece work its way into your soul.

Download if you choose, again at your own expense. I'm sorry!)

BOLERO, MAURICE RAVEL.

LIVE PERFORMANCE,

LONDON PHILHARMONIC ORCHESTRA.

MAESTRO VALERY GERGIEV

Holy hell! What an amazing thing to witness. A flash mob. After the last note is played, the musicians gather their instruments and walk off the plaza the way they came without saying a word to each other. Wherever they met afterwards, the man can only imagine the high they must be feeling. It truly is a magical piece of music.

The crowds of people gathered at la Sol Plaza are milling about listening and laughing, enjoying Easter Sunday out. There are women in black shawls everywhere handing out sprigs of rosemary. Something to do with the holiday, the man assumes. He is tired of the crowds. He is lonely. He must walk sideways once again as he heads up Calle De Alcala to the Regina. There are too many people around now. He needs to get quiet. He has to stop walking shortly after he begins, he is nauseous. He is suddenly hot. A sweat bead from his head travels down the center of his back and is stopped only by his belt at the top of his hips. Deep breaths. The nausea subsides in a few minutes as usual. The man continues to the Regina.

"Will you bring ice to 321, por favor?" he asks as he enters the lobby of his hotel. The staff members have been different each day so far as the man can tell. They look at him with annoyance at the request for ice. The man does not care really. Not only is the ice request tiring and irksome, he is a bit moody after the visual spectacular of the flash mob. Once again, his body is sending signals of hunger and thirst. The fourth day with very little food, water, and sleep has begun to tinker with his head.

Lying down on the hotel bed, he stares out the doors. It is very cold in the room. Just as he likes it. The sky is becoming a dark friend. It is near 5:00 p.m. in Madrid.

The soft chime that can only be Edward is heard on his phone.

Edward: Hello. How are jou?

Man: I'm fine.

It is becoming more and more difficult for the man to not show his disappointment in Edward's insouciant attitude towards him.

Edward: All good?

Man: Yes.

Edward: I come now to see you?

Man: Yes

Edward: I use uber.

Man: Its fine.

He cannot help but wonder if Edward is using his Uber account for other trips around town without the man's permission. He could find out easily enough he supposes, but he lets it go. Like so much of this once in a lifetime trip to meet Edward, he does not want to deal with more disappointment.

Edward lets himself in surprisingly. The man left the door open a crack for him. They greet each other stiffly. Edward sits down at the table, shivering.

"Close the doors if you're cold, Edward."

He is wearing what looks like the same shoes and pants as usual. His pea coat is singed up tight. After he closes the French doors, he sits back down. The man turns the heat on in the room. It heats up quickly.

"Are you more comfortable, Edward? Why don't you take your coat off and relax? If you would like a beverage, you know where they are."

Edward chooses bottled water, removes his coat, and sits back down. The man immediately notices Edward is not wearing the watch his mother gave him. He has never seen Edward without this timepiece on his wrist. It was first noticed by the man in the videos Edward sent to him early on. His pale face and green eyes and cool hair and, of course, nude. The watch was always on in those videos when he was naked.

"Where is your watch, Edward?"

Edward retrieves the watch from his coat pocket. The man then notices Edward is wearing the whale bracelet. Edward hands the watch to the man. It is broken at the connection of the leather band to the face of the watch. Torn.

"You just need to get another watchband and a pin to hold it in place."

"Jes, I think so," replies Edward.

"If you like, leave the watch with me and I'll stop at a shop somewhere and have it repaired for you. If you like?" said the old man.

"Thank you very much." Edward hands the leather band to the man.

They chat idly.

Edward asks how his day has been. "How do you like Spain," he asks.

The chatting is uncomfortable. The man can tell Edward is ready to leave.

He looks at his phone. "My brother is here to get me."

One hour is all the man will get today. "Okay, Edward. Goodbye!"

"No say goodbye," says Edward. "I see you later, okay?"

The man does not respond to Edward. He can tell Edward can sense how he is treating the man.

"Okay, enjoy you evening," Edward says. "I work now," is his excuse for leaving, so the man lets him out.

The man does not wait for a hug or kiss. He shuts the door to Edward. The man turns off the heat and opens the doors to the cold breeze drifting by. He stares out the open space at the iron sculpture of the conquistador proudly atop a chariot pulled by four magnificent horses. This marvel sits on the top of the building directly across the street from his hotel room. Banco Bilbao Vizcaya. The man can sit in his chair and see the entire structure. He stares and dreams, almost trance-like, for an hour.

He decides he will go out and find a watchband. There really is nothing else to do. Or anything the man wants to do. His heart is heavy. His knees are as old as he is.

He wanders the city of Madrid again. A watchmaker is found and, oddly, his shop is open on Easter. The watchmaker investigates the watch and the band. He informs the man this particular watch requires a pin that is difficult to find. He does not have one that will work. The kind watchmaker then writes an address on a piece of paper and hands it to the man along with the watch and band he has placed in a little bag.

"This man can fix problems," the watchmaker says.

"Today?" the man asks.

"No. Monday, tomorrow."

"Gracias. You are very kind."

The man is tired of wandering. Of exploring! At least by himself. He wonders why he came here, to Spain. It certainly is not going as he imagined. It rains the rest of the evening as the man attempts to kill time showering, listening to music, anything to take his mind off the narcissistic ass he has come to meet.

Chapter Thirty-One

Three hours of sleep. That's better than the last four nights. The man feels better this morning. Hopeful and very hungry. A bowl of fruit will do nicely, he decides. There are many things to do today. It is Monday. Looking out the doors, the day is gray and moody. Will there be no sun? No warmth at all? Not even one iota?

The man is excited to start his volunteer work with the homeless shelter. He knows exactly where it is. The shelter was found days ago. It is very near the hotel. Across the street from the shelter is the immigration building. There are many South Americans of this country, or that, standing in what looked to the man to be an enclosed cinder block patio area. There is a large opening in the wall. However, it has iron bars as if to hold the migrants in, or to keep the dispossessed out. He does not know.

The director of the shelter stated via email to the man to "Just show up on Monday anytime!"

It feels wonderful to the man to have something structured to do since Edward has no intention of spending anytime with him in Spain. He felt a sense of purpose. Of promise. Of possibility.

After eating a bowl of fruit from the bar and a sip of water, he sets off for the shelter. The man is worried it is too early in the day. It is 9:30 a.m. Many Spaniards will not be mobile for several more hours.

It is raining again. Holy hell. The rain in Spain does not stay mainly on the plains, he sarcastically says in his brain. Again.

The shelter is unlike any the man has seen. He has worked with many shelters in America that do not look like, nor operate, like this one in Madrid.

The structure itself is very old and obviously looks very Spanish. The only indication that he is at a shelter is the plaque on the front gates. The gate opens to a courtyard where much of the internal buildings are accessed. The man expected to see men and women lying about in makeshift camps protected only by a tarp and a shopping cart. Not so. At least not in this particular shelter. There are one or two people chilling in the courtyard. There are no homeless or indigents he can see.

After walking around for thirty minutes, he finally located the man's office with whom he has been emailing. He is nowhere to be found. The man waits near the director's door for another half hour. No sign of the man. No one seems to know who the old man is asking for. He decides to leave the shelter and find those who need more help out on the streets.

After purchasing sandwiches and bottled water, the man's bag is as stuffed as a Baptist ministers wife at an all you can eat breakfast buffet. There is no one in the courtyard across the street at the immigration building. So, he moves on. As he walks, he is looking down darkened alleys and near garbage cans. Darker places where the homeless might be sleeping or hiding.

In America, the homeless problem is a juggernaut. Many hundreds commune together in tents and makeshift encampments. They walk right up to your car when you are stopped at a streetlight and knock on your window to ask for money.

In Spain, these indigent human beings are not as brazen as those found in North America. There definitely are not as many gathered in clusters spinning tales as they warm themselves over a makeshift fire in a garbage can. There are fewer homeless than he expected, frankly. In fact, very few.

Eventually, he comes upon a man lying on a darkened stoop in front of a building that stands vacant. This man is covered in filthy clothes and old newspapers. Everything he owns is in the shopping cart positioned close to himself as he sleeps, or attempts to do so.

He opens his eyes. He stares at the man.

The old man asks him when he ate last. The communication between the two is not working. The language barrier is too tall and made of ancient stone. The man retrieves a sandwich, a bag of chips, a cookie, and a bottle of water. The indigent man's eyes become very large. A large grin pops up on his face — face that has not been washed in months, it appears.

The man offers the items to him. "May I wash your face for you?" The man pulls at a moist towelette and puts it to the homeless man's face. He makes no attempts to stop the old man. There are tears in the old man's eyes as he cleanses the man's face and ears. The old man tells him he is going to clean his feet and hands. He does not understand a word of what the old man says. Or maybe he does? It does not matter.

The old man dumps some water on his feet and cleans them as best he can. He moves on to his filthy hands. He tries to clean the cracks. The nails. The knuckles. He does what he can.

The homeless man simply smiles at him.

This is the best kind of payment a man can receive, thinks the old man as he returns the smile. Contagious. Now that his soul coffer is restocked a skosh, the man travels on to search out other hungry and lonely indigent Spaniards.

And so, it goes for the better part of the day. The man stops wherever and whenever he sees another human who may be hungry or thirsty. Often, they need only to be touched. The man is happy to oblige.

On two separate occasions, the man purchases shoes and socks. Both men have bloody feet. Layers of scabs from walking without shoes. He catches a case of the giggles trying to determine these men's foot sizes. He cannot take either of them into the shoe store, so he guesses at the size.

The store clerk seems to have an attitude, because the man cannot decide what size or color. Her attitude makes the man laugh harder. She is not amused. The man returns twice to the shoe store. Once to get a smaller size. *(HE WAS OFF BY SEVERAL INCHES WITH THE FIRST PAIR, READER.)* Both the old man and the homeless fellow have deep belly laughs when the shoes are placed on his feet and he attempts to walk in shoes three inches too big. The man then returns again to buy the other homeless man shoes. *(Which, yes, reader, these were the correct fit.)*

There was another occasion on this day that must be recorded and put to paper forever.

As the old man is walking toward the immigration center to see if he can assist in any way before he ends his day, he comes across a man standing on the sidewalk under an awning. His age is undeterminable. His clothing is dirty and bedraggled. His hair is greasy and in need of a good shearing. He wears the insoles of someone else's shoes on his feet, from the look of them. These insoles are tied to this mysterious man's feet with dirty string bits made of cotton. Perhaps they are from his own worn-out shoes. Who can say?

This homeless individual seems to sense somehow the old man approaching, as evidence by the lifting of his head in the direction of the man. He then steps out in front of the man. He does not speak. He prostrates directly in front of the man. He leans up upon his knees, opens his eyes, and looks upward toward the blackened sky. His eyes are milky white. Completely glazed over. He is blind. He begins to pray.

This is another moment in the old man's life where no words can accurately describe to you, reader, the quiet soul of this man that is kneeling before him. The simple truth that he was!

The old man begins to cry. Big tears. Tears that could be heard as they splash on the sidewalk. Both men can hear them land. The blind man reaches out his hand to take hold of the old man's. The old man gives it freely to him. Neither man speaks. They hold each other for several seconds. The old man is sobbing as he places food, money, and water into the blind man's hands. He will not accept any of it. This moment, here in Spain, dear reader, will forever be the closest the old man has ever felt to his maker.

(Let us have a break. You and me. We shall listen to something light and free, as these last moments weigh heavily upon my soul. You heard this song earlier in this scribe, dear reader. Now listen to it again with new ears.

> Music Download
> "Oh Heavenly Day"
> Patty Griffin
> Children Running Through album

Feeling very tired and thirsty, the old man begins to find his way back to his hotel. His brain is racing ahead of him at mach.

The work today has been very cathartic for him. He feels close to humankind as he walks onward. He is cold and wet again. The sun is lazy and dark at the horizon. The sun has been on vacation for many days. How the man wishes to see the sun.

MUSIC DOWNLOAD
"SEE THE SUN"
LISA GERRARD AND PETER BOURKE

Back in familiar territory now, he continues walking. His knees and feet have paid a high price today for their help with the displaced in this beautiful city. His heart is light. It seems to be what the man is using for fuel.

The immigration center is a few hundred feet from him now. As he approaches the enclosed courtyard area, it is full; at max capacity, it appears. These immigrants are processed here before leaving for whatever lies ahead for them.

Men.

Women.

Children.

Families.

Grandmothers.

Grandfathers.

Aunts.

Uncles.

Cousins.

Yours.

Mine.

Tired.

Lonely.

Displaced.

Hungry.

The man offers what he has left in his bags. He reaches through the iron bars and places all the water he has left. He leaves all the remaining food as well. Not much. Many of these beautiful people of foreign lands rush to get what they can. The offerings are gone in seconds. The man has a pocket full of one-dollar euros. He hands them out through the gate. Smiles are free and it shows.

Hotel Regina is just around the corner to the right. He leaves these moments with such gratitude inside his deepest place. He is crying as he enters the Regina. He makes no eye contact with the staff. It's an effrontery to his senses to be thrown back into reality so soon. Back to his reality. It's late in the day; 5:30 p.m.

Edward called the man on his phone at five to say he wanted to come and see him. The man assumes Edward is working again tonight as he doesn't mention anything about dinner. He is really not in the mood to feel sad about Edward. Not after the beautiful day he has had.

Edward comes into the hotel room shivering. His nose is red. Rubbing his hands together as he comes in, he says, "Is freezing."

"Come in and sit down, Edward. I'll turn on the heat for you."

Edward takes a small piece of candy from his pocket and hands it to the man as he sits down. "For jou," Edward says. "Chocolate."

"Thank you, Edward. I love candy."

The conversation is brief. A bit strained. Nothing is mentioned or asked about regarding the volunteer work the old man did today. Within an hour, Edward says he must leave. The man makes no protest. No emotions. No pleading.

"Goodbye, Edward."

Edward leaves without hugging or a kiss.

There is a feeling deep inside the man's soul. He knows it well. It is building and rolling in like a storm on the sea. He is becoming depressed again. The Edward he has met in Spain is not the same Edward he knew in the beginning. He is not kind. He is not sweet. He doesn't talk. There are no more engaging conversations like the hundreds in the past. The feelings of detachment, of being undesirable, are creating a fissure in the old man's heart.

What to do with the rest of the evening? The day was such a high and now it's as low as the cloudy sky. He decides to go out again. He really must eat something. He has had little water today. The realization that Edward does not desire him sits constantly in the back of his thoughts. It has removed the desire for food and water.

The man is dressed warmer for a change; long-sleeved cotton pullover and the new jacket. It is still cold and wet when he steps outside. There has been no sun. No Sol. Not even a peek of a ray delivered the man's way this entire trip. *Nothing like the cold and dark to lighten your spirits,* the man is thinking.

The man does have one errand in mind to address. This morning before his work with the homeless he dropped Edwards watch off to be repaired. The shop of the repairman was not easy to locate. The man had to ask for help in finding the shop. The address was written down on a post-It note. It was not entirely readable nor accurate to the man's dismay. Nevertheless, the shop was eventually found. The directory on the wall in the lobby area of a six-story old structure that was most likely a wealthy Spanish family home informed him that the repairman could be found on the third floor. Avoiding the grand marble staircase just ahead of him the man chose the elevator. Rickety, old, and made of open iron scrollwork the man gingerly gets in and manually closes the gate. He selects the third floor. The pulleys and wheels begin to grind and protest the movement.

The top half of the elevator is open. This is the only time he will get to ride in the great glass elevator that he loved so much as a child.

The repairman was located and given the watch for repair. He looked young and healthy and genuinely happy to help. He told the man to leave the watch with him and to come back that afternoon.

It is now after 7 p.m. as the old man returns to the very spot, he met the repairman. The shop is still open. The man is pleasantly surprised. The repairman greets the man as he hands over Edwards watch. He is grinning. He knows that his work is excellent. The watch is perfect in every way. Polished even. The man pays, tips, and thanks the young artist then exits the building.

The man is examining Edwards watch as he walks back to his hotel.

The new band matches the old one exactly. Edward will be pleased. The man has an overwhelming urge to talk to Edward. Intuitively, he knows he will not be given what he needs. Yet, he cannot help himself. He sends Edward a text. He tells him that he is lonely. That he is bored alone here in Spain. He tells Edward he wants to see him.

A very short time later, Edward replies to the man. Not with a call, but a text. Edward tells the man he should go out to a bar and meet another man. "Find someone to go to dinner with," Edward says. "Take someone back to your hotel," he suggests.

The man is sickened as he reads these text messages from the very person he is here to see. The man cannot see clearly as he walks. After reading these messages, he is crying. He is heartbroken by Edward's suggestions to his loneliness. His knees feel weak. The muscles in the legs have turned to rubber. The old man is dizzy. He feels old indeed. This pivotal moment in Spain, alone in the rain, he will finally face what is in front of him.

Rejection.

Loss.

Rain.

Cold.

Thirsty.

Hungry

Watch.

Embarrassment.

Age.

Sadness.

Youth lost.

Advantage taken.

The man sits in front of the French doors staring out at the bronze conquistador atop the magnificent chariot pulled by four horses situated on top of the building directly across the street from his room. Several hours pass as he sits, trance-like. The night turns into day as it has for millenniums. The man has not slept.

Conquistador

Chapter Thirty-Two

Tuesday morning. The sun has declined its presence once again. The soft drizzle caressing the windowpanes is yet another reminder to the man as he stares out from bed he is not in charge.

The memory of what Edward texted him last night hits him full force suddenly like a driver running a red light only to be hit by an oncoming car.

The man has no desire to get out of bed. He is losing will. The light in the room shifts suddenly. There is bright yellow and gold and purple coming through the drapes. *This must be seen,* he thinks as he jumps out of bed. Sure enough, there is a large break in the gloom of the last five days. It is enough to rouse the man. He can feel the entire room fill up with warmth and light. Holy hell! Dressed and combed, the man heads outside to face the Sol.

It is surreal walking now in Spain with the sun in its full glory. The gold and yellow reflect from every angle on every building and sculpture. Holy hell! He is giggling out loud with the sun. It has been too long for these two compadres. The sun and the man know each other well.

There is a stirring in the stomach as the man walks.

Pastry.

Coffee.

Pungency.

Green.

Garlic.

Bread.

Old Women.

Kneading.

Needing.

Chocolate.

Ah, the very thing. Some chocolate, any chocolate will do for the man. His mouth is wet for the first time here in Madrid!

It is a chocolatier the man has entered. Close to ninety percent of the items on display the man has no idea what they are. He does recognize lemon, lime, almond, coconut. "Holy hell, two of each, por favor," he orders. These delights are placed in a brown paper package tied up with a string.

(DO YOU REMEMBER, READER, HOW MUCH WE LOVE BROWN PAPER PACKAGES TIED UP WITH STRINGS?)

The man must be alone with the chocolate. He briskly walks to the first spot void of people he can find to savor the smoothness. The cocoa. The burst of lemon. Tart and fresh. The man may very well need to locate a moist towelette to swab himself. He is so excited. It's bitter, not too sweet. Then the grapefruit citrus. Oh my. Another moist towelette for the man, please.

Semi-nauseous, but completely satiated, the man walks on toward the famous landmark, Victory Arch. The arch is of Roman design erected in 1950 as a celebration piece of the Francoist triumph in the Spanish Civil War. It is an amazing stone structure that rests in the center of what the man has come to know as a round-about.

This area of Madrid City the man has yet to see. It is another beautiful display of architecture, wealth, and power.

The phone in his pocket rings and vibrates. Holy hell. It's only 1:00. It cannot be Edward.

"Hello! As you wake?"

The man smiles every time. "I slept fine thank you." He feels no need to inform Edward he has not slept at all. He knows Edward would not offer concern or a show of affection.

Edward tells him he is coming over to the hotel now. The man is shocked really. They will have a day together, or at least half a day. The man is overjoyed at the prospect of walking around Spain with Edward. Seeing it through his eyes. He will ask Edward to show him his favorite spots, nooks, and crannies in the city. They will get to know each other more. Holy hell!

He races to the hotel to freshen up. *What would you like to do today?* the man texts Edward.

Edward responds he will do whatever the man wants. In fact, the exact words Edward uses are, *As you wish.* Edward is nonchalant, passive, and uninterested.

Let's do some shopping. I need a new watch, the man texts. I don't really know where to go for that. Maybe you can help?

Edward texts he will show him where to find a watch. The man pins his location and tells Edward to have the Uber driver drop him off there. Edward arrives within ten minutes. As he approaches the man near the arch, he does not smile nor show any sign of affection toward the man. Edward informs the man they will need to call for an Uber to take them to buy a watch.

After an Uber ride of twenty minutes, they arrive at a mall that could easily be found anywhere in a North American Mid-Western town. Not in Madrid surely.

The mall was an insult to the man; a mall complete with a food court and all. Edward spoke nothing during the Uber ride there. He was on his phone texting. He received an audible message every few seconds which he immediately opened and responded to.

The mall is a bust. Neither one of these men wanted to be there. Anyone watching them would think they are bored or fighting. No conversation. No kindness. No smiles.

The man buys them lunch at the food court, primarily to see what Edward chooses and if he actually places the food in his mouth and swallows it. He does.

An Uber is called to return them to the city centre. The man waits outside the mall at the curbside. Edward is cold so he goes inside to wait.

It is surreal to the man. He came over 5000 miles to meet this jerk, and he is outside not twenty feet from him while he is on his phone inside.

Sitting on the bed back at the Regina now with Edward, the man is angry. He is angry with himself. At Edward for his lack of interest. Most of all, he is angry at Edward's meanness, his cold heart.

The man is lying on the bed fully clothed with Edward lying, not quite next to him, but askew, positioned away from the man.

The thing the man wants most on this trip is to lie next to Edward and hear his breathing as he drifts off. To hold him. This is as close as he will ever get. Lying fully clothed and not touching.

"Let's listen to some music," the man tells Edward. "I'll play you one of my favorite songs! It's called 'Bolero'."

As the piece starts, Edward says, "I love classical."

The man smiles and closes his eyes to listen. The man is remembering the flash mob as the music is playing on his phone.

Edward reaches over and takes the man's phone from his hand. The man does not resist. He assumes Edward is looking at the video of the orchestral work of Bolero. The man can sense Edward is texting or typing something on the man's phone. The man intuitively knows Edward is leaving the man a message somewhere on his phone. He lies there on the bed, fully clothed, listening to his favorite piece of music, with Edward in the flesh lying next to him, yet he is not there. The man can see the futility in his efforts to get to know Edward. He simply will not open up to the man. With a sad heart, the man dozes off hearing Ravel's masterpiece while also hearing the soft clicking sound his phone makes when it is being typed upon.

The man is awakened by Edward standing at the foot of the bed texting someone.

Edward can see the man is awake. "My brother sends me a text. My boss fire me now. My brother will come at six to get me."

"I'm sorry, Edward," is all the man can say.

Edward is texting furiously on his phone. He clearly has no interest in being where he currently finds himself. At the Regina with the old man.

The man has no idea what is happening to, or with Edward. His brother is a strange influence on him. Wouldn't the brother of someone who has a visitor from an entirely different country make some attempt to meet him? Invite him for dinner? Apparently not.

The whole thing leaves more questions than answers for the man. He spends the rest of the night, many long cold hours alone, staring out the open doors, sitting behind the bars on the balcony railing. He has become a prisoner of himself. The man looks, searches, and tries everything in his limited arsenal to find the message Edward left on his phone a few minutes ago. The man is quite sure Edward has written something to him on his own phone. Alas, he does not locate it that night.

Chapter Thirty-Three

Today is much colder and windier than any thus far. The man wanders and explores more of Madrid, alone, sad, and in a kind of daze. He sleeps two hours last night and is never able to achieve the R.E.M. stage of sleep. He is becoming bored. He takes no pleasure in what he is seeing anymore.

The man assumed Edward would spend last night with him, since he was out of a job. Not the case. He has no idea when he will see Edward today. He does not confide in the old man anymore about anything.

The man has managed to kill most of the day. Almost as if he were in a haze. It's 3:00 p.m. in Madrid. He heads back to Regina. As the man walks into the hotel, Edward is standing in the lobby. They head to Room 310 together.

"What are you doing, Edward? Why did you not call me?" the man said.

"My brother, he drops me off. Is okay?" Edward asks.

"Yes, it's okay. Are you hungry? Would you like to eat?"

"No, I fine," Edward says.

They both move over to the table next to the bar near the lobby to sit. Edward rarely speaks unless prompted. Or perhaps he simply is just stoic. The man does not know anymore. The idle chitchat goes on for a few minutes. Edward then tells the man they should get going.

"The appointment is at four."

The man totally forgot he told Edward he would go with him to the plastic surgery clinic today. "Oh, yes, Edward, sorry. Give me five minutes."

The man quickly seeks the elevator and pushes the third-floor button. As is often the case, the elevator is waiting at the lobby level so he does not have to wait for it to lower floors. Once inside Room 301, the man brushes his teeth briskly and changes his shirt. One final check in the mirror in the beautiful bathroom and he is prepared to announce his readiness to Edward.

It is a short walk to the clinic. It is raining, of course, the duration of the walk. Edward locates the address, and they both enter. Edward speaks in Spanish as the man sits down on one of the uber small cushioned stools. The clinic is about what the man expected. It is very small. Three rooms in what must be highly overpriced as it is directly in the heart of the city. The waiting area consists of a reception cubicle and four small overstuffed ottomans. The room appears to be very clean and sterile to the man.

Edward sits next to the man to wait for their scheduled time. They are ten minutes early. Edward and the beautifully dressed receptionist begin speaking in Spanish to one another. The man can get the gist of their conversation by way of their hand gestures. The man hears his own name referenced in the conversation.

After several minutes of talking and form signing, the receptionist informs them both the doctor will be with them soon. The old man inquires how long the procedure will take.

"About an hour," the gal behind the orderly desk informs him.

The man turns to Edward and asks if he needs him to stay while he is being treated. Edward is on his phone. Texting. Non-stop. The man becomes annoyed. He tells Edward he will return in one hour.

Edward simply says, "Okay."

Just as the man gets up to walk outside, the receptionist speaks to Edward. After A brief conversation with her, Edward turns to the man and tells him the doctor is ready to speak to them.

"To us? What do you mean, Edward? As you are well aware, I do not speak Spanish. Why does the doctor wish to involve me?"

"No, it good. I splain to them and they bring English speaking doctor for jou."

"For me? For what? Edward, please tell me what it is you want me to hear from your doctor. What is it you want me to do here? You have to communicate better with me please."

Edward simply looks at the man as if he expects him to read his mind.

"Do you want me to talk to the doctor to see exactly what the procedure is?"

"Jess," is all Edward says.

The clinic is very small. There are two employees working the phone system and the doctors are on call. A polished young woman enters the waiting room and introduces herself to Edward. "Please follow me." She says to him. The receptionist then arises from her computer and informs the man that the doctor will consult with him first in another room.

Edward is texting with someone on his phone as he walks behind the assistant.

"Edward" the man says, harsher than he intended. "You must come with me to consult with your doctor. You must be proactive in this. This is your face, not mine." The man is aware that the word "proactive" is lost on Edward.

They both have a seat in a small clean examining room. There is no conversation between them. The doctor gently knocks on the door and steps into the room. "Hello, I am Dr. Marianne" she announces with an outstretched hand to the man. She does not offer her hand to Edward. Her English is impeccable.

"This is Edward Arias, your patient." The man says almost accusingly.

"How can I answer any questions you may have?" she says as she looks the man directly in the eye.

"Well, I do not know, honestly. My friend will tell you what he wants. My role here is to see that he is not receiving something he did not ask for, and that the procedure is safe and effective. I work in the medical arts and beauty industry in America. I believe Edward may feel better if I hear all you have to say to him. Are you comfortable with that?" the man asks the doctor.

"Yes, of course, I'm happy to do so!"

There is a moment of silence. The man turns to Edward and asks him if he wants to speak to the doctor about the procedure he has read about. The man can clearly see Edward is not interested in the details of the procedure to remove the dark circles from under his eyes, he just wants them gone.

"Talk to her, Edward, not me. Think of any and all future problems or complications. How long it lasts. Ask her now."

Somewhat embarrassed, Edward begins to talk with Dr. Marianne. They speak in Spanish, of course. After Edward seems to be finished with his questions, the doctor looks at the man.

"I'm sorry, Doctor, as you have been made aware, I do not speak Spanish. I apologize for that," the man says a bit irritated. "Would you mind telling me what you just discussed?"

The doctor explains the procedure to the man. The man is well aware this is a scam and the procedure will do nothing to relieve the pigmentation problem around Edward's eyes.

"So, you will inject a chemical subcutaneously around Edward's eyes, is that right?"

"No, it is not a chemical, it is co2."

"Oh, I see. May I ask how co2 changes the melanin levels Edward is unhappy with?"

"It's a reaction under the skin to the co2 that may cause the hyper-pigmentation to change."

"I think I heard you say *may*. Why do you say it *may* change?"

The doctor begins a ramble of policy and procedure and that nothing is a guarantee. This procedure may "give Mr. Arias the results he is looking for, but it may not."

The man knows pigmentation that is hyper will not change with co2. It requires a bleach of some kind. Many South American countries market it freely under the heading of anal bleach to change your dark skin to a Caucasian tone surrounding your anus. The doctor must know this.

"Is there not a bleaching product that would be more effective for this situation, Doctor?" the man asks.

"Yes, however, it is not available in Spain."

Ahh. The answer the man has been trying to get out of her. The man asks the doctor if she would excuse Edward and himself while they decide what Edward wants to do.

After the not-so-good doctor leaves the room, semi-irritated, the man asks Edward what he wants to do.

"I want," is Edward's response.

"Okay, you know they will inject a solution in your orbital socket in five to ten locations. You will be swollen, and it may be painful. You will most likely bruise. To be honest, Edward, I happen to know this treatment will not give you the results you desire. You have a very large amount of skin around your eyes to correct and this procedure is effective on a much smaller scale, at best."

"I want," Edward replies.

The man has no idea if Edward understands anything from what he just said. "Okay, do it. I'm happy for you!"

"Problem is, it's more money," Edward says.

"More money than what, Edward?"

"I keep money you gave me. But need more to do this," Edward says with eyes down.

"Edward, is this something you really want?"

"Jess, my whole life I hate my skin. Friend tink I sick always with dark circles."

"Okay, I'll go out and take care of it. You stay here and I'll send the doctor in."

Edward has not put his phone down once during the entire event. The man tells the receptionist he will be paying for the service and inquiries how much it is.

"Well, it is a five-week treatment, so the total will be over 700 euros."

Holy hell. That, of course, was never mentioned by anyone. "Will you accept American currency?" the man asks.

"Si, of course."

"Please tell me the total in dollars. I must find a Western Union or ATM, so tell the doctor to proceed and I'll return shortly."

The man leaves the clinic with full knowledge he is being used once again by Edward, and by this ridiculous clinic. Yet, he retrieves the extra money. Close to 1000 dollars and returns to pay the debt.

When Edward emerges from the treatment room, he is a bit shaken and pale, but none the less the same. He smiles softly at the man as he stands to open the door for Edward to exit the clinic. It is raining; *surprise*. Edward is, once again, on his phone texting who knows who as they walk back to the hotel.

"Edward, would you mind not texting or whatever you are doing on your phone when you are with me, please?"

Edward's reply is he has family he must respond to. The man lets it go. Edward is hugging the sidewalks as he walks. As close as he can get to any awnings or rain protection he can secure. He is holding one hand over his face. "The rain will not hurt your procedure, Edward, I assure you."

"No, I don't like it!"

"Are you in pain, Edward?"

"No bad."

"There is no swelling yet, that is good."

"Si," Edward mumbles.

At the hotel, Edward is pensive. Is he worried about money? Is he worried his brother will not be pleased he did the face treatment? The man can only guess. Edward is not talking as they sit in the hotel room ten feet apart.

"Why don't you go home, Edward? Put some ice on your face. You do not look comfortable here with me."

Edward hesitates as if he wants to say something then he changes his mind. He stands up to leave. "Thank you very much for today."

"Si," replies the man.

Edward stands uncomfortable for a second then leaves.

The man stares out the prison bars on his balcony till morning light. Often crying. Mostly just staring and thinking about his life. His choices. How wrong this choice was, coming to meet Edward.

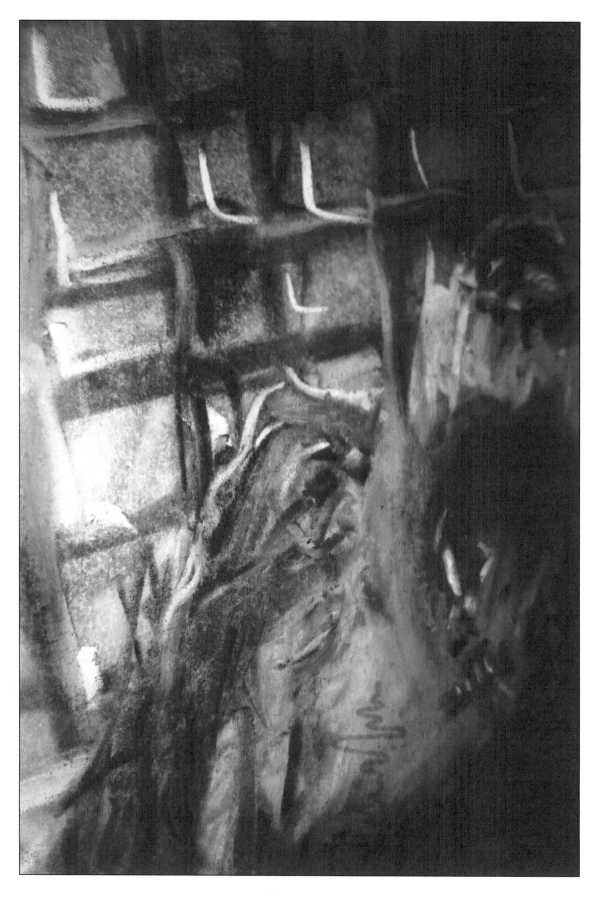

The Prison

Chapter Thirty-Four

It is the old man's last day in Spain. *What place can I find?* wonders the old man. *A place where I can ponder. Where I can be alone with my mistakes.*

The sun is shining. Not one cloud in the sky. Ironic. The last day in Spain and the sun comes to visit.

He must go now. To a place where the stone turns to grass. Ah, he finds such a place. An oasis just past the Victory Arch. A park, it appears. Vast. Very few people wander this early. What an amazement this city called Madrid is to him. Old, new, young. Oddly, it feels like home to him. He feels as though he has been away for many years and just returned home.

Near the gates of the park's entrance there is a woman. At least the man assumes it's a woman from her ample hips and pendulous breasts resting in each armpit. She is homeless. She is passed out on the cement. Covered with an old newsprint and several bedraggled coats. As the man approaches her, he can see the yellow of her eyes peeking out beneath a cap. The cap is crocheted and matted and stained. Actually, it looks like it was once someone's carpet remnant. He touches her lightly on the shoulder. She responds with a smile the size of the St. Louis Arch. She has no teeth when she smiles, the corners of her eyes turn to crepe paper 1000 years old.

The man opens one of the water bottles he carries with him for these precise moments. He holds it up to the woman's lips. They are as old as time. Cracked and fissured. A deep purple, her lips are. The man pulls out his soothing lip balm he is never, ever, ever without. He removes the lid, unsure if this woman will allow him to apply the moisture she desperately needs. He moves toward her lips, she does not object. He layers a heavy amount on her lips. She smiles. It is a smile that need not be communicated with the spoken word. There is a new sparkle in the corner of her left eye that was not there before. He then puts the water to her lips and pours a teaspoon amount in her mouth. She swallows it. Again, he nourishes her with aqua. She accepts. He takes one of her hands in his and makes her hold the bottle as he pushes her hand to her mouth. She drinks. Very slowly, but she drinks. The man begins to cry again. Why? Who knows? This creature lying in front of him is human. She has a soul. It shines if you do not step around her when you pass by. He has not brought the lotion he needs to help heal her hands. So, the old man holds them in his. No words. He does not dare to look at her feet for he could do nothing for them. He is unprepared.

He hands the woman a fifty-euro bill. She does not look at it. He closes her hand around the bill lest the wind carry it away to the undeserved. As he walks off, he cannot know it, but she is watching his every move.

The sun is bright and high in the sky, yet it is very cold. The sun on the man's face makes him think of the shop roof as a child again. Worlds away and yet still the memories of his childhood haunt and chase him. They seem to have a motive. They need to be put on a shelf but, alas, the man has no shelf.

The man is void of energy. There is nothing in his stomach other than its lining. His lips now bleed where the flesh meets the face. The sun that was moments ago a warmth on his back is gone, replaced by sweat. That familiar tingle. Chills. Then it is gone. Replaced again by feet and knee pain. This is how the man finds his life to be. One trouble traded for another without his permission.

The man thinks upon Edward. Thinking about all he has forfeited since Edward lost interest months ago. He has lost all perspective since then.

The man has given himself away. He never had much self-respect. But it is completely gone now, with the sun.

Gone

Money

Time

Affection

Deliverance

Continuity

Faith

Hope

Green Eyes

Travel

Lips

Skin

Soft

Velvet

Moist

Dew

Olive

Pale

Dark Circles

Haunted

The man wants to fix it all. Everyone except himself. Little food. Little water. Six days.

There was a time the man remembers, when thirst was quenched with water. That was months ago.

He lies on the hotel bed in Room 301 at the close of his last day in Spain. Edward is not working. He knows the man is leaving for North America in the morning. Yet he has not contacted him today. The man is no longer expecting anything from him.

(NOTE TO READER: A BIT LATE, DON'T YOU THINK?)

He can smell Edward on the pillow next to him as he dozes in and out of consciousness. It smells of cigarettes and cheap cologne. The room is thick with the smell of shame. The man feels ancient, suddenly embarrassed by his heart's demands. He assumes the fetal position and retracts in his mind.

There is a sudden shift in the room's energy. The man stirs from under Edward's pillow, and Edward is standing at the foot of the bed. He is holding something in his petite fingers. An octagonal box of sorts with a smashed royal blue ribbon atop. The man is so startled he screams. No, more of a deep guttural moan of protest. The man jumps off the bed in fight or flight mode with his hands clenched in fists. He has yet to realize what is happening. Edward is terrified. He stumbles two feet backwards and announces himself to the man.

"I am Edward. Are you okay? Please, do you know me?"

The man wakes from his stupor which, by the look on Edward's face, is a relief to both men in Room 301.

"I'm sorry, Edward, I was dreaming. How… Where did you come from? Who let you into this room?" The man's heart is still beating to the sound of loneliness. He is angry.

"I knock. I open door," Edward replies.

"The door is locked automatically when shut. It's a hotel not an apartment," the man briskly informs Edward.

"Door is no locked," Edward says with a frightened, pale, childlike look upon his face.

The man cannot figure out in the brief few seconds that followed this conversation how Edward got into his hotel room. He leaves it for now.

"Edward, sit."

He does.

"What are you doing here? What do you want?"

"I want noting. I see jou."

The man is so utterly moved by the child he now sees in Edward, he cannot help but begin to cry. It has all been too much. This day. This week.

"No cry please. I no see jou smile tis week," Edward pleads.

The man simply can't believe the narcissism in this Colombian. In the man's head, a reel is playing over and over. *No shit, dumbass. I 'no smile' because you no see me.*

The man sits down on the other side of the bed as Edward sits next to him. The smell of tobacco is nauseating. It actually burns the man's eyes.

"Do you smoke, Edward?"

"No, I never have."

The man leaves it.

Edward stands up, moves in front of the man, and begins to undo his pants. The man takes Edward's hands and pushes them away.

"Stop it, Edward! You don't want me! I know you don't! You have given me nothing of yourself this whole trip!"

"I do want," Edward half-heartedly admits.

"No, you do not, and I know it as well as you do." The man stands, puts his button back where it belongs and tells Edward to leave.

"NO. I no leave you. I stay for hour and half. I leave at nine."

"No, you leave now. I've had enough."

The man opens the hotel door and motions for Edward to leave. Edward attempts to hug the man, but he is pushed away. The man shuts the door behind Edward and takes two steps before he completely loses it.

(NOTE TO READER: YOU MAY BE CURIOUS AS TO WHAT EDWARD WAS HOLDING IN HIS HANDS WHEN THE MAN AWOKE TO HIM STANDING AT THE FOOT OF THE BED. THE MAN FOUND IT LYING ON THE FLOOR NEAR THE FOOTBOARD. INSIDE THIS OCTAGON BOX? THREE ITEMS. TWO CHEAP TOURIST NOVELTIES. ONE LETTER HANDWRITTEN IN ENGLISH. THE MAN DID NOT READ THE LETTER NOR DID HE OPEN THE NOVELTIES MOST LIKELY RE-GIFTED TO HIM.)

Solace in the Park

Chapter Thirty-Five

The man rolls out of bed after two hours of half sleep. It is five in the morning. He immediately throws up all over the dirty linens he has placed in a pile for housekeeping. Dry heaving for ten minutes, his stomach feels torn from his ribcage. It is time to go. The flight home is not for several hours, but he cannot deal with this sadness. Kicking Edward out of the hotel last night gave him some self-respect back. That felt good.

The room is put together. He is packed and calls for a car to take him to the airport. He makes it to the curbside at the airport when he begins to vomit again; vile bile. The car and driver quickly speed off. The Man locates his carrier and checks in for the long flight home. He must linger for five more hours before boarding. Still semi nauseous, the man finds a restroom to brush his teeth. This simple act makes him feel a little better. He takes a handful of water and nervously swallows it. "Deep breaths," he tells himself. He instantly feels bloated, but the water stays down.

After sitting for four hours the Man decides that the only thing worse than flying on an airplane is waiting for an airplane. The wait is down to an hour now. *Holy hell. I need to be alone,* he thinks.

The flight home from Spain to North America was brutal. Several children onboard. Hot as Hades inside this tube of death. The air is stale and pungent.

The man cannot walk after sitting for fourteen hours on an airplane that went from Spain to Amsterdam and then on to home. His knees have become swollen beyond recognition. His feet are numb. It's sort of a dentist numb feeling. However, being numb does not alleviate the pain, it intensifies it. The man's hips hurt because his knees hurt, as well as his feet. His lower back is deeply pooled in a dull ache that will only be alleviated with a hot shower and four more pills. He has none.

The Dutch gal at the exit of the fuselage can clearly see the man cannot walk as everyone tries to exit this hell. She instructs him to stand down and let others pass and she will attend to his needs semi-directly, spitting in every direction like a rain bird on an early Saturday morning, as she spoke.

Her solution is a wheelchair. The man is mortified. However, he cannot walk at all now. So, he acquiesces to the lovely wheelchair. Another age-related insult. The man looks like hell. He is pushed as far as the end of the corridor we all know as the tunnel to adventure, doom, a death, or home!

The old man has arrived in North America. The state of the righteous. The Dutch woman hands the man off to a Delta crew member. She wheels him through customs and kindly asks if he would like her to see him the rest of his journey to the parking and the luggage area. The man declines. He is not up for conversation. Polite or otherwise.

He finds his luggage and performs the necessary tasks to be allowed back into the country of his residence. The man is numb. He does not belong here anymore. He knows it. He felt it inside the corners of his soul when the plane first began its descent. A melancholy, deep loss. Oddly, it is not for the child he left in Madrid, Edward. No, it is for Spain itself. He recognizes this feeling. Spain felt like home. He is homesick for Spain already.

The man limps toward long-term parking. He is becoming emotional. The memories of this journey are ever-present. He is stuck between two continents. Two worlds. The man can feel a long deep cry session coming upon him now. He cannot get alone fast enough. He feels sick. The man's back is sweating with memory. With smells of cigarettes and denial.

He finds his vehicle as he left it. Dusty and smelling of anticipation. He can feel the excitement, the mood, the energy the car has retained while waiting for the man's return. There is no more anticipation. No more energy. No excitement. The man is spent.

As he drives home, the sky above is a dark pewter with charcoal streaks across the entire skyline. Clouds hover over the mountain tops with a weight that matches the man's mood. He is oblivious to the world around him. Jetlag. No sleep. No water. No food. No energy.

The man suddenly begins to sob. He must pull the car off the road. The tears come harder than ever before. He is utterly lost in his head. He no longer knows who he is. He has become a shell. His emotions have him hostage. He is trying to stand outside of his pains but it will not let go.

Twenty minutes later, the man drives the remaining miles to his apartment. He cannot remember ever feeling this low. *Low as a child is not the same as low in adulthood,* he thinks as he pulls into his complex.

Home.

Stairs.

Knees.

Hips.

Feet.

Holy hell.

The white couch.

He begins the ascent to garlic and onions. Fuck! The keys are in his left pocket! The man enters the apartment to silence and must. He is bedraggled with thoughts of his mediocrity. Normally, he would be ecstatic at the thought of his California king awaiting his friend after a journey. He feels no comfort in home now. He lies down on his king. The flight has delayed his watch by many hours. It is late in North America. The end of April. It is dark and wet. The sun has bid adieu. The man will not sleep again for many days. There is a madness that seeps into his body and brain due to lack of food and water and rest.

The man is awake. Wide awake, several hours later. The man makes a decision at 4:46 a.m.

It is still black outside as he gets out of bed to retrieve his laptop. Jetlag is weighing heavily upon the man. Sitting on the corner of the white couch, he opens the device. It is actually funny to him now, the word "laptop." He has no idea what a frickin laptop even is really. It is yet another indication to him of his obsoleteness. He does not care. He wonders, as the thing powers up, about the young and their fascination with all things tech. For he will certainly never understand. There is a push among the young he does not get. *The thing is*, he thinks to himself, *it's not even interesting. It's like Trig 101. What the hell is that?* He sees no joy or art in Trigonometry 101 or 201 or 10.00.

He is irritated with the sidetrack his mind is taking. He is having trouble with clear thinking. He remembers college. Math, NO! Absolutely not. Art? Yes, definitely. Drama? Duh. Social hall? Probably not. The man can see his mediocrity now in all life endeavors. If there was a picture to be painted, he painted it. If the man wanted to understand anything that did not have to do with his rightful place on earth, he figured it out. The trouble was he could not share it with anyone.

The man accomplished many things great and small in his years, others would say. He became bored. Once a challenge was met. The man was on to something that challenged him more than the last easily performed task.

As a young boy, he was eager to please his mother. His father frightened him. His siblings had no idea who he was. He did not know them.

In thinking about his mother now, the man understands there is a peculiar thing that happens between a mother and a gay boy child. A bond. A genetic need for each other perhaps. His mother did not know who her child was and from where he came. Nor did his father. The siblings were busy dealing with their own awkward growing to be concerned with the boy. It's spectacular how heterosexual mothers can see the sheer genius of anything that catches the light the same as homosexual boys do. The man's mother showed him light and sparkle and reflection in many ways. She also gave him darkness and piss in the pants.

(NOTE TO READER: AS WE MOVE FORWARD TO THE END OF THIS TALE, THERE WILL BE MANY SONGS FROM THE MAN'S PERSONAL PLAYLIST. THE SONGS WILL COME AT YOU FAST AND IT WILL NOT ALWAYS BE KNOWN TO YOU, WHY THIS SONG, WHY THAT SONG. AGAIN, IF YOU CHOOSE TO DOWNLOAD AND LISTEN WITH THE OLD MAN, YOU MAY BECOME CLOSER TO HIM.

Mother shows her son light

Chapter Thirty-Six

Two weeks later, the man is on a plane bound for Madrid, Spain, Alcalá 19 Centro 28014 Madrid. Hotel Regina. The man has no reservation. It is a twelve-hour production to arrive. One that he is the sole actor.

As the man walks down the aisle to his ridiculous sized seat, (even for a diminutive sized fellow) it is an embarrassment. The man cannot walk on the plane with erect posture. His head is continually pecking at yet another object his genetic profile dictates without consultation.

The man has not booked comfort class as he did on his first visit to Spain. He has no concern for comfort. Extreme comfort seems to be an embarrassment of the American people who claim there is no caste system. Just get on any plane in America bound for anywhere and walk past those sitting smugly in first-class. Or as it is now called, "business class." The man has an uncontrollable urge to drop a can of Raid in the aisle and watch the self-entitled passengers in first-class all scurry for the nearest Whole Foods.

The man has no luggage. No change of clothing. Nothing to place in the overhead bin. He does, of course, have his earbuds in as usual. He has worn them every day since he arrived home on that wet, cold day from Spain.

He has lost the ability to communicate in America. Particularly with anyone outside of his work.

The man had to keep moving. He could not sit around his apartment. It reminded him of Edward when he spent any amount of time there.

In the short time since returning from Spain, the man has had a nervous energy. A need to keep moving, lest he hole up in the apartment. (*THE ONE WITH THE WHITE COUCH, READER. YOU KNOW.*)

No, the man has other plans. The earbuds give him an autonomy. He wore them at full volume at the grocery store. At the bank. In the apartment after he returned from Spain.

The ironic thing the man discovered is most people are so bored with their mundane occupation they did not even expect a response from the man when asked a question. He couldn't give an answer anyway. He was lost in his music. The music soothed him. It allowed him complete escape from the thoughts and endless unimportant chatter of the working masses around him. There was a feeling then the man recognized. It was how he survived his childhood. Hiding in plain sight. Keep your head down. Pretend you like sports so you will fit in. Talk to girls. Tell every testosterone-infused redneck how much it turns you on. All the while you're thinking how you might get into the pants of the fuckhead you are pretending to impress.

These thoughts come frequently to the man now.

He remembers his past. It makes him nauseous. There is a continual nausea that visits the man now. He has not eaten again in many days. The man has no desire for water. It seems a spoil to him now. His lips are fissured. The man has lost some twenty pounds since his return to the country of his birth. Try as the man does, food is a poor replacement for memories.

His memories are now an uncertain friend. So many things the man now thinks as he adjusts his seat buckle on this jetliner that matter not. Simple joys of life. The word "joy" in itself is a conundrum still to the man. Something natural? Perhaps. Something achieved? Probably. Something given? Something lost? Joy is a three-letter word. The man chuckles as he thinks of the word.

The plane begins to taxi.

> MUSIC DOWNLOAD
> "YULUNGA"
> SPIRIT DANCE ALBUM
> DEAD CAN DANCE

(NOTE TO READER: THE WISH IS THAT, WHEN YOU DOWNLOAD A PIECE OF MUSIC, YOU LISTEN TO IT IN SURETY BEFORE READING ON.)

There are no Dutch on this sojourn. The man adjusts the air vent above his head. He is nauseous again. His back is beginning to sweat. The adult next to him is annoyed the man's shoulders reach beyond his ticket price. This also makes the man giggle. *Fuck you,* he thinks as he smiles to himself.

The man can smell sweat on himself. His shirt is visibly darkened with the filth of memories oozing from every pore. The man could not care less as the plane has reached cruising altitude.

> MUSIC DOWNLOAD
> "STORMS IN AFRICA"
> THE VERY BEST OF ENYA

> MUSIC DOWNLOAD
> "TELL ME ON A SUNDAY"
> SARAH BRIGHTMAN
> ANDREW LLOYD WEBBER COLLECTION

MUSIC DOWNLOAD
"MARLENA DIETRICH'S FAVORITE POEM"
PETER MURPHY
DEEP (1989)

The rest of the flight is unremarkable other than the two-year-old who walks, laughs, and screams at the top of her lungs and farts unattended up and down the aisles. Clearly, she has an incident in her britches.

This also gives the man the giggles. Why? He is not sure. Ordinarily, he would want to choke the little bastard.

The plane begins its descent. He cannot remember when he slept last. His face is gaunt. He is hungry. He is thirsty.

Somehow, he has lost his ability to take care of his basic needs. The man senses the landing gear loosen and lower. Beads of sweat pool at the man's lower back. The man is home. Flashes of memory infiltrate his brain.

The homeless

The queen's palace

El sol

Edward

The Regina

Watches

Passover

Easter

Wandering

Sadness

Coldness

Wet

Jesus

Mary Magdalene

(READER, CAN YOU SEE THE GOLD? THE GUILD. THE CHARIOTS. THE SWEAT OF ISABEL'S LEGIONS

THAT LOST AND STOLE AND CONQUERED THE WORLD FOR HUNDREDS OF YEARS. THIS IS SPAIN! MADRID, SEVERAL MILLION IN THE CITY. THE BLACK HAIR. THE LIGHT-COLORED EYES OF EUROPEAN SPANISH. THE ELEGANT HIP MOVEMENTS. MOTHER MARY ON A FLOAT.)

The old man begins to cry. He cannot control it. He has arrived in Spain. Espana. He exits the plane.

> **MUSIC DOWNLOAD**
> **"EMPTY WATER"**
> **LISA GERRARD**
> **ESSENTIALS**

> **MUSIC DOWNLOAD**
> **"BRING HIM HOME"**
> **JOSH GROBAN**
> **2015**

The old man finds a taxi at the curb. He directs the driver to Calle de Alcala 19 Hotel Regina. It is cold and wet. The man expects nothing less from the weather as he sits in the back of the car in great pain. The rain collects the light from other vehicles' headlights and creates drops of illumination on the window beside the man's head. The driver attempts to chat with the man. He does not bother to respond to one word the driver says. No one shall ever know what the driver said to the man. It is lost with the speed limit. It is a short drive from the airport; eighteen minutes, forty euros this time.

The man is dropped off at precisely the location he was dropped off on his first visit to Spain. The train construction is still active on the street, of course. It has not been that long since he left Spain. The new underground rail system appears to be a slow-moving turtle. One can only hope the trains are the hares upon completion.

The man cares not. It is an insult to all who came before on these six-hundred-year-old streets. The man has nothing in his hands other than what was lost.

His feet are swollen. His knees are not his. The man has a visual limp. He walks past the ATM that stands in front of the Regina. A landmark for him only a few weeks ago. The man reaches El Sol Plaza.

> **MUSIC DOWNLOAD**
> **"STAY ALIVE"**
> **JOSE GONZALES**

He stops to listen to his earbuds. He tears. The man does not make eye contact with anyone.

There is no need. There is no offering for the man now. The sound of the man's shoes on the cobbles is melancholy.

The path has begun to lower in elevation.

MUSIC DOWNLOAD
"SAVEAN"
DEAD CAN DANCE
LIVE AT THE MAYFAIR

There are uncontrollable tears in the man's eyes as he remembers the time he spent here wandering around this city a short time ago. And, of course, Edward is ever-present in his mind.

The image of this unresponsive, narcissistic ass is so strong the man must stop and catch his breath.

The music in his ear is all he needs now to add to the revelations these months have stirred in his soul. He moves forward beyond El Sol. Plaza.

MUSIC DOWNLOAD
"SONG TO THE SIREN"
THIS MORTAL COIL

It's raining. It's cold. The sun has gone. The man has no coat. He walks on. Farther and farther. Small streets give way to tiny streets. Alleys lead the man to fewer streets. The man stops at what would be the equivalent of a small hardware store in North America. He finds what he needs. It is getting colder now, very cold.

Edward is now three miles from him. Edward does not know the man has returned to this place. Edward would not care.

Cold.

Wet.

Alone.

Choice.

The man can see a barricade ahead in his path. He remembers it from his first visit here. The sidewalk lowers itself in elevation as he walks. There is only one sound to be heard coming from the man as he moves.

A rattle of sorts. Coming from his pocket. There is also something bulky under his left armpit. From his pocket comes the sound a prescription bottle of medication makes in the plastic container when carried in the pocket of someone too thin. Under his armpit is his purchase from the hardware store just a few moments ago.

MUSIC DOWNLOAD

CURSUM PERFICIO

ENYA

The man is in much pain. He has walked far outside the Centre of Madrid city. Both of his knees have swollen to extremes. Tongue tied and knobby knees. An aunt or uncle or teacher somewhere along his move to adulthood used to say that to him. Memories come at him. Almost as an attack as he walks on.

Edward, the selfish dick is ever-present. At least the memory of him is. The smell of Edward on the pillow at the Regina is as vivid as if he had smelled it not one minute ago. Cigarettes. Tobacco smoke. Stale and covered with some European scent. The man must stop and process this memory again. Catch his breath and then release.

It is raining once again. The man wonders as he leans against the familiar white church wall, if the sun really comes out to play with anyone anymore. Or is this simply spring in Spain? It seems to him to be intentional.

The elevation continues to lower as the man's knees and feet protest their current predicament. The man is shivering. His shirt is soaked through with rain and sweat. There is a bird perched on a wire just ahead of the man. As he nears the fowl, he can see the white in the eyelids as it blinks away in guilt. The bird has been seen many times by the man and the child within. Here in Spain. In North America. Cranny's. Nooks and sky. It squeals in the darkness. A familiar echo that brings with it a churn of the man's stomach and the memory of a numbers game.

The man's mother comes to him as he walks now. An image of a beautiful young girl cooking in a magic kitchen. Cinnamon rolls. The smell is carried to him by the wind and rain. Lemonade. Tart and full of sunshine. The man's little brother visits next. The brother is a child when he makes his presence known to the man as he continues to walk. He has no words to say. The child within himself attempts to reason with the old man now. He tells the man to turn around and walk back home.

The man can see a familiar object just ahead. The very thing he has come back to Spain for. The juniper tree! The same tree he stumbled upon several miles outside Madrid on that first day he met Edward. Edward had one hour for the man, he said then.

The old man walks toward the tree. It's raining. The man is cold. He is hungry.

The man is unaware he is crying. He cries at car commercials these days. The last time the man visited this tree he was lost and pissed and incredulous at Edward's disinterest in his visit.

The man now does not care. He places his hand in the pocket of his wet jeans. (The right pocket!) He takes out the bottle of pills. There are thirty sleeping pills. A month's supply for the old man. He has added twenty opiates he purchased from Pioneer Park in North America. The man has no water. He no longer cares for water. He empties the contents of the bottle into his cracked brittle mouth. He is used to chewing pills without water. He chews and gnaws at the bitter relief. He swallows and gags. The medicine stays down. The man is lying down under the massive juniper tree several miles from the city of Madrid. There is no one around. The tree is in a small secluded area.

The man pulls the small hacksaw out from under his armpit. He notices he is bleeding as he removes the hack. It has created a laceration as he walked.

The man is becoming dizzy. He cannot feel his body. He removes his shoes and socks. The blade of the hacksaw is small and streamlined. As the man begins to remove his left foot, he is unaware of the existence of anything. The blade tears the top layer of his epidermis. He can see fatty tissue around the blade. It is whitish and pink. The fat creates a lubricant for the blade and now is moving more easily. The man reaches bone. Then major blood vessels. There is a popping sound as he continues to saw. He can feel pressure from the blade but no pain. Halfway through the ankle bone he hits his gristle. The blood spatter is warm against the man's face and chest. The foot is not cooperating with the saw now. It flops left and right as the final push removes the albatross that has put the man under this tree.

The man is losing much blood. He will not leave this mortal coil with feet. The right foot was much easier to remove. The combination of blood loss, medication, lack of sleep, starvation, and dehydration are all now in line with willingness to take the man's soul away.

Tired.

Cold.

Hungry.

Bleeding.

The man is being called home. He begins to chain stoke. The man is fifty years old. He is not an old man. He allowed the attraction of a child to make him feel old.

◎◎

Three days pass before a left foot is found. Shortly thereafter, a right foot. Then the remains of what the Spaniard's call, "A large American was discovered at peace under a large juniper tree."

Edward never knew.

> **MUSIC DOWNLOAD**
> **"NOW WE ARE FREE"**
> **LISA GERRARD**

Self Portrait

Goodbye

CPSIA information can be obtained
at www.ICGtesting.com
Printed in the USA
JSHW040044220623
43426JS00002BA/4